EL ALAMEIN
Ultra and the Three Battles

Alexander McKee

SAPERE
BOOKS

EL ALAMEIN

Published by Sapere Books.
24 Trafalgar Road, Ilkley, LS29 8HH
United Kingdom

saperebooks.com

ISBN: 978-1-80055-971-4.

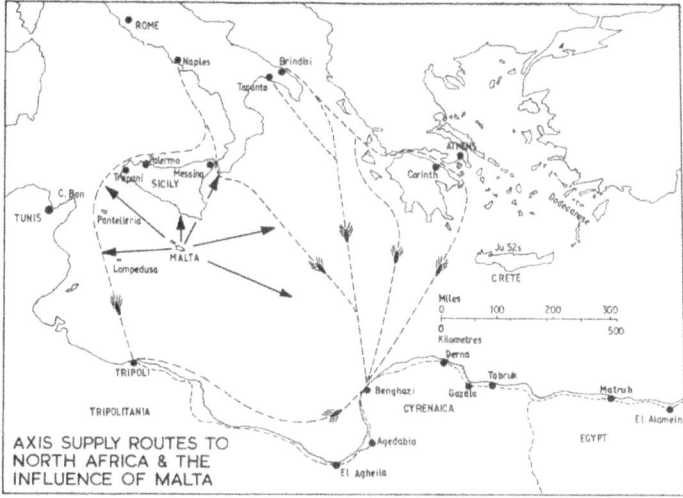

AXIS SUPPLY ROUTES TO
NORTH AFRICA & THE
INFLUENCE OF MALTA

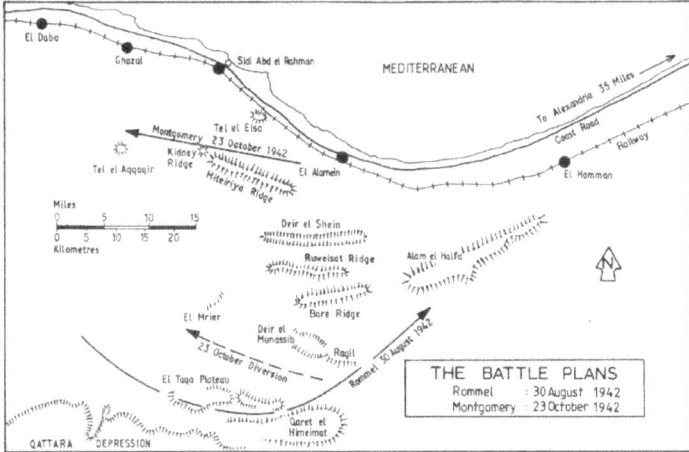

THE BATTLE PLANS
Rommel   : 30 August 1942
Montgomery : 23 October 1942

TABLE OF CONTENTS

1: AMBUSH UNDERWATER

Large submarines did not last long in the Mediterranean, where the water is often deep but dangerously transparent. A lurking submarine can on occasion be seen even 100 feet down. Underwater a diver can frequently see for that distance, although a wind ruffling the surface above may mask a submarine to aerial search. When it dies away the boat is left exposed to the aeroplanes which normally circled all convoys. A flotilla of the big T-class boats, operating from both Malta and Alexandria, lost nine of them in the last half of 1940, when Italy entered the war.

They were replaced by boats of the U-class — small (191 feet long) patrol submarines designed for operations in the shallow North Sea area, they had a surface displacement of 630 tons giving a positive buoyancy on the surface of 90 tons. With a maximum beam of 16 feet and a crew of some 30 men, the hull was packed with weapons and machinery — four 21-inch torpedo tubes in the bow plus four torpedoes stowed as reloads; diesel engines for surface running (10-12 knots) and electric motors powered by heavy batteries (maximum 8 knots, 2 knots at slow cruising speed), giving a submerged endurance of only 60 hours — the vulnerable point of all submarines prior to the introduction of nuclear propulsion. Their designed diving depth was 200 feet, but if antisubmarine vessels could keep a boat down long enough, the crew would gradually pass out or be forced to surface where they would most probably be instantly destroyed.

During 1940 13 U-class submarines were launched. Among them was *Unique*, which reached the island fortress of Malta in

January 1941. The island is a great rock, only lightly covered with soil, rearing out of the Mediterranean between Sicily and what was then Italian North Africa, in a choice position to ambush or raid the sea routes between Italy proper and the ports in the Italian colonies across which the desert war was being fought. Aircraft based on Malta were in a prime position to harry those routes, but for slower vehicles such as submarines, the best technique was to lay an ambush line of U-boats across the likely or known approach line of a convoy.

In August 1941, while her former captain was being rested for one patrol, temporary command of *Unique* was given to Lieutenant Arthur Hezlet. It fell to Hezlet to be in command therefore when a convoy of four fast Italian liners carrying troops to North Africa was reported. *Unique* was to be teamed with two other boats — David Abdy's P 32 and Robert Whiteway-Wilkinson's P 33.

The convoy loading at Naples consisted of the four passenger liners *Oceania* and *Neptunia* (both nearly 19,500 tons and 19½ knots), *Marco Polo* (12,300 tons) and *Esperia* (11,398 tons). They were to be escorted by four Italian destroyers and a number of aircraft. Helmut Huber, a junior NCO, was a reinforcement on his way to join 104 Infantry Regiment under the command of Major the Reverend Wilhelm Bach, who became a popular hero even in England for his defence against the New Zealanders in 1941, surrendering only when he had neither ammunition nor food left. Huber was a passenger in the *Esperia*.

Most of the soldiers in this ship were Italians. Out of a total of 3,000 men (more than double the number the ship would have carried in peacetime) some 450 were German. Like Huber, they were all reinforcements. Popular war films and books, in which naturally the hero cannot die in the first act (although allowable in the final act or chapter), have obscured the basic military fact that most men do *not* go all the way — they are in fact consumed by the battle. Consequently, the military meaning of a reinforcement is of a man who is stepping into a dead man's boots and very probably will soon become a casualty himself. They all knew that, but like most of us in a similar predicament blindly believed that they were immortal. The German reinforcements had been drawn from units stationed in Italy and in Greece, which in 1941 had fallen to the Wehrmacht.

The convoy left Naples at ten o'clock in the morning of 18 August, 1941, with its destroyer and aircraft escort, soon leaving Vesuvius and the Salerno peninsula behind. At 1030 a.m. on 20 August, only an hour away from their port of destination, Tripoli, they were hit by three torpedoes; seven minutes later, the *Esperia* had gone. Huber recalled:

> The ships were loaded with troops (no weapons, ammunition or other equipment). All had life-jackets and jumped into the water. Lifeboats were launched by the destroyers and while the three other liners continued to Tripoli, the rescue action was started immediately. Rescue by the Italian seamen was courageous and exemplary. I was rescued after two hours in the water. At about the same time several fishing boats arrived from Tripoli to assist. 270 men were lost, mainly Italians, many of whom were crew members and below decks during the attack; only about 12 Germans were drowned. Immediately after the attack the destroyers and aircraft counter-attacked with depth-charges on what seemed to be just one submarine, but the results were not known.

Hezlet with *Unique* was the only British boat to score. Because the escort concentrated on saving life, no really determined attack on the submarine was made on this occasion, although she was leaking oil. Soon after, *Unique* sailed back to Scotland, and when she returned was under the command of Lieutenant R. E. Boddington. His orders were to spend some time patrolling off the coast of Northern Spain before entering the Mediterranean. On October 1941 he parted from his escort and next day another submarine on the same patrol, the *Ursula*, heard underwater explosions which she connected with an attack on *Unique*. Boddington and his boat were never heard of again, and although the Germans made no claims to have sunk a submarine in October, it was accepted that the detonations heard by her sister boat on the 10th must have been fatal. There were no survivors. Hezlet had commanded on only one patrol on a temporary basis to relieve the previous captain, and fortunately for himself was not on board *Unique* when she returned from Scotland under Boddington; so despite all the odds against, he survived the war and became an admiral.

The most successful of the Malta-based 10th Submarine Flotilla was *Upholder*, under Lieutenant-Commander M. D. Wanklyn, who after a disappointing series of failures as a submarine commander (which almost cost him his job), finally got his eye in and began to sink ships at a phenomenal rate. He was 'quiet and modest, but his eyes penetrated everything', recalled his First Lieutenant at the time, N. L. C. Crawford, now retired as a captain after getting his own boat. 'Wanklyn was nearly fired after five dud patrols, but the crew were one hundred per cent behind him. That's leadership.' The first lieutenant is responsible for the running of the boat; usually the captain is the only one who looks through the periscope.

'On this occasion we were recalled suddenly from shore leave in Malta to form part of a line of three submarines to be put across the expected line of a convoy, with *Upholder* in the centre of this line, timed to intercept at night.' A fourth submarine was put out to the south-west for what was left of the convoy at dawn.

> During the night we had a message from *Unbeaten*, the submarine to the eastward — Convoy Sighted. Ten minutes later we saw them. Two large two-funnel liners escorted by five or six destroyers. There was a fairly heavy swell and *Upholder* was only a little submarine. Normally the submarine tries to attack at right angles to the target and the spread of the torpedoes is caused not by swinging the boat but by the movement across the submarine's bows of the target. But with this heavy swell and the bows swinging... Wanklyn allowed time for his order to reach the bow of *Upholder* and got an overlap on two liners, firing first at the bows of the one ahead, then at the stern of the ship behind her. The third and fourth torpedoes were fired across the centre of this double target as the submarine's bows swung back with the swell.

Usually after an attack, bound to bring retribution, the drill was for a submarine to go down at once. But on this occasion Wanklyn said: 'No, I'm going to stay up a bit.' While they waited for the counter-attack they heard two detonations — a torpedo hit on one ship? or on two? When no counter-attack came they reloaded the four empty tubes and hung around until it was light enough to see through the periscope.

> We saw one ship lying stopped and several destroyers circling. We closed and were just about to get two more torpedoes off when a destroyer came at us and we went deep. Wanklyn went *under* the target liner, *Oceania*, then turned and fired from the other side. He managed to hit and she went down pretty quickly.

The two troop-carrying passenger liners this time, on 18 September 1941, were the two which had evaded *Unique* when she had attacked the four-ship convoy on 18 August, a month earlier, and sunk the smaller *Esperia*. They were the *Neptunia*, 19,330 tons, and the *Oceania*, 19,405 tons. Wanklyn had fired only minutes before another submarine in the ambush, *Unbeaten*, was about to finish off the damaged *Oceania*.

But the slightly bigger and faster *Vulcania* got away: although the *Ursula*, positioned to finish off any cripples at dawn, saw her and fired torpedoes, she missed; it seems likely that no allowance had been made for the greater speed of this liner and an estimate had been based on the known speeds of the *Neptunia* and *Oceania*, which were in fact slower. However, it was thought for a time that she had at least been damaged, because when sighted later she was moving slowly and had a great list. In fact the overloaded destroyers had been transferring survivors, and a joyous committee of welcome had rushed to one side to greet the saved men, causing the *Vulcania* to heel over.

There were some odd things about these ambushes, ordered in a hurry without prior warning. On this last occasion, *Upholder*'s men had been ordered off shore leave in Malta on the afternoon of 16 September, and sighted the convoy in the early hours of the 18th, southbound for Africa. Crawford noted at the time that 'the convoy was exactly along the track we were given and on the course given'. It seemed uncanny, as if the Allies had a spy highly placed in the enemy command. In effect, they had.

To conceal the real source of such information, wherever possible 'accidental' overflights of convoy departures and passage routes were arranged, so that the enemy would blame the all-seeing eye of RAF photographic reconnaissance or perhaps the stealthy glance of a submarine's search periscope. Just as often, he blamed traitors in his own midst, the unknown 'watchers on the quay' or the careless talkers in the ranks.

The Malta boats which set these ambushes were supposed to number ten submarines but were subject to a continual drain of losses. In April 1941 *Usk* was sunk, in May *Undaunted* was lost, in July *Union* went, and in August two more U-class boats as yet unnamed and known only by their numbers, P 32 and P 33, failed to return. By the end of 1941 only three of the original ten were still operating from Malta, although they were now officially a flotilla under Captain 'Shrimp' Simpson. The 10th Submarine Flotilla as it was now called consisted then only of *Upholder*, *Urge* and *Unbeaten*.

Upholder under Wanklyn carried out 25 patrols during 1941 and 1942, sinking three U-boats and one destroyer, damaging a cruiser and another destroyer, sinking or damaging 19 supply ships engaged in supporting the Axis forces in North Africa, totalling 119,000 tons. Wanklyn was awarded the Victoria Cross. Undoubtedly, good intelligence regarding the movements of enemy convoys often put him in the right place at the right time. Important though that was, it did not make him immortal nor his submarine indestructible. In April 1942 *Upholder*, having landed Allied agents on the African shore, was ordered to join a patrol line with two other submarines off Tripoli to intercept yet another convoy for Rommel. On 14 April the submarine *Urge* heard heavy depth-charging and the Italian torpedo boat *Pegaso* reported attacking a sonar contact pin-pointed by the dropping of smoke bombs by an Italian seaplane. When the echo vanished, the *Pegaso* rejoined the convoy she was protecting. Neither *Upholder* nor her crew was ever heard of again. Captain Crawford survived only because he had been ordered home to take a submarine CO's course.

2: ENIGMA

Enigma is the Greek for puzzle, but it is also the name of an automatic code and cypher machine, of about the same size and of somewhat the same appearance as a large office typewriter, invented for commercial purposes in Germany in the 1920s and subsequently taken up by the German armed forces in a more complicated and secure version. Its purpose was the passing of orders and reports at high speed during wartime in such a fashion that they could not be read by any outsider. Each message was typed, automatically scrambled by the machine, transmitted by wireless, received and unscrambled by a similar machine or machines by the recipients. The 'scrambling' process, which was mechanical by means of wires and wheels, gave millions of variations, so many that any ordinary attempt at code-breaking would require years of work by enemy mathematicians; even if successful, their efforts would be merely of historic interest when passed to the military.

Not all these machines were of the German Enigma type, nor was their use confined to the Germans; this was a game at which many could play. The code word used by the British to describe the decoding and deciphering of enemy wireless messages sent using automatic machines was known as Ultra. Technically, many messages involved both codes and cyphers, the first referring to words, the second to numerals; but for the general reader it is often convenient to use 'code' or 'decode' as a simplification. Of course, many military messages were sent not by wireless which the enemy could overhear, but by landline or by despatch rider. An Army headquarters was noisy with the clacking of the teleprinters, the shouting of staff officers down a bad or suddenly cut telephone line or the revving of Don R's bikes. Messages not sent by wireless were fairly secure. The messages sent over the air by automatic coders were believed to be impenetrable by any enemy who might intercept them; often, this was true, but not always.

The introduction of this rapid and supposedly secure communications system implied a fast-moving method of warfare for which Germany's chosen enemies were not prepared. This has gone down to history as the blitzkrieg — the war of rapid and daring manoeuvre rather than the slow avalanche of blood and the thunder of bombardment typical of the Western Front of 1914-1918, which all nations now dreaded.

Formerly, Intelligence matters were considered to be secret for all time. A ruse could thus be used more than once, and in more than one war. Soon after the end of the Second World War there was a change. Some surprisingly highly placed people began apparently to let cats out of bags. 'The Man Who Never Was' is one example, the so-called 'Traitor of Arnhem' another.[1] Sometimes these stories contained elements of the truth, in others, none at all. They tended to generate

---

[1] *Operation Heartbreak* by Duff Cooper (Hart-Davis, 1950) told in fictional form of how a uniformed corpse, carrying documents showing that the Allies after clearing North Africa in 1943 would attack in Greece, was planted on the Germans, when their actual target was Sicily — see *The Man Who Never Was* by Ewen Montagu (Evans, 1953). The supposed 'Traitor of Arnhem' was a Belgian Resistance man who was said to have gone over to the Germans and told them all about the Allied airborne assault in September 1944 — just another easily believable tale whereas the truth was that the airborne planners in London made a number of second class decisions leading to a first class defeat. See *The Race for the Rhine Bridges* by Alexander McKee.

controversy and indignant counterclaims. The breaking of Enigma was no exception. The Poles, the French and the British all claimed to have played a major part, and as documentation was necessarily sparse or even non-existent, the ground shifts underfoot. Short of bringing the dead to life and reactivating the racks in the Tower of London, there is little possibility of uncovering the definitive story.

A 'garbled story' (according to the British official history) was given in Michel Garder's book *La Guerre Secrète des Services Spéciaux Français, 1935-1945* (Paris, 1967), which claimed the credit for France in 1937. This work sparked a reply by General Gustave Bertrand, a former head of the cryptanalytical section of French Intelligence. He gave an earlier date, 1932, and the detail that the French contact was a German (whom he referred to as Asché), an employee of the German Army's cypher branch until 1934 and thereafter in the Forschungsamt of the Luftwaffe, dealing with signals intelligence.

In turn, this revelation spurred Colonel Paul Paillole, ex-chief of French counter-espionage, to back his colleague by adding that the German's name was Hans-Thilo Schmidt, a playboy whose motive for treason was the money to support his life-style. He added that he was prompted to this action by anger at the 'false claim' made by Group Captain F. W. Winterbotham in his book *The Ultra Secret* (Weidenfeld & Nicolson, 1974) that it was really a Pole who had worked in Germany in an Enigma factory and had been brought from Poland to Paris by the British organisation SIS, who had first revealed the secrets of the machine. To rub it in, in his preface to the book — the first to lift part of the veil on Ultra — Winterbotham patriotically claimed 'the laurels for the Enigma Operation' for the wartime code-breakers of Bletchley Park in England.

General Bertrand's counter-blast supplied a valuable corrective to this enthusiasm. From their German source inside the Wehrmacht communications system, he claimed that the French had had sight of 303 documents concerned with the Enigma machine, which included instructions for one type and 'keys' or settings for 1932, 1933 and the first half of 1934, plus two texts — one in clear, the other of the same message 'scrambled' by the machine. The main lack was the absence of data concerning the internal wiring of the wheels or drums which actually did the 'scrambling'.

The French general went further. He claimed that he then contacted the British, the Poles and Czechs, but the Czechs did nothing and the British showed little interest. The Poles, he added, had been working to break Enigma since 1928 with a team of mathematicians. British records show that the French provided them in 1931 with photographed documents regarding the Enigma Mark I which the Germans began using in 1930; they also reveal the reason for the small interest shown by the British. The Government Code & Cypher School (GC & CS) was forbidden to supply this information to Allied foreigners until shortly before the war. As usual in Intelligence, things are not always what they seem.

In its turn, the French general's book produced reactions, notably from the pre-war head of Polish Intelligence, S. A. Meyer. He did not mention the work of the German traitor employed by the French. His claim is that the Poles simply bought the commercially available model of the Enigma, set up a team of mathematicians, and put them to finding out how it might have been improved and modified for the Wehrmacht.

A rival story, which could also be true, suggests that some daring Polish skulduggery resulted in the snatching of an Enigma machine from a lorry delivering a batch of them to

German Army units. Frequently in Intelligence either the left hand does not know what the right hand is doing or, more often, it is decided that it might be safer not to say.

But Enigma machines were bound to be captured, once war had begun — as indeed they were to be — and the Germans, accepting this, had made their code system so complicated that even an actual Enigma specimen would not provide an enemy with the means to read the messages it could send. The main contribution to the long-term breaking of the various German codes seems to have been the Polish assumption that, if a man could invent a machine to make and transmit a puzzle, another man might make a machine to solve the problem. The Poles produced what they confusingly called a 'bombe' (a word shortly to have sinister meanings in Europe); it appears to have been an electro-mechanical high-speed scanning machine.

The British were not entirely innocent in this matter; they were merely holding their cards close to their chest, not giving away how much they knew before they had established that these friendly foreigners really had data of value to swap. As early as the spring of 1937 they had broken the early type of Enigma used in the Spanish Civil War by Franco's forces and by his German and Italian allies, but they had had no success with an improved model being used by the German Navy. For their part, the Poles recognised that they themselves lacked the resources to crack this problem, for the naval Enigma had defeated them too — and war was close.

What was taking place then and was to continue throughout the war was a struggle between the code-makers on one side and the code-breakers on the other, a conflict which initially saw successes for the Poles, the French and the British. But when war began in 1939 the Poles lasted only three weeks; and when the Germans in 1940 attacked France in her turn, they achieved total victory in six weeks. Their use of a still-secure high-speed communications system was an important factor in their success.

Necessarily, this is a simple summary of what was in fact a fiendishly complicated and ever-changing process, but this book is concerned with what information was made available to certain military commanders and with the use, or otherwise, which they made of it. Those interested in the technical details of the operation — known as Ultra — can do worse than read *The Hut Six Story* by Gordon Welchman, one of the code-breakers of Bletchley Park (Allen Lane, 1982). There are many others.

This work would be totally unbalanced if it was not revealed that people other than the Germans had modern cypher machines too. The British machine, as used by the Foreign Office, the Army and the Royal Air Force, was known as the Type X. The Admiralty, deciding after trials of Type X in 1936 that the machine was not good enough, retained their system of recyphering and recoding. Catty suspicions have been voiced that this was because the machine, although highly thought of by Lord Mountbatten, had been recommended by the RAF; and inter-Service jealousy (by no means exclusive to the Navy) was a prominent feature of Britain's preparations for war and may have contributed to her long run of initial defeats. But it could simply be that in the First World War the Admiralty had contained a code-cracking organisation of brilliance known as 'Room 40' (although it was not always intelligently used by admirals who did not believe that commodores and captains knew enough about war to allow them to interpret the broken enemy messages), and that this tradition of success made them complacent.

The Germans however had learned from their defeat by Room 40 and in the Second World War devoted considerable resources to listening to their enemy's messages on the air and trying to decode them where necessary. They had in fact broken one British naval code, so that the position in this war was reversed.

The only perfectly secure code is the one which is used once only. There is nothing to get hold of for comparison. But if a mass of material has to be transmitted, the more there is, the greater the likelihood of the messages being understood. A moment's thought shows why. The addressee's name, rank and appointment has to go on it, and that of the sender; and the date; and the file references; and a great deal of other necessary information which will be exactly or almost identically repeated in coded message after coded message. And an outburst of British naval code and cypher followed the outbreak of actual operations, of which the German B-Dienst (wireless interception) Service took advantage.

Right from the very beginning also ordinary radio listening stations were overhearing the clear speech chatter of RAF fighter controllers; and from at least as early as 1939 the operators soon built up considerable understanding of their opponents' organisation and methods. When it became clear that secret matters were no secret to the enemy, the presence of spies or traitors tended to be suspected, or idle talk in pubs or railway carriages, rather than operational chit-chat on the air where, it was assumed, there was no enemy. Bomber Command, for example, with its strict sense of terrestrial security, would close bomber stations before an op was prepared, regardless of the fact that all the chatter of pre-raid flight-testing was being broadcast to interested listeners on the other side.

One more thing needs to be realised. Even if a message was made in clear without the use of code, no ordinary Englishman or German would understand a wartime message written in their language. The reason: for economy and speed all Services in all countries wrote and frequently also spoke in authorised abbreviations. For instance, the British abbreviation A/Tk (anti-tank) was matched by its German equivalent PAK. The British used abbreviations for units and formations — Bn, Bde, Div and so on. In speech, Div was abbreviated too, and rfts (reinforcements) spoken as 'ruffs'. And also, a Bn is a unit, whereas a Div is a formation. And what's the difference?

In very bald terms, just decoding the enemy's messages was simply not sufficient. One needed a staff who by continually studying the enemy's communications could 'read' them deeply, seeing information which at first sight seemed not to be there. There was no substitute for informed interpretation of decoded messages. 'Raw' information was not enough. But this realisation came late. To begin with, the Foreign Office, the Admiralty, the War Office and the Air Ministry were advised by four separate security sources, who did not even get together among themselves. Further, while the breaking of foreign codes was 'offensive' and had glamour, looking for weaknesses in our own system was 'defensive' and therefore inglorious.

The exotic lady who profited from amorous pillow-talk by careless generals and so obtained the plans of the fortress had very much been superseded in the twentieth century by a complicated technical organisation. Flag-waving and pigeon-fancying had likewise been downgraded by the ever-increasing use of wireless, now known by the abbreviation Sigint (for Signals Intelligence). Its first component was what in Britain was called the 'Y' Service, the interception of signals, including where possible their origin, by DF (Direction Finding). In the USA this was called RI, for Radio Intelligence Service. Next in the chain came TA, for Traffic Analysis, the study of communication networks, involving call-signs, procedures, low-grade codes and plain language. The results of the work of analysts or processors finally went to operations branch. These were the facts arrived at after digestion and placing in context by people who from long day-to-day study of the enemy's organisation and signals were intimately familiar with him, thus avoiding the muddled handling by inexpert staff which had for instance marked the Admiralty's control of the Battle of Jutland in the First World War in spite of the good work of Room 40.

Sigint, particularly in its 'Y' manifestation, is nowadays regarded as vitally important, and various incidents have occurred abroad where information-gathering ships have been either captured (by the North Koreans) or 'taken out' (by the Israelis). In both these cases the 'innocent bystanders' were US Navy ships. In Britain the role presently played by Sigint hardly surfaces, except when some politician mentions Cheltenham or a holiday-maker queries the purpose of all those weird aerial arrays in Cyprus.

Although the importance of conventional espionage has been downgraded, other forms of information gathering, some traditional, have retained or even improved their value. The art of interrogating prisoners of war has included many subtle approaches, as well as the more traditional and direct brutal type of questioning, where in a battlefield situation very rapid answers of life-or-death importance to the interrogators are required.

Perhaps one of the greatest developments has been in aerial reconnaissance. Even at the start of the 1939-45 war, the traditional old, slow Somme-type aerial 'banger' was in vogue, to be soon replaced by the extremely fast stripped-down and unarmed high-flying fighter.

The commanders of the Second World War had all these means of information gathering at their disposal. They could not merely, as Wellington so often wished to do, look over the summit of the next hill, but study photographs of the enemy's back areas and Lines of Communication (L. of C.), and even hear him talking hundreds or even thousands of miles away.

3: MONTGOMERY IN ENGLAND

> The Desert War continues to exercise its fascination over British writers, whether veterans or historians. Why? It is true that the battle area was romantic and unique. It is also true that the British have a bad conscience about the campaign. All accounts, including General Tuker's, come down in the end to trying to explain, excuse, or assign blame for the fact that the best Army the British Empire could put in the field was never as good as a couple of spare panzer divisions and a scratch light division shipped to Tripoli at short notice.

I thought this paragraph from a book review of 1963 so much to the point that I cut it out but, alas, without noting its author. Although nearly thirty years have passed since then, I feel it is still valid as a comment. But where is the explanation?

The fascination of the Desert Campaign is easy to explain. For years it was virtually the only war we had, a long-running, cliffhanging serial. All the others were short and definite with identical endings: loud cock-crowings from the gutter and sometimes even the quality press at the prowess of our untried but totally irresistible forces, followed shortly after by the thump of a German of Japanese boot connecting sharply, followed at once by an evacuation of such British forces as had escaped death or capture. This was the pattern for the first half of the war, from autumn 1939 to late summer 1942; such hatred as was felt was directed mainly at the over-boastful media — including the supposedly impeccable BBC — rather than at the enemy. Who did they think they were kidding?

In the first flush of eventual victory there was a spate of war books, particularly of a revelatory nature, such as *I Was Hitler's Chauffeur*. Forgery was still to come in the shape of totally fabricated diaries more to the taste of modern streetwise readers, almost all of whom could be hoodwinked almost all of the time. Of course, there was a need for revelations because few of the millions of cogs in the military machines knew anything like the full story — and some aspects, especially the Intelligence side, have remained secret until recently. It is also true that in wartime it is not a good idea to tell the whole truth, because it will interest the enemy exceedingly.

However, at the risk of having this chapter retitled *I Was Monty's Anti-Tank Rifleman*, I must first give some aspects of the Desert story as they appeared to the audience waiting in the stalls — that is, to the British Home Army which had a special interest in these events because sooner or later they were destined to meet, not the shadowy Wehrmacht who are nightly and effortlessly defeated on all our television screens, but the real thing: the professional people whose job was to kill you if you didn't kill them first.

I chose quite the wrong time to join. Having tried and failed to get various air-crew jobs, from RAF to Fleet Air Arm, I chose a unit for which one could still volunteer — the London Scottish. The process took a little time because I had to prove Scottish background (not difficult) and a London area residence (which involved a small deception). I reported for duty to their training company in Southampton on 2 February 1942, which was not quite the nadir of the war so far as Britain was concerned. But nearly.

On 12 February there was activity in the Channel nearby — three major units of the German Navy made Drake turn in his seabed grave by breaking out from Brest and parading up-

Channel past Dover under strong Luftwaffe cover. Nothing as offensive as this had happened since the French Admiral Tourville had defeated an Anglo-Dutch fleet in 1690. And on 15 February, the far-off fortress of Singapore fell to a Japanese force outnumbered three-to-one by the British.

Instruction in fieldcraft, including crawling in the snow, was varied with route marches and night operations in which one was supposed to kill silently, mixed with late lectures. On 5 February I noted merely 'Lecture by Austrian refugee on concentration camps' and on the following evening 'Lecture by Angus on tank operations at Halfaya'. This was relevant and I made copious notes, especially of Angus's preliminary warning that his talk was 'strictly private, as if revealed the general public would lose all confidence — if they still have any — in High Command.'

The story told was of chaos and incompetence, generals with no real idea of what to do and no co-operation at all between tanks, infantry and artillery — except in one instance, which I shall come to. Then the slides, and the biting comment: 'All British tanks except Matildas just scrap.' The Matilda was slow and short-ranged, but heavily armoured; the gun however was a 2-pdr with a range of 500 yards. The German Mark IV was nearly twice as fast and had a 6-pdr gun, 'very good tank'. The slides showed a typical British tank — a big, bulky vehicle with a matchstick protruding from the turret — the 2-pdr gun; then a typical German tank — a bloody great gun with an ordinary size tank attached.[2] And I never forgot the comment about the

---

[2] At this time the Mark III tank was the German 'workhorse' in the desert. In early 1941 it had a 37 mm gun firing an approximately four pound shell. In the autumn of 1941 later models appeared with a short-barrelled 50 mm firing a five to six pound shell. The Mark IV which appeared in France in 1940 was designed to break through infantry defences by use of a 75 mm or three-inch gun which fired at

Boys anti-tank rifle with which we were equipped —
'guaranteed NOT to pierce the armour of any known type of
German tank; but will stop a Bren carrier.' The one successful
attack had been made with artillery preparation to make the
Germans keep their heads down while the tanks got in range.
'Infantry should keep right up with tanks.'

One day we were taken out on a range to witness the Royal
Artillery demonstrating the frightening power of the awesome
2-pdr gun which was so special that only the RA could handle
it; infantry need not apply. And there it was — a matchstick
between two wheels poking out of a shield. I understand now
that the 2-pdr was recognised as out-of-date and ineffective,
but that production was continued in order to produce
impressive numbers of them, instead of re-tooling the factories
to make the 6-pdr which was available. A lot of people are
unnecessarily dead because of that decision. The procedure in
Africa was, I am told, that 'Jerry sees you coming, has a brew
up, then shoots you; and you still aren't in range to shoot him.'

On 31 March that year the Chief of the Imperial Staff,
General Sir Alan Brooke, confided his worst forebodings to his
wife. He deplored the British lack of good military
commanders — half the officers commanding corps or
divisions were unfit for their jobs, but if he got rid of them, the
replacements would be just as bad. That was one big worry. An
even larger obstacle to success was that the government had
only one big man in it and he a 'grave danger in many respects'.
Party politics overrode the real issues of the war, and the
politicians' influence created a confused tangle because they
sought to interfere without fully understanding. For the last
fortnight (mid-March 1942) the CIGS had the feeling, for the

---

far longer range than any British anti-tank gun. Like all German tanks
at that time, it was fast.

30

first time, that Britain was likely to lose the war unless this situation was altered. (See *Alanbrooke* by General Sir David Fraser, Collins, 1982.)

Worse was to come; nadir had not been reached. The losses of merchant shipping to the U-boats during the first half of 1942 had been 'appalling'. And it was at sea, most of us felt, we could certainly lose the war. But public relations people and propagandists generally may care to note that the absolute, ruthless honesty of the Army lecturer led to a belief in what we might be told by that source later; and it did not depress us.

It would be absurd to give the impression that all we were worried about was the war; on the contrary we all had individual lives and preoccupations of our own. People like Churchill, who lived for, through and by the war, were the exception. Ours was a wholly volunteer battalion, but the British Army, like the German, was largely conscript; unlike the German soldier who had pride as a warrior, the British generally were uninterested in the war except on those few occasions when it touched them directly.

My memories of those days contain nothing romantic or dramatic; instead a great deal of boredom, plus an immense amount of extreme physical exertion — and exhaustion. In this I expect we were like millions of others of all nations mobilised to kill each other.

We did I think a one-week route march through the New Forest, and I noted in my rough diary, 'McGlashan walked into a hedge, asleep on his feet.' I remember having live ammo fired over us, and the only man who stirred was an NCO known even in the Sergeants Mess as 'Neanderthal Man'[3] — he

---

[3] The 19th century German spelling seems much more neolithic than the modern German 'tal'; by courtesy of the British Army I was later to see the river valley where the skull was found.

scuttled off like a crab, while the raw recruits, who all had had fairly extensive experience of bombing by real enemies, stayed where they were. I remember the ceremonial 24-hour guard mounting which used to take an hour and a half — even the backs of one's buckles were inspected for a bright shine; while, if you were lucky, you lined up behind them as part of the cliff-top patrol arrayed in what the Army delicately calls 'Shit Order', with everything darkened, '36' grenades in your pockets and a Tommy-gun (the original Thompson — the gangster weapon) slung over your shoulder; alas only a silly little 20-round magazine, about three seconds' worth of fire-power. Most unlikely to meet a German trying to scale those cliffs at Barton-on-Sea, but there were usually a few German aircraft wandering about to remind you there was a real war on somewhere. Probably they were interested in the invasion craft being used by the Canadian Division training on the Isle of Wight opposite.

I remember the name of the Company Commander, but not that of the Colonel, nor of the Brigadier, nor of the Divisional Commander (although it was the Bow Bells Div, I think). The Colonel-in-Chief, however, was certainly the lady who is the present Queen Mother, whose influence got us our kilts and a unit magazine (to which I contributed, of course). Less pleasantly, we were put through a gas chamber (without gas masks) and exposed to various gases, but notably phosgene, to accustom us to the smell of danger; and I must have breathed in more than was good for me. Anyway, I was downgraded to B.1 for a while, and this may or may not have saved my life, for in July we were all lined up for a draft for overseas to be picked, and the first command was, all light duty men, two paces (it may have been three) backward march! I had a bad feeling about that draft, whereas when later it came to

Normandy I was certain that I would survive, although I now sometimes wonder how many men, believing they are immortal, die with a look of surprise on their faces.

I expect that those chosen sailed on a convoy for Africa and served at Alamein under Monty. I can't say I'm sorry to have missed it — flies, desert sores, heat and thirst, the khamseen, no thanks. But I didn't miss Monty all the same. I remember the usual sort of 'scheme' we carried out, lying under hedges on a damp, probably Wiltshire hillside and watching below in the valley a long line of Bren carriers trundling past pretending to be a panzer division. No one explained what we were there for or what we were supposed to do; it all seemed perfectly pointless and haphazard.

But the 23 June affair was different. After it was over we were told: 'Forget what you have seen.' So in my original ink diary I wrote: 'Reveille at 2.15 hours, for an interesting "scheme". As we groped for our rifles in the darkened tent, we heard a Jerry overhead.' This time we were briefed, we knew what we had to do, where and why; and the whole thing went like clockwork. I don't know who did the staff work, but Monty was certainly there, as were Mountbatten of Combined Ops and Paget of Home Forces. It was at Monty's request because the previous exercise had been a total shambles — mainly owing to Navy difficulties with the new, awkward and necessarily unseaworthy large landing craft — and so he had been unable to see how these craft handled during beaching, how the tanks coped, or not, with the shingle beach, how the engineers dealt with the problems of getting them over the sea wall, how long the infantry took to vacate their assault craft and the rest of the necessary nitty-gritty (an expression not then coined).

At dawn Monty was on a hill overlooking the site together with the rest of the 'top brass', which included the Canadians McNaughton and Crerar, when a 2-inch smoke bomb fired from a mortar landed between him and another officer.

'That one was aimed up here deliberately, let's get out before they try again,' snapped the future field marshal.

Much as one understands how tempting a target that collection of august individuals must have made, I am not convinced it was a mere spiteful joke, for we got the same treatment. When I came to type my written diary I added the previously secret detail.

> This turned out to be the rehearsal for the Dieppe Raid. We [2nd Bn The London Scottish] were supposed to be German reinforcements hurrying to Dieppe and, after many weary hours in the lorries, we came in sight of the sea and the invasion armada lying off shore. We jumped out of the lorries on the start line, and headed for the 'enemy', passed through a sudden smokescreen and after brief street fighting, 'Dieppe' was ours.

The place was West Bay and Bridport in Dorset. I drew a quick sketch of our attack and there, sure enough, you can see the platoons spread out in a web-like advance with the usual 15 feet between each man, and a large smoke canister falling from the sky among us, obviously from a mortar. With that spread there was little danger and anyway, as in the days of Blenheim and Waterloo, you could see the projectiles coming.

I remember running along by the sea wall into the town, after coming out of the smoke, seeing the landing craft, flying balloons and already backing off the beach with the Canadians embarked. Obviously they didn't want to risk a clash between the two forces (although the London Scottish were a well-educated and non-brawling species of soldiery). I had never seen a tank landing craft before and was rather surprised that we had anything so advanced, although the infantry assault craft were moored in many local waterways and presumably the reason for the continual overflights by Luftwaffe aircraft at that time.

In history books this scheme was 'Yukon II', involving mainly the Canadian 2 Div. Both McNaughton and Paget criticised the smoke cover as 'inefficient' and 'amateurish'. The last major assault on defended beaches had been at Gallipoli in 1915. The technical means of putting troops ashore had improved since then, but no one even realised the nature of the problems of successful assault, let alone solved them. The plan was Montgomery's because the assault division was from his South-Eastern Command, but no one man was really in charge and Monty was the wrong man anyway to deal with Allied forces, particularly as he would insist on treating Canadians as part of the British Army, an idea surely scotched by Vimy Ridge in 1917, when a mainly Canadian force won a notable victory and Canada came of age.

Because once given a job, he thought you should get on with it without 'bellyaching', Montgomery did not balk as the props were knocked away from the plan. There was — there had to be — a heavy preliminary bombardment to stun and overwhelm the defenders immediately before the assault; the use of heavy bombers in mass was first ruled out, partly because Air Marshal Harris said that he had neither planes nor crews to spare for useless sideshows from his prime objective of bombing Germany; and partly because there was a veto then on such bombing of French towns when weather conditions ruled out accuracy. Then the use of a battleship was ruled out because the Navy had changed its mind about the invincibility of battleships since the Prime Minister had sent two capital ships to their doom in the Far East. It is probable that political pressures lay behind the decision to go ahead in spite of the two unsatisfactory exercises.

Nevertheless, Montgomery's plan for Dieppe was similar in outline to his eventual plan for Alamein — a frontal assault on a strong defended position. Mountbatten urged attacks on the flanks rather than the head-on attack. Indeed this was the traditional way of taking a port — land on an undefended locality near by, push inland then drive round behind the port and assault from the landward side.

The Dieppe raid was postponed, then cancelled; then it was on again; but by that time Montgomery had left his 'South-Eastern Army' to become the commander of the Eighth Army in the Desert.

In retrospect, Montgomery was most fortunate in that he was shifted before the exercise could become an operation; and it seems that he himself was beginning to have doubts. If so, they were fully justified by the event, which took place on 19 August 1942. It was yet another nearly total British fiasco, of the kind the Canadians were to call a FAFU. In an adult England this can now be revealed to stand for 'Fearful Army Fuck-Up'.

The Luftwaffe followed the retreating landing craft all the way home to Portsmouth and one bomber, in trying to hit a train, blew the roof off my parents' house. The massacre of the Canadians and Commandos may — who knows? — have influenced Montgomery in the care, preparation and deception which just about turned the scales at Alamein, when combined with the heaviest bombardment of the war up to that time.

4: 'AN OBSCURE GENERAL'

> Detachments of a German expeditionary force under an
> obscure general, Rommel, have landed in North Africa.
>
> British Intelligence Summary, 1941

Leutnant Heinz Werner Schmidt read this captured document
during the last days of the campaign in Eritrea, before he was
flown out to safety. Eight days later he was face-to-face with
the obscure general in question. During the flight he had
remembered why the name was familiar. It belonged to the
leader of the so-called 'Ghost Division' which had run amok
behind French lines during the campaign of 1940.

The general was short and strongly built, his eyes blue-grey,
with a hint of humour in his face, forceful and energetic. He
did not like Schmidt's appreciation of the situation in Eritrea,
that it was bad and that there was nothing to be done about it.
He lifted his chin and glared. Then he told the young officer to
report to the Chief of Staff for a job.

So Schmidt was present when Rommel outlined his plans to
the officers, most of them wearing the black uniforms of the
Panzertruppen, highlighted by decorations won in Europe. He
spoke in bursts, pausing between sentences, abruptly and
precisely. The task of the expeditionary force now forming was
to stabilise the situation, to restore the confidence of the
Italians in victory. Tripolitania *would* be saved from the British.
The front *would* hold. To disguise their present weakness,
pending the arrival of two more promised divisions, all
German tanks already landed, plus the armour of the Italian
Ariete Division, would parade through Tripoli, to cheer up the

local population and to mislead the enemy's spies. 'Thank you, gentlemen. Heil Hitler.'

The parade took place next day, the German tanks clattering and squeaking along the streets, splinters flying, watched by surprised but silent Italians, normally an exuberant people, and to the amazement of Schmidt who had not realised that so many panzers had been landed in Africa — until he noticed a track defect on one tank which seemed to be repeated on other tanks at regular intervals; and then the penny dropped! The chosen route must be circular...

Then came the Italian armour, and what a change in the demeanour of the crowds. There was wild cheering and cries of 'Viva Italia!' Their tank commanders played up to it by assuming bold, audacious expressions. A speech by Rommel, translated sentence by sentence into Italian, followed; he was cheered only when he referred to the brave deeds of Italian troops.

The first fault Rommel found with what was to be called the DAK, the Deutsches Afrika Korps, was with their headquarters. It was in a luxurious villa with luxurious conditions, iced lemonade on tap all day and crisp white summer uniforms worn. He got them out right away; into Eastern Tripolitania, nearer to the enemy and among their own units living in spartan desert conditions, and where also the HQ was harder for the enemy air force to pin-point.

Schmidt was at the capture of Mechili when Rommel dropped in, literally, in his Fieseler Storch, a slow-flying aircraft which could put down on a sixpence and acted as his personal battle taxi, for the obscure general, soon to be famous, believed in leading from where the hottest action was and the 'front was frontest', as the Germans put it. The Germans took three British generals that day, plus their enormous command vehicles. Rommel appropriated one of them for his forward HQ. In it he found a pair of sun-and-sand goggles. 'Loot is permissible even for a general,' he said, and wore them ever after. The Rommel image was complete, preserved and projected by the photographer and reporter serving with him.

Although the British record against German and Japanese armies had been dismal thus far, rapid and hassle-free victories had been won in Italian-held territories in Africa. The Duce's boast that he offered the democracies an olive branch supported by eight million bayonets was a gross exaggeration; Italy was not ready for war, indeed it could be argued that any nation lacking coal, iron and oil will never be capable of effective war-making. Only a handful of Italian divisions were fit for war, their armour was much inferior to the British, let alone the German. Also, many Italians believed that they were fighting on the wrong side, for an atheist cause.

When the Mediterranean exploded with German violence in the spring of 1941, Ultra was but of slight positive use to the British Army and packed a decidedly negative effect as a result of the urgings of Churchill in London, based upon undigested decrypts there, for immediate aggressive action. The Prime Minister, who had played a part in the Room 40 work of the First World War, thought he had discovered through Ultra a magical means of controlling the Second. Two broad factors affected his judgements. Firstly, his instrument, the British Army, was not at that time a very good one; and secondly, he greatly overrated his own abilities as a strategist, favouring always the bold, romantic stroke of the would-be cavalryman recalling his Fuzzy-Wuzzy-fighting days in the Sudan and the bright-uniformed cannonades of his ancestor Marlborough, and ignoring the prosaic, businesslike side of real war. Indeed,

Rommel would have suited him better as a commander than Generals Wavell, Auchinleck and Montgomery.

Commanders were still generally cautious of the value of all intelligence work, as potentially unreliable and inferior to battlefield information. When you are actually in contact with a real enemy you soon get to know a great deal about him and his capabilities. And to start with, only a few top people had been indoctrinated and knew about Ultra — for valid security reasons — and most assumed just that we had a good spy on the other side. They did not realise that Ultra information came from listening to Germans talking to other Germans on an official basis.

Those who did know did not at that time understand the limitations of Ultra. Both coverage and context were often incomplete. They were getting only part of the picture from the enemy's side, by no means all of it, and a lot of the essential background might be missing. Above all, the eavesdroppers tended to assume that the Germans were always telling each other the truth, the whole truth, and nothing but the truth; and yet the fact was often otherwise. This was incredibly naive, for surely they all must have known of the old Army (and Civil Service) trick of indenting for twice what you really require in the certain knowledge that half of it will be disallowed. Or did they think that Germans were above that sort of thing?

In the event, however, no one could have guessed at the breathtaking lack of candour with which the ambitious Rommel initially regaled not only the German High Command but also the Führer, who could be far more deadly. His brief was as he had stated it to his officers: prop up the Italians, keep them in the war. His role was to be limited to no more than counter-attacks, like a hound on a leash. Hitler wanted no rash adventures to dissipate Wehrmacht strength from the imminent tremendous assault on the USSR which must decide the war. On 21 March 1941 Rommel was ordered to prepare by not later than 20 April a plan to reconquer the Italian province of Cyrenaica, in eastern Libya, from the British. The plan would then be considered by the professionals in Berlin before being approved. Rommel was not an aristocrat and had not taken the Staff College route to high command, although he had instructed at the War Academy at Potsdam and had published a book on infantry tactics. At first the British press called him 'von Rommel', in the belief that all German generals had to be high-born.

The British high command's appreciation of Rommel's situation and intentions matched that of the German high command: Cairo and Berlin were as one. He was not ready to attack, some of the divisions assigned to him had not yet even arrived in Africa. Both high commands were in for a shock.

On 31 March, nine days before the date on which his plan was to be submitted, Rommel was off. Sensing now that there was little in front of him, he took the advance elements of the Afrika Korps to the frontier of Egypt. Just as the British had swept the Italians out of Cyrenaica, so the Germans drove the British back. On 3 April Hitler advised caution, telling Rommel not to risk a counter-thrust from Benghazi and to wait for 15 Panzer Div to land. But he already had Benghazi. Tobruk however was held at General Wavell's orders by Australians, and they did not take kindly to Rommel's plan to 'bounce' them out of the port; the attempt was a minor disaster, often quoted by Rommel's opponents on the German side as an example of rashness.

In fact there were two rival theories of war conflicting not only in the desert but throughout. One was the Blitzkrieg idea

— don't worry about your own troubles, bash on regardless and make the enemy think only of his own plight. Rommel was the most prominent practitioner, but many other German commanders thought in the same way. The British idea, of which Montgomery is the best known practitioner, was the exact opposite; always keep balanced so that you are not deflected from your purpose by anything the enemy does ('a balanced army proceeds relentlessly with its task regardless of what the enemy may do'). Like Rommel, Monty had been a lecturer at a Staff College and was a thoroughgoing professional.

In this case, Rommel had judged correctly. After much contradictory advice, Wavell had been ordered by Churchill and Eden to forget about the desert; instead his small but hitherto victorious army was to be landed in Greece and to take on a great German army not yet engaged in Russia — an absurd, doomed expedition however much one needed to support the Greeks against the coming German attack. Wavell loyally supported his political masters, as soldiers are supposed to do. The Germans followed up their rapid conquest of both Yugoslavia and Greece in April 1941 by launching what was at that time the most ambitious airborne assault of the war. And here Ultra worked.

Decoded messages pointed to a build-up of air-landing and parachute troops, one division each, with bomber and fighter support, and the target as Crete. On 6 May another message hinted at 17 May as the date and named the three airfields to be attacked and captured. To preserve the security of Ultra the commander in Crete, General Freyberg, was forbidden to strengthen the airfield defences, although he was told the sense of the decoded messages. A seaborne invasion was also planned, and here the British Navy was allowed to intercept —

with fatal results to the invasion forces; although a warning of planned German air attacks on the Navy around Crete did not and could not prevent losses of ships. The air landings began on 20 May and by the end of the month Crete had fallen to airborne assault alone — but by a very narrow margin.

The result is difficult to assess because the 'garrison' of Crete consisted almost entirely of the survivors of the Greek campaign, disorganised, lacking much in the way of weapons and radios. But certainly, if only a fraction of the material lost in Greece so rashly had instead been sent to Crete, the island would have held. In crude terms, the Germans lost 6,000 men killed, wounded and missing and the British, Dominion and Greek forces 3,500 only — but they lost 12,000 men taken prisoner, defeated by a much smaller German force. For the air-landing and parachute troops, however, it was a massacre so severe that afterwards the Germans carried out only minor airborne operations, such as that in the Dodecanese in 1943 which succeeded, and that in Holland at Christmas 1944 which failed.

Full warning via Ultra had not given victory after all. But the fight put up prevented Hitler from authorising an invasion of Malta later on, when that island was a decisive factor in the savaging of Axis convoys to Rommel, and so contributed to the victory at Alamein in the following year. On the other hand, London had not been able to make up its mind about Mediterranean priorities until far too late, and then put Crete way down the list.

Ultra, together with Churchill's impulsive reading of it, played a large part in the continual British defeats in the Desert.[4] Here one has some sympathy for the Prime Minister,

---

[4] The present Churchill mythology, created partly by his firm, forcefully expressed defiance of Hitler in the aftermath of the British

locked up in London, accountable to Parliament for the conduct of the war, attempting diplomacy from a weak, indeed disintegrating hand, knowing something of war but not enough, reading decoded and decrypted German messages giving Rommel's plight — lack of tanks, lack of food, lack of fuel, lack of men — and seeing no reason not to accept all this as the whole, gospel truth.

Moving an army is rather like moving a small town, including its workshops, hospitals and so on; but notoriously Rommel disregarded this aspect of an advance, regarding it as the province of the quartermasters. A modern, missile-firing, petrol- or diesel-driven mechanised and motorised army operating in a desert waste without natural water or fuel supplies and ill-served by a road and rail network is in military technology a world away even from the disciplined Zulu impi fighting close to the kraal, in the empire-building phase of British military history with which Churchill had been acquainted when young. He has been accused of being a romantic lover of war, but it might be truer to say that he was a lover of romantic war — and cavalry charges were certainly that. His references to desert war as being like war at sea

---

disasters of 1940, partly by the version he gives in his own books, and partly no doubt due to political considerations, has resulted in the belief in a simple, lovable old bulldog. This exists in the popular mind alongside criticism openly expressed at high level in which, although his great gifts of energy, innovation and wide-ranging interests are acknowledged, these must be set against that 'restlessness' and 'constant interference' which according to Lord Selborne as early as 1923, faulted Churchill's system of control. The same criticisms are met with in the Second World War, especially from admirals and generals. For simplicity's sake, I have quoted only General Alan Brooke, CIGS, but many other senior commanders present this alternative picture of a gifted but highly-strung individual under great strain and acting too impulsively.

express the same concept — Beatty and his battlecruisers tearing into action, 30,000 tons of power going to battle at 30 m.p.h. Anything less like the tightly integrated battle group of German armour, antitank guns, artillery, infantry and soft-skinned transport which roamed the desert can hardly be imagined.

But the Germans also had a bold and coherent doctrine of war, understood by all — unlike the British with their pride channelled off into inter-Service and inter-arm rivalries of devastating unimportance. And the Germans had the means of modern command to control all this effectively — and inadvertently tell their prime enemy in London of what they intended and what were their wants requiring urgent remedy. Who can blame him if he grew impatient at what seemed to be missed chances by his own forces?

One main reason why the British high command doubted that Rommel could be ready to attack was their own experience of driving forward against Italian opposition for some 700 miles: even with small forces, the attack was difficult to sustain at such great distances. In ancient times, there used to be a saying that in desert wastes small armies met defeat and large ones starved. Even in Europe in 1944, close to the UK base, the Allied Blitzkrieg by British, Canadians and Americans slowed perceptibly after some 250-300 miles; to take just one instance, petrol tankers would tend to consume much of their useful load just moving from the base port to the forward area. And the larger the army the greater the problem and the more pressure for sizeable ports with deep-water quays. The North African ports had no great capacities. And there is one thing not widely recognised — in no Army during the Second World War did everyone ride; quite a fair proportion had to walk. All these factors together explain why the war in North Africa went back and forward across the desert with no final decision either way until Alamein. On the British side, the troops bitterly referred to the Gazala Stakes or the Benghazi Handicap.

Early in April 1941 Luftwaffe HQ in Berlin signalled that they were sending no more Junkers 88s to Tripoli as they were needed elsewhere. The code-breakers cracked this one quickly — Luftwaffe material was usually easier than Army or Navy — and Churchill thought it so important that he had a complete text sent to General Wavell, as it seemed to hint that Rommel had only weak forces and that Wavell should try his utmost to drive the Germans back. On the same day Rommel was fibbing to his Italian superiors that he had been given complete freedom of action by Berlin. This was not known in London.

The decrypts which followed all seemed to bolster Churchill's reading of the Luftwaffe message. German GHQ (OKW) reminded Rommel that his advance had been made without orders, and another intercepted message was from Rommel referring to his shortages of petrol and ammunition. On 4 May the RAF sank three ships carrying petrol and this, it was fairly assumed, must have worsened Rommel's plight.

What Ultra did *not* suggest was the basic fact: that Rommel intended to disobey his orders outright and that he intended with a handful of unacclimatised troops to race across the borders of the Italian colonies and on into Egypt. This was so totally incredible that not only did the British not believe it, but nor did the German war leadership; they sent Paulus, a senior general and also an old friend of Rommel, to Africa to restrain Rommel's impetuosity. The report Paulus made was sent by Luftwaffe Enigma and was broken. This told London that Rommel had been ordered to halt, due to the exhaustion of his men (true enough, Rommel did drive his men to total exhaustion), and that even when 15 Panzer Div arrived, he was not to advance unless ordered to, and was to prepare a layback defensive position at Gazala. Anyone reading this could hardly be blamed for thinking that Rommel was unlikely to advance and might be ripe for counter-attack.

This was exactly what Churchill urged on General Wavell on 5 May, and on the 7th he reminded him that he was being sent in the 'Tiger' convoy due to arrive on the 12th more than 200 new tanks which he playfully referred to as his 'Tiger Cubs'. Clearly Churchill did not realise the poor condition in which these tanks arrived nor, even when repaired, their inferiority to the German armour and vulnerability to the 88-mm flak guns which Rommel was using as extremely effective anti-tank weapons. Even in 1944 these still tended to dominate the battlefield and decimate even the improved and modernised Allied armour.

Although these new tanks were not ready until workshops had been able to repair deficiencies, Wavell ordered General 'Strafer' Gott to attack Rommel on 15 May with what it is now clear was insufficient preparation. That offensive met the repulse it deserved. Churchill would not accept this verdict and at the Prime Minister's urging, in mid-June Wavell launched Operation 'Battleaxe', which was also defeated.

British intelligence via Ultra was simply inadequate. It gave no idea of what Rommel actually intended, nor did it at this stage of the war, because German Army Enigma could not yet be read, give full information of Rommel's strength in tanks, a key factor. At the same time, unknown to the British, German Intelligence was highly efficient and gave the Germans an accurate picture of the situation on the British side.

There were two ingredients here. From the start in 1939 the Germans had realised how much information could be had from listening to ordinary operational radio traffic and how over a period of time experienced staff could become highly proficient at reading the enemy's mind in this way. The information could be classed rather as tactical than strategic (for want of a better definition) and in Britain is sometimes referred to as the 'Y' Service. The CO of Rommel's radio intelligence unit was Hauptmann Alfred Seebohm, who soon developed brilliant skills, aided by British chatter made in bland ignorance that an intelligent enemy was listening and — worse — understanding.

For the high-level strategic information, Rommel had to wait a little longer. There are two stories regarding this. The first tells that the beginning was in Rome in August 1941, when an old and trusted Italian servant working in the American Embassy stole or copied a key to the safe which held the details of the American Black Code (so called because the documents were bound in black), which Italian agents were thus able to extract, copy and return unnoticed. A rival story from the German side says that it was not the Italian spies who gave the Axis the code but its breaking by German experts in the autumn of 1941.

From Rommel's viewpoint the most important man who used the broken Black Code was an American military attaché in Cairo, Colonel Bonner Frank Fellers. The Colonel was not of course a spy in the pay of the Germans, but he might just as well have been, for his duty was to transmit to Washington full information including the substance of British briefings at the highest level. Taken together, Seebohm and Fellers kept Rommel fully informed on enemy capacities and intentions for almost a year.

When one couples this with the realisation that London's information via Ultra during the same period was singularly partial and ineffective and that the Prime Minister, on inadequate information, was ordering his Middle East commanders to carry out unwise or impossible moves, one can hardly be surprised that the sacking of the first Commander-in-Chief, Wavell, and his substitution by Auchinleck produced no improvement, or that Churchill became even more enraged. As the British Army had many serious defects, this is understandable; but it was unwise. Some of the defects were of material and could have been remedied; simply urging all-out offence was no substitute for patient enquiry and clear thought. But by this time, so badly had the war gone for Britain that Churchill's own position had been in doubt.

5: UNCONQUERED ISLAND

The German armed forces had a military, battery-operated improved version of the commercial Enigma machine invented by Arthur Scherbius, himself a German, in the 1920s. The Italian Navy used a modification of the commercially available Swedish C38 machine. This had first been intercepted in December 1940. From the summer of 1941 the British had broken into the cypher which carried the bulk of the Axis radio traffic concerning their Mediterranean shipping. In conjunction with continued possession of the island of Malta as an air, sea and undersea base athwart the Axis supply lines to North Africa, this knowledge was vital if good use could be made of it; and it was.

The British Navy was always certain that Malta dockyard was essential and that the island must be held; between the wars there was much discussion about building underground fuel tanks and other secure installations. The RAF proclaimed Malta helpless before the Italian bombers which could be based on the much larger island of Sicily only 30 minutes' flying time away (at 1930s cruising speeds). The Army believed that Malta, heavily fortified in the sixteenth century, could not resist a modern invader. All this on the basis that Italy would be the main enemy and that the French Mediterranean fleet would be fighting on the same side as the British. Because of the divergence of views, the island was not abandoned but neither was it adequately prepared for defence. Its survival, when France fell and the French Navy was neutralised, was consequently of a hair's-breadth nature.

In practice, Malta was at its most dangerous to the enemy (now German as well as Italian) and at least risk when the battles in North Africa swept westward across the desert towards Tripoli, for then the island came within range of fighter cover; and it was possession of the airfields which was the chief prize of desert victory to either side. When Rommel swept forward to the Egyptian frontier and beyond, Malta became isolated and vulnerable; for a time in 1942 without power to hurt.

The battle raged back and forth across the desert half-a-dozen times in two years of conflict:

Dec. 1940-Feb. 1941: WESTWARD to El Agheila[5] (Wavell & O'Connor)
April 1941: EASTWARD to Egypt (Rommel)
Nov. 1941-Jan. 1942: WESTWARD to El Agheila (Auchinleck)
Jan.-Feb. 1942: EASTWARD to Gazala (Rommel)
May-July 1942: EASTWARD into Egypt (Rommel)
Oct.-Nov. 1942: WESTWARD towards Tripoli (Montgomery)

Only the final westward offensive overrode the inherent braking effect of trying to support winning-size forces at a great distance from local bases.

A further logistic factor was the distances and difficulties of supply from home bases to forward bases in Africa. When Britain had only the Italians to face, resupply to Egypt could be through the Mediterranean past the mid-sea base of Malta; later supplies had to come some 12,000 miles round southern Africa. For the Afrika Korps resupply from Germany was less than simple, either via mountainous Italy or via the rugged

---

[5] A strongpoint west of Benghazi.

Balkans and Greece, and then by sea, where it was open to Ultra-directed jabs at Axis shipping by submarines, surface craft or the RAF and Fleet Air Arm.

In October 1941 Force K arrived at Malta to take advantage of the new source of information, camouflaged by sending out reconnaissance aircraft to make apparently the initial sighting of the convoys. Even so, the interceptions seemed miraculous. The force was small and compact — the two light cruisers *Aurora* and *Penelope*, fast, new and well-armed, and the two excellent 'L' class destroyers, *Lance* and *Lively*. This action had been taken as the result of two messages. On 23 August the C.-in-C. Mediterranean had made a suggestion which had crossed with a brisk minute by the Prime Minister to Admiral Pound in London made the previous day. Ultra's value for military intelligence was still doubtful and incomplete, but supply ship sailings, routes and ports of arrival, with timings, were simple and obvious. Winston Churchill asked the First Sea Lord to ask the C.-in-C. Mediterranean what he was going to do about it, bearing in mind that there was still a war on. It was an unnecessarily rude message, particularly as the cruisers required had to come out from the UK.

Force K's first two runs towards Benghazi, the main port serving the Axis in North Africa, were fruitless. The third, when they again sailed from Malta on a Saturday, was led as usual by Captain Agnew in the *Aurora*. The sailing was at very short notice, and unusually unwelcome in the *Penelope* because her bridge had just been painted light green and the paint was still wet. The crew were told that a Maryland aircraft had sighted six merchant ships escorted by four destroyers 40 miles east of Cape Spartivento at 1400 hours that day, 9 November 1941. Then they were told that the radio of the aircraft which was to guide them to the target had broken down and so they 'went dashing into the night without much hope of success' according to a book written by her ship's company, subject to wartime censorship, which I bought in the year of publication, 1943.

The captains of all four ships had discussed the best means for annihilating such a convoy, and therefore *Aurora* made three signals only on sighting. 'Enemy bearing 030°', 'Reduce speed', and 'Don't waste ammunition.' Captain Agnew stalked the enemy by leading round to the north to silhouette them against the moon, relying on the recently applied light camouflage to hide his ships until they came to within 6,000 yards.

The cruisers first engaged the Italian destroyers steaming astern of the convoy, and then deliberately exterminated the merchant ships. These seemed to burst into flames the moment they were hit. A tanker turned into a furnace-like wall of flame, an ammunition ship produced a vivid firework display before blowing up. Soon the night was lit by the flames of eight burning vessels, with a great pall of smoke marking the grave of the ammunition ship.

The anonymous author in *Penelope* admitted: 'Of course, we were lucky... Lucky in finding the enemy... particularly lucky in having a task that was successful for our first taste of action.' They also found that there was less new green paint on the bridge, but quite a lot of it on their uniforms. Back in harbour, the Padre said prayers of thanksgiving and they prayed for the men they had killed and those they had had to leave in the water. Force K as a whole had suffered only a few men wounded and in *Penelope* the casualties were 'limited to six canaries, who died of heart failure when the guns fired.' Later drafts of canaries were tougher and sang defiantly during violent actions.

Another convoy was intercepted on 24 November and *Penelope*, being nearest when a column of smoke was sighted over the horizon, did the job alone. The escorting destroyers screened the two merchantmen with smoke, darting in and out again to fire at the cruiser, but hitting her only with shell splinters; totally outgunned, eventually they had to leave the cargo ships to be sunk at leisure; both caught fire and drifted, blazing furiously, with frequent explosions, so were probably carrying ammunition as well as petrol. Churchill sent a special signal to Captain Agnew, congratulating the force on the 'very valuable part they had taken in the great battle now raging in Libya'.

Early in December they went out again on a successful interception and sank a supply ship, a large tanker and the gallant Italian destroyer *Alvise da Mosto*, which engaged both cruisers and on being hit by salvoes from both, blew up and sank with all hands.

On 21 March 1942 Force K sailed to bring in another convoy to the island, for Malta itself had to be supplied constantly with fuel, ammunition, torpedoes and spare gun barrels for its ships and aircraft, ammunition for its own guns, food, and the thousand miscellaneous items a garrison needs. Two days previously the island had acclaimed the arrival of Spitfires, a fighter in the same class as the Messerschmitt 109 (the latest mark, the 109F, was now coming into service in the Mediterranean). This day they witnessed a portent — a massed raid by the Luftwaffe from its many dispersed bases in Sicily only 50 miles to the north. The British crews thronged upper decks in the harbour to watch. An apparently endless pattern of bombers passed over amid the puffs of shellbursts and the bright streaks of tracer bullets; huge dust clouds rose up from the target, obviously an aerodrome.

The last British victory, for some time to come, had been on 13 December off Cape Bon, in Tunisia, when four destroyers directed by Ultra ambushed two Italian cruisers, the *Alberto di Giussano* and the *Alberico da Barbiano*, lying in wait for them inshore, where they were unseen against the background of the land. Both cruisers were carrying a deck cargo of cased petrol for Rommel, relying on speed and stealth; both were torpedoed, caught fire and sank. An American diplomat reported the nearby beaches strewn with corpses afterwards.

Force K did not take part because of lack of fuel, but shortly afterwards lost a cruiser and a destroyer when the force ran into a minefield. This was but one of a series of British reverses at sea. To aid Rommel, Hitler sent U-boats to the Mediterranean; in November they sank the aircraft carrier *Ark Royal* and the battleship *Barham*, the latter with heavy loss of life. In December Italian frogmen riding underwater vehicles immobilised inside Alexandria harbour the two battleships *Queen Elizabeth* and *Valiant*, the depth being too shallow to allow them to disappear beneath the waves. In February 1942 a relief convoy for Malta from Alexandria was turned back; in March two ships out of another Alexandria convoy got through but were bombed and sunk in harbour before their cargoes could be fully unloaded — a black mark for the British organisers, which *Penelope*'s diarist was not allowed to mention in 1943 but was not overlooked by the official RAF historian in 1975, who recorded that the Malta RAF descended on the two ships and removed all cargo consigned to them with praiseworthy rapidity. When the ships were sunk by the bombers, only 5,000 tons out of 26,000 tons had been unloaded.

Some may regard this as indolence, others as a stubborn stupidity in refusing to accept any possibility of defeat and therefore thoroughly praiseworthy. London cannot have been amused.

The 'great battle now raging in Libya', brought about by Churchill's impatience, did not go well; Malta's isolation increased. German technical assistance to Italy's anti-submarine forces resulted in considerable improvements and, finally, the mining by German E-boats of the approach channels to Malta's naval harbours, combined with German air superiority, which meant that they could not be swept, spelt a temporary end to the operations of the British 10th Submarine Flotilla from Malta. On 26 April 1942 the submarines began to leave and were not to return until July. The surface ships, including the badly damaged *Penelope*, were also forced to depart. Few aircraft now remained operational on the island.

The campaign against the Axis sea routes waged by the 10th Submarine Flotilla from Malta ranks as one of the most intense undersea conflicts so far. Losses were high. Wanklyn's *Upholder* almost certainly fell victim to the improved Italian escorts while engaging a convoy for Benghazi in April. Others simply did not return. In one case there was a single survivor to tell the tale, so far as he knew it.

Perseus was patrolling north of the Greek island of Zante in the Ionian Sea, after an unsuccessful attack. Just before midnight on 6 December she struck a mine which broke the submarine's back and sent her 170 feet to the bottom in a steep plunge canted over to starboard. Of course, the lights were out, and the crew were hurled forward and to one side before she struck the seabed and settled nearly upright.

Leading Stoker Capes and five others were still alive in one compartment. With the aid of a torch they unclipped the hatch and rigged the escape trunking which should allow them to get out one by one. While this was going on the hull began to list to starboard and only two men now showed signs of life. The emergency breathing sets supplied oxygen, which rapidly has toxic effects much below 30 feet, and they were at 170. Capes got clear of the shattered, listing hull at a depth when even the Greek seas are dark or at best twilit by day, and then remained sufficiently in control of himself to unfurl the apron of the set which acted as a water brake to prevent too rapid an ascent, which can be fatal, particularly near the surface. On the way up, still 15 feet down, he passed a moored mine. On the surface, which he reached without bursting his lungs, Capes found himself alone; and then, the sole survivor and in the middle of the night, began the ten-mile swim to shore. The Greeks on Cephalonia sheltered him until he was picked up by a caique in June 1943.

The great battle demanded by the Prime Minister had taken place and movement in the desert was rapid — but in the wrong direction. Preparations were begun for the evacuation of the fleet from Alexandria and the demolition of the base. On 29 June the 14,650-ton submarine depot ship *Medway* and the Greek submarine depot ship *Corinthia* left for Haifa in Palestine at *Medway*'s best ten knots, escorted by the cruiser *Dido* and seven destroyers. Next morning U.372 put two or three torpedoes into the lumbering *Medway*, hitting the engine room and cutting off electrical power. Seventeen minutes later, she rolled over and sank, taking 30 men down with her. Forty-seven of her store of 90 scarce torpedoes floated to the surface and were picked up by the escorts.

WRNS are not supposed to go to sea in wartime, but there was one on board *Medway*, Third Officer A. S. Coningham. She gave up her life-jacket to a rating who was struggling in the water. The gallant Wren survived.

Vic Henley was an able seaman at this time aboard the auxiliary *Glenroy*, lying in Alexandria after being torpedoed while carrying Australian soldiers to Tobruk. They could hear the desert guns and were told that if the Germans broke through their task was to sink the *Glenroy* in the harbour entrance. The signal to block the harbour would be the sight of the floating dock leaving Alexandria. The fast 'Glen' ships, together with the *Breconshire*, made many hazardous runs through Luftwaffe-dominated sea space, and the *Breconshire* still lies off Malta.

Howard Ogle, who was in Malta dockyard during the siege, recalled priority supplies being brought in by the fast minelayers *Welshman* and *Manxman*. Now, hundreds of soldiers were assembled to unload them at once, covered by smokescreens, with Germans bombers aiming into the smoke. Once a smokescreen drifted over a Maltese village with regrettable results; the airmen took it to be shrouding the fast supply ships. By now Malta had received 25 times the tonnage of bombs delivered on Coventry and they were high explosive, for the buildings of Malta, of concrete on iron girders to resist earthquakes, could not be fired so easily as those in British or German cities.

Rations, even for Service people, were reduced still further. One tin of bully beef among three men per day; half a small loaf per man per day, one egg every fortnight, one slice of bacon every five days. Matches were split in four and everyone tried to light from someone else's cigarette. The Maltese — those who were not serving in the ships or at the guns that is — took shelter in underground tunnels, some of them new, others as old as Christ or even prehistoric.

By mid-April 1942 the number of fighters serviceable had been reduced to six, the guns were reduced to 15 rounds per barrel per day. The dockyard and the airfields were a wilderness, the great city of Valletta, rising between the Grand Harbour on one side where in peace the battleships, aircraft carriers and cruisers moored, and Marsamuscetto Harbour on the other side where the destroyers lay and the submarine base was, showed broken walls like exposed bones. On some days, the great dust clouds rising from the bombed buildings reached prodigious heights and drifted away for miles across the blue Mediterranean.

Ultra became progressively less useful; warning of air attack was either too short or there was too little force to take advantage of it. Italian C38 gave advance notice of a southbound Italian convoy; it was attacked unsuccessfully and five of the few strike aircraft remaining in Malta were lost for no gain. That was on 14 April. On 10 May four destroyers were sailed from Alexandria without air cover in a desperate attempt to ravage a similar southbound convoy; two days later the German Fliegerkorps X sank three of them in an attack revealed too late through Luftwaffe Enigma.

The invasion of Malta was thought by London to be a possibility, somewhat on the lines of the successful conquest of Crete by airborne troops. The Luftwaffe build-up in Sicily and the escalation of the bombing perhaps pointed that way; so too did rumours obtained from POW interrogation and diplomatic sources, and there was talk of troop movements in southern Italy. But there were contra-indications — air reconnaissance revealed no significant signs of invasion preparations; Sigint generally showed nothing positive. The British staff concluded that only if the Luftwaffe's assault failed to neutralise Malta might the enemy contemplate trying to capture the island.

This was believed until on 7 February 1942, Luftwaffe Enigma revealed that Fliegerkorps XI was setting up a supply base in Reggio Calabria, in southern Italy. Fliegerkorps XI was the formation of parachute, air-landing and glider-borne troops which had conquered Crete in little over a week the previous year. Further information from Luftwaffe Enigma revealed that General Ramcke, who had fought in Crete, was now in Rome and there were indications that parachute units were being moved from the Russian front. Another source altogether claimed that Hitler had ordered the capture of Malta in April. But air reconnaissance continued to show no signs of invasion preparations; nor did signals traffic hint at it.

In May there were direct references from decrypts: an 'intended operation' had been postponed and as a consequence a particular battalion should be retained in North Africa. A second decrypt even revealed the code name, referring to 'exercises in connection with Operation "Hercules"' which required the return to Italy of two ferry barges. What did this mean?

Wireless code-breaking was not enough. Germans and Italians were indeed discussing an invasion of Malta, but they were doing it face-to-face (with no Allied flies on the wall) or by landline (which the Allies could not tap). All that went over the air was partial, incomplete, useless.

'Smiling Albert' Kesselring, commanding all Luftwaffe units in the Mediterranean, believed that bombarding Malta was not enough; the island had to be taken. Admiral Raeder, head of the German Navy, thought so too. On 12 March 1942 he put the matter to Hitler, who explained that the Italians were already planning such an expedition. He would shortly be discussing this with the Duce, and clearly the Luftwaffe must take part, one way or another.

Rommel himself had originally agreed with this, but his success over Auchinleck's forces encouraged him to believe that, with the supplies and reinforcements now reaching him across the Mediterranean, he could capture Egypt. The British, quite properly, had plans for that eventuality; they were prepared to lose Cairo, even Alexandria, because the really vital area to hold was that of Abadan and the oilfields. They therefore had to be concerned with the French in Syria and the Persians in Iran, then as now an unstable area. Little-known battles were taking place there. The great chimera of course was that the German armies now driving for the Caucasus might meet another German army under Rommel in a vast (and probably impossible) pincer movement. Off centre stage was the fall of the Italian naval base on the Red Sea, Massawa in 1941; soon to be available to take the great convoys of soldiers, guns, armour and supplies sent out on the 12,000-mile journey from England round the Cape to reinforce the Eighth Army.

In late April Spitfires on reconnaissance over Sicily began to report construction of exceptionally long runways on the plain of Catania; by 10 May three such strips had been completed. Clearly, they were for the use of gliders and their tugs. Mussolini had visited Hitler at the Berghof at the end of April to co-ordinate operations; but the Allies had no microphones in Hitler's mountain home. Face-to-face they decided the order of attack, there being insufficient forces to prevail everywhere. Operation 'Theseus' in May or June — complete the capture of Cyrenaica. Operation 'Herkules' in July or August — the capture of Malta. Next, date unspecified — invade Egypt and drive to the Nile and the Suez Canal.

Kesselring's bombers — up to 300 sorties a day — almost but not quite neutralised Malta. But they did serve to take much of the pressure off Rommel's supply routes. And Rommel now thought he could reach Cairo without waiting for

Malta to be captured. Apart from some harbour craft, virtually the only vessel which could move was HMS *Beryl*, a 90-ton coal-burning converted trawler turned minesweeper. When *Penelope* was bombed in dock, *Beryl* was steaming up and down the creek making smoke to hide her from the bombers. The fuel tanks on the Marsa at the end of Grand Harbour had been destroyed and no fuel was coming in, but there was enough coal for her to sweep the entrance and make approach less hazardous for the handful of fast ships or supply submarines to risk the mines. They brought only top-priority cargoes in limited quantities. What faced Malta was not so much invasion as paralysis from lack of supplies and then surrender from starvation. Another convoy had to be got in even if the cost was exorbitant.

The strain on the British Navy was intense. For political reasons — in case Stalin might make another pact with Hitler — Churchill ordered convoys to sail to Russia even during the summer when days were long and losses must be heaviest; militarily it was madness, but the Prime Minister ordered it. Then there was the need to reinforce the remnants of the Far East fleet. It had always been likely that if Britain went to war with Germany both countries might be ruined and the British Empire in Asia left immediately at the mercy of Japan. Now the worst had happened.

The Luftwaffe too was stretched. Hitler found that he needed more aircraft for the Eastern front, more bombers for revenge raids on England, more bombers and fighters to support the Afrika Korps. Spitfires flown into Malta took toll of the Luftwaffe also, though their own losses were heavy. Reichsmarschall Goring became impatient with Malta. Adolf Galland, general of the fighters, was ordered to Naples as were all the unit leaders, to hear the Reichsmarschall playing the old song he had sung during the Battle of Britain — it's all the fault of the fighters that we lose so many bombers, they aren't aggressive enough. There were harsh words spoken. It must be the fault of the fighters, it couldn't be that the high command had fundamentally miscalculated. Great war leaders are never wrong.

On the British side a similar but if possible even more absurd conflict was being argued out, with Ultra (then highly imperfect) as grounds for it. Whitehall was trying to claim, on inadequate and incomplete evidence — and most acrimoniously — that Rommel had so few tanks that the Eighth Army ought to attack now if not before and overwhelm him. Cairo argued that he probably had more than that, if you took into account — for they could not now be counted, the British having retreated — the number of disabled German tanks repaired on the battlefield and put back into action. And you must add into the equation the fact that British tanks were inferior to German tanks and required a numerical superiority to offset this: and don't forget, the Italians had some tanks too. The Prime Minister, perhaps rightly, ignored the probable 138-odd tanks of the Littorio Division and told Cairo that as the enemy had 100-110 tanks forward and the British 160, with substantial superiority in the air, what was keeping them? In fact, Rommel was now obtaining substantial tank reinforcements across the Mediterranean, but the German Army Enigma which would have revealed this had not at this time been broken. This was irritable guesswork, both in Cairo and in London, but the dispute went on pointlessly for many months in the spring of 1942.

Even when at last one of the appropriate codes had been broken, this did not stop the vendetta which had developed between Churchill and Auchinleck. GC & CS in England were able in April to read half the traffic with a delay of a week or more between Rommel's HQ and his supply bases in Africa and Europe and to Berlin. Two tank returns were read, the first referring merely to 161 unspecified serviceable tanks, far below Cairo's estimate of what Rommel must have according to reconnaissance, including that on the ground by the Long Range Desert Group (LRDG), which actually saw the tanks they counted. The second return was dated the following day, 22 April, and was closer to Cairo's ideas (although not to Churchill's): 264 German tanks, helpfully broken down into types, for while the Mark IIIs and Mark VIs were formidable the Mark IIs were not, plus a round figure for Italian tanks of 151. Grand total 415 for Rommel. But this did not stop the Prime Minister firing off a personal signal to his Commander-in-Chief, throwing in his face the unspecified 161 German tanks (compared to Cairo's accurate estimate of 265 runners and 45 in workshops: a total of 310 for Rommel without counting Italian armour).

This illustrates how misleading partial and unspecified evidence can be; and also how unwise it is to feud with subordinates. From this time, although his estimates were right and later confirmed by better Ultra, Auchinleck was doomed in Churchill's eyes. But that Malta at this time was on a knife-edge of risk, there could be no doubt; and the Prime Minister was determined not to lose one more fortress of the British Empire.

In June 1942 a double convoy was run to Malta: one of six merchant ships from Gibraltar to the west and one of 11 merchant ships from Egypt in the east. The hope was that the enemy might concentrate on one and so let the other through. The hope was vain. The Italian Navy, a much better service equipped with well-designed modern ships, was not to be compared to the Italian Army with its poor little tanks. The British now had no operational battleships left in the eastern Mediterranean; *Queen Elizabeth* and *Valiant* were sitting on the bottom of Alexandria harbour, whereas Italy had fast modern battleships plus rebuilt older capital ships which the British could only oppose with cruisers now. It was not realised how much the big Italian ships were in practice hampered by shortages of fuel.

The 11 merchant ships sailed from Egypt with an escort of seven cruisers, 26 destroyers, some corvettes and a submarine screen of nine boats out and the old demilitarised *Centurion*, a pre-First World War battleship converted to a radio-controlled target vessel, lumbering along behind pretending to be a real battleship to frighten the opposition. To combat the Italian battle fleet was a small force of shipping-strike aircraft. The result was an Axis victory.

The convoy never reached Malta. It was turned back with the loss of one cruiser, three destroyers and two merchant ships sunk plus three cruisers, one corvette, three merchant ships and the old *Centurion* damaged during two days of German air attack.

One of the Stuka pilots was Hans Drescher, Staffelkapitan of 5 Staffel II. SG3, specialising in pin-point accuracy in support of the Afrika Korps, usually against tanks, trucks and guns. They were now equipped with the JU 87D, in which the rear-gunner handled twin machine-guns instead of the single gun which made such a poor show against the heavily armed fighters of the British and the South Africans. Drescher himself had been shot down on 29 May 1942 by a Curtiss fighter after an attack on British tanks near Tobruk; he crashed near a British A.A. battery and was taken prisoner, but escaped that night while being driven to a POW camp.

On 14 and 15 June 1942 he led his Staffel in attack after attack on the relief convoy south of Crete, claiming hits on an 8,000-ton ship, a cruiser and a smaller ship. They usually operated as a Gruppe consisting of three Staffeln of nine planes each plus a staff flight with three planes. The complete Schlachtgeschwader was made up of three Gruppen.

> Mediterranean convoys were reported to us by reconnaissance. The merchant ships, protected by cruisers and destroyers, always travelled in the centre of the convoy. It was our task to sink those, so we approached high up at about 5,000 metres. After we had established the position of the ships we wanted to attack, we eased out into a loose chain, line ahead, and when we met the enemy flak we began to weave towards the centre of the convoy, losing a little height all the time, before finally diving on various merchant ships, each unit taking its turn, with one 500-kilogramme bomb per plane. When we had dropped our bomb, we evaded the flak by flying very low over the sea. We always estimated that we would have five to ten per cent losses during such attacks against ships.

Although it was the Stukas which inflicted the ship losses, the distant presence of the Italian fleet was the main factor in the decision to abandon the hopeless enterprise, although the RAF strike aircraft intervened with some effect.

During 13, 14 and 15 June RAF aircraft were out searching, having been moved forward to Malta as a base (the Stukas were flying from Derna in North Africa). On the 15th, 217 Squadron Beauforts from Malta crippled the 10,000-ton cruiser *Trento*, watched by the as yet unnamed British U-class submarine P 35. With periscope up, her CO found himself 'in the centre of a fantastic circus of wildly careering capital ships, cruisers and destroyers ... of tracer shell streaks and anti-aircraft bursts'. He was tempted to keep his periscope up and just watch open-mouthed, but submerged and sank the crippled ship shortly after. In this chaos the Beaufort crews thought they had also hit both the battleships but were mistaken.

Four-motor Liberators, most with American crews, were sent out from North Africa and one of these hit the battleship *Littorio*, 35,000 tons, on her forward turret, the most heavily protected part of the ship, and did little damage. 38 Squadron despatched a flight of Wellington ICs carrying two Mark XII torpedoes to Malta on 11 June to take part in the hunt for the Italian Navy. For H. A. (Bertie) Taylor it was his first operation, his pilot being Flying Officer Michael Foulis. They twice drew blanks and once made an interception, which Taylor found exciting:

> I remember the attack quite vividly, possibly because in my previous 20 years no one had shot at me in anger! Mike found the fleet (about 3 large vessels and 6 destroyers as I remember) and went in low over the destroyer screen. They opened up, as did the capital ships, but he held his position and dropped his torpedo, and escaped below the flak. I learned at that moment that I was a mere beginner at the art of low flying.
>
> He then circled to attack again by which time a destroyer was laying a smokescreen on the down moon side (we always attacked with the target silhouetted by the moon). That did not deter Mike in the slightest; he simply went in through the smokescreen as though he could see through it (which I certainly couldn't), got right down on the deck and ran in with all hell breaking loose. I am not certain when he dropped that torpedo but I do remember looking up at a battleship as we shot past it.

A hit was scored by 38 Squadron on the *Littorio*, the torpedo being dropped by Pilot Officer Hawes. But for one cruiser sunk and one battleship damaged, the Italian Navy had nevertheless done its job and turned back the eastern convoy.

The relief convoy from Gibraltar consisted of only six merchant ships with a heavy escort initially until the Sicilian narrows were reached: the vintage battleship *Malaya*, the old aircraft carriers *Eagle* and *Argus*, three cruisers, 17 destroyers. Air attacks began off Tunisia, with one merchant ship sunk and the cruiser *Liverpool* damaged by an air torpedo. When the covering force turned back at the narrows, the Malta Beaufighters took over — a handful against the massed power on the Sicilian airfields dominating the final stretch. Two Italian cruisers and five of their destroyers were sighted; and were attacked by five British destroyers which made smoke to screen the convoy. An Italian cruiser and one destroyer were damaged, as were two British destroyers. Stukas of a special anti-shipping strike force sank a merchant ship and damaged another when, low on fuel, the Malta Spitfires had to leave. Finally there were only four merchant ships left afloat, two of them crippled. To save the others, the cripples were sunk after their crews had been taken off. In what should have been the swept channel on the final approach to Valletta, five destroyers hit mines; one was lost but the other four struggled into harbour. Malta could hold out for just a little longer.

A factor in Malta's survival was a division of opinion in the German camp. Rommel had previously agreed with the general all-service consensus that the capture of Malta must precede final victory in Africa, for in German hands its effect would be decisive. The Luftwaffe commander in the southern Mediterranean, Field Marshal Kesselring, still believed that; but Rommel, finding that he had Auchinleck's army apparently routed and in flight, changed his mind. One more push, and he might be in Cairo (although Mussolini would insist on taking the credit).

Consequently the forces gathered for Operation 'Herkules' — the capture of Malta — were diverted to the Afrika Korps instead. They included the German parachutists of General Ramcke's brigade and the Italian parachutists of the Folgore Division whom the British, to their surprise, found to be of high quality. Italian formations praised by the Germans included, as well as the Folgore, the Young Fascist Division and the Ariete Armoured Division. Whether or not the German and Italian airborne forces could have succeeded in taking Malta is another matter; they would have had to be supported by follow-up seaborne forces, a matter of great technical difficulty when facing a large, battle-experienced garrison instead of a mass of khaki-clad refugees as in Crete. I lived in Malta for two and a half years during my childhood; the ancient fortifications still appeared formidable, and when I revisited the island with a diving expedition in 1985, fifty years later, with the benefit of ten years' service with the British and Canadian armies, the maze of fields hemmed in by stone walls impressed me as a tough nut for lightly armed infantry to crack. That 'Herkules', if tried, would have succeeded, seems highly questionable.

The opposite policy, which was Rommel's and was tried, definitely failed. As Staffelkapitan Hans Drescher noted:

> The position of the English at El Alamein could no longer be penetrated. This made it possible for the British to make their strategic position of Malta completely capable of defence once more and to destroy the German supply routes for Africa. The basic principle of Rommel's plan — which depended on sufficient reinforcement — became invalid.

'You have to hand it to Jerry, he's a stubborn old bastard,' was a typical Normandy comment on the German Army fighting against long odds. The Germans might have said the same about the British defending Malta. When the Germans relaxed their attacks even slightly, immediate advantage was taken of it. The old governor had gone and a new governor, Lord Gort, had taken over; Malta itself had been awarded the George Cross. The submarines of the 10th Flotilla, which had left in April, were coming back at the end of July, although because pre-war parsimony had prevented the construction of submarine pens in the easily cut rock faces, submarines in harbour had to spend their time submerged to lessen the risk of damage by bombers. Blast pens and shelters for the aircraft, bomb dumps, fuel and personnel had been hastily built on and around the airfields. Ethelred was no longer entirely unready, even though such veterans as the carriers *Eagle* and *Argus*, which should have been in a museum for historic ships, had had to be resurrected for convoy escort duties. But despite all this, the threat of surrender forced by starvation was soon only one or two weeks away.

The Prime Minister was well aware of it, as was the Navy. At all costs fuel, ammunition and food had to be got through in quantities, with the odds all against the ships because Rommel held the nearest North African airfields. So the epic convoy of all time sailed for Malta from Gibraltar in August. It was as much an epic of the Merchant Navy as of the Royal Navy, with the pick of the modern fast merchantmen selected, three of them American, and massively escorted for much of the way by two redoubtable battleships, *Nelson* and *Rodney*, each with nine 16-inch guns, plus three aircraft carriers, six cruisers and 24 destroyers now available from the Home Fleet after the fatal PQ 17 convoy to Murmansk.

James Reid Forbes sailed as a young petty officer in one of the escorting light cruisers, the 33-knot, 5,450-ton *Sirius* armed with ten 5.25-inch guns. She commissioned at Portsmouth in May 1942, acquiring a horde of big black Portsmouth rats and a suppression force of two cats named Taganrog and Stuttgart; on their first trials in the Solent they were attacked by an Me 109, so their initial battle experience was in June. When fully worked up they went north to Scapa Flow, base of the Home Fleet, then out into the Atlantic in July to join the escort to PQ 17, which was shortly withdrawn and the convoy told to 'scatter' from what proved to be a non-existent threat: an object lesson in how not to interpret intelligence material. Only 11 out of 35 merchant ships reached the Soviet Union, the rest were sunk.

From this Admiralty fiasco and the cold of Iceland they were sent south to the Mediterranean heat in August to join at Gibraltar the escort for the 'Pedestal' convoy to Malta; and there many of the crew became incapacitated by sunburn, a disciplinary offence in all Services, but rather unfair in a Navy which was shifting you about between contrasting climates. To ensure secrecy they sailed from Gibraltar at two in the morning, to find in the Straits outside thousands of little lights — the Spanish fishing fleet, doubtless reporting by radio to the enemy.

The vicissitudes of 'Pedestal' have been the subject of books. Forbes's recollections are of a great force led by the three aircraft carriers and flanked by the two battleships, and a spirit of determination. The *Eagle* torpedoed — a huge carrier heeling over, figures sliding down her deck. Another carrier, the *Indomitable*, burning. A horde of torpedo bombers attacking, the *Rodney* opening up on them with her 16-inch guns, so that the pilots had to fly through an inferno of splinters and huge gouts of water.

> The convoy never faltered, not even to pick up survivors. We brought an Italian submarine to the surface and massacred them all, didn't pick any of them up. It was a grim time in the war. Sink, burn, destroy. A kind of madness came over us at that time. The *Nelson*, *Rodney* and the remaining carrier had to return. It was a pitiful sight to see the convoy go on in the dusk off Cape Bon.

Now attacks came upon the convoy with its reduced escort from all directions. Only one merchant ship had been damaged so far. Then came U-boats, German dive bombers and torpedo bombers, and during the night Italian motor torpedo boats. Of the three cruisers, the Germans got the *Nigeria*, damaged and forced to turn back; the Italians sank the *Manchester* and four merchantmen, damaging a fifth. One day's steaming close to the Sicilian airfields separated the remainder from Malta. When ships were damaged they slowed, and soon the convoy was a convoy no longer but a procession of scattered, limping ships. Some were damaged again and again, stopped, repaired damage, carried on; and were hit again. And again. The cruiser *Kenya* was damaged also, the A.A. cruiser *Cairo* sunk. But four cargo ships reached Malta, together with the American oil tanker *Ohio*, very nearly broken-backed, assisted by tugs and a destroyer. Her British master, Captain Mason, received a well-deserved George Cross. And Malta was saved.

Naval historians tend to regard this convoy as the turning-point in the war. Petty Officer Forbes thought otherwise. A few months later *Sirius* was in Bone in Algeria, as a base for harassing Rommel's convoys; but now the Afrika Korps was retreating, and for the first time in the war Forbes saw something he had never seen before — Germans. Thousands of them, sitting on the jetty, all prisoners. This for him marked the true turning-point of the war.

But to get there the British Army and Air Force had had to fight three battles at Alamein: one defensive/offensive under Auchinleck, one defensive under Montgomery, one the final offensive which went all the way, also under 'Monty'.

6: AUCHINLECK

THE TROUBLE ABOUT RUNNING THIS WAR IS
THAT THERE ARE TOO MANY POLITICIANS WHO
THINK THEY ARE GENERALS AND TOO MANY
GENERALS WHO THINK THEY ARE POLITICIANS
AND TOO MANY JOURNALISTS WHO THINK THEY
ARE BOTH

Notice on the Press Censors Office, Cairo

Denis Johnston was a radio war reporter newly sent out to the
Middle East, who found himself busy unpacking while it
seemed everyone else in Cairo was doing the opposite. He was
of course convinced that he would be able to do a job of free
and objective reporting, quite free of propaganda (which
showed how new he was to the game). At his first press
conference, keyed up to report on the air the stirring news of
what was happening in the desert, the Military Spokesman told
them: 'Developments in the battle have resulted in certain
areas losing their former tactical importance. Accordingly, the
garrison of Knightsbridge has assumed a mobile role.'

The hearty roar of laughter which resulted caused the
Colonel to delete that passage from the subsequent
communique. But at least it was a change from the Battle of
France in 1940, where our forces were always retiring to
prepared positions according to plan. And it worked. Kind old
ladies would tell you, smiling confidently and confidentially,
that 'Tiger' Gort was lurking to a flank, waiting to strike. It was
patriotic to believe them. What the Military Spokesman was
really saying was code for admitting that a disorganised, beaten

army was fleeing for the Nile as fast as it could go. In this situation Denis Johnston made his first visit to the desert. Behind the party of correspondents he was with, drove an elderly American general, riding up in a jeep to appraise the way the British were fighting the war.

What Johnston described was 'a roaring, rattling caterpillar of battered trucks and dirty men', transporters shouldering broken-down tanks, RAF recovery lorries towing wrecked aeroplanes, churning dust and spewing out petrol fumes. Everyone in their party was soon covered from head to foot in that dust. From some of the lorries came the noise of voices raised in song:

> Oh they've shifted father's grave to build a se-war,
> They've shifted it regardless of expense.
> They've shifted his re-mains
> Just to lay some bloody drains,
> To glorify some Toff's new res-i-dence.
> Gor Bli-mey!

'Most of them were dirty and tired yet they were not looking particularly distressed — only bored,' reported Johnston. When filling up with petrol, he spoke to one of them.

'Things must be pretty serious?'

'Hope it puts the wind up Cairo,' was the dusty answer.

And of course no one knew where anyone else was, not even Main Army HQ, they'd lost that as well. Although I missed the desert I experienced an almost identical event in Normandy, right down to the cloaked-in-dust bit and the loss of Army Main HQ. In that case it was our side that was doing the pursuing and the Germans, until shortly before under the command of Rommel, who were doing the fleeing. Their Army was perhaps slightly more disorganised than ours because we were travelling at 30 m.p.h. and most of them at 5 m.p.h., but there was not much in it.

Johnston in the desert was still green. He was looking for the 'front' (an obsolete 1914-18 concept) and consistently failing to find it. They came to a point where there was a battered, bullet-pocked railway station and the road crossed the rails. There was no one there. The signal arm stood at *Safety* but the name on the front of the platform building read:

ALAMEIN

The war correspondents reset the signal at *Danger* and driving off towards the sea found some dugouts where the HQ of the 1st South African Division was supposed to be. As indeed it was. Johnston overheard a conversation on the telephone between General Dan Pienaar, the divisional commander, and some unfortunate RAF officer. In a thick Afrikaner accent, Pienaar was speaking frankly at a dramatic moment in the war.

'If you've got to bomb my trucks, you might at least hit them, but you missed every bloody one.'

An agitated South African staff officer tried to get rid of the war correspondents, but Pienaar waved them to stay and went on speaking to the RAF.

'Who's talking about the 10th Hussars? I hear you bombed them four nights ago for four hours. I suppose you'll say they never gave you the recognition signal?'

'But they didn't, sir,' whispered the staff officer. 'Nobody knew what it was.'

'OK, forget the 10th Hussars,' went on Pienaar to the RAF unfortunate. 'That still doesn't explain why we were shelled from the rear yesterday.'

Agitated yapping noises came from the telephone. Pienaar went on remorselessly.

'See here. My father fought the British in the Transvaal, and all I want to know is, what side I'm supposed to be on now. Because if I'm on Rommel's, say so, and I'll turn round and have him in Alexandria within twelve hours. Just work it out, and let me know as soon as you've decided.'

The conducting officer then introduced Johnston as the new correspondent, at which the general's face momentarily distorted with fury.

'Well, I haven't much time to read the newspapers, but so far as I can judge, some people are very misinformed about the war.'

Johnston made a fatal error, explaining that he was not really a newspaper man. He worked for the BBC.

'Oh! Just the fellow I want to see. What the hell do you mean by saying that we had air cover back at Gazala? I heard it myself on the radio. The sky was full of planes, I agree, but not one of them was ours.'

Pienaar paid no attention to disclaimers that Johnston was new to the desert and had not been at Gazala when Rommel began his drive for Cairo.

'All I'm saying is that when the men hear that sort of thing it makes them very annoyed with the BBC. And judging what they tell me Churchill has been saying in America, he must be very misinformed too.'

'In what way, General?' ventured Johnston.

'He says he doesn't know why Tobruk was lost. Everybody here knows perfectly well it was lost because certain people couldn't make up their minds whether it was to be held or not. So Rommel made it up for them. You can't blame the men for doing nothing when they know they're being buggered about. Can you?'

This war correspondent's first important interview on the battlefield was failing to produce really usable stuff designed primarily to hearten a home audience. Johnston tempted fate by saying that he understood that Mr Churchill had seemed certain that Rommel could be kept out of Egypt. This was to wave a red flag under the very nostrils of the bull.

'Yes, I heard that too; but I don't know what he supposes we're going to keep him out with. I've got no artillery and no armour. For weeks I've been asking to have my transport repaired, but now they tell me I shall have to indent for it through the proper channels. Yet I can't move on the blasted road for vehicles piled up with all sorts of rubbish.'

Johnston had nearly lost his first battle. Could he give the bare facts in a stirring press message?

OUR REPORTER, SPEAKING FROM THE ALAMEIN BOX, QUOTES GENERAL PIENAAR AS STATING THAT THE LINE CANNOT POSSIBLY BE HELD AND THAT THE PRIME MINISTER IN WASHINGTON IS TALKING BALLS

No. So he fell back to a previously prepared position.

'Maybe you could say something about the men?' he asked, always a good gambit with generals, who invariably declared that the men were 'splendid' or 'in good heart'.

'What men?' said Pienaar.

There were the South Africans, of course. There were the Indians, poor fellows, God help them. And the New Zealanders if they could make it back to Alamein (which they did) and supposedly there were some Free French but he had not seen them yet.

'Where everybody else is, I don't know. Probably getting ready for the Second Front.'

In the latter case, the general was quite wrong. In the UK we were still practising sub-unit battle drill without any effective antitank weapons whatever and even the Royal Artillery still equipped with the silly little 2-pounder. We were not to be properly equipped until after Monty took us over in 1943.

Remorselessly, General Pienaar went on. He explained the deficiencies of the Alamein position, which ought to be further west, and in any event had a hole in it seven miles wide and apart from that consisted seemingly only of stores and good underground shelters, no defence positions as such. Because it was so close to the Nile, once Rommel broke through he was in the clear right away.

'Then you think it *will* break, sir?'

'Unless something more is sent up to me damn quick, it certainly will. I can't hold with what I've got now.'

'Then that means the retreat goes on?'

'No, sir. Not so far as I'm concerned. I've retreated far enough and here I stop whether we hold the damn thing or not. So my advice to you is, get out while the going's good, and off that bloody road. Goodbye, Mr What's-your-name.'

At that moment up rolled the jeep and out stepped the American general with outstretched hand.

'Gee, Gen'ral Pienaar, I sure am glad to meet you! I know some of your waffle-asses back in Cairo.'

'Waffle-asses?' enquired the South African.

'Yes, sir. Those guys who sit all day on chairs until they get patterns on their backsides.'

Then Johnston saw an amazing sight. General Pienaar laughing.

The correspondent's story was a lifelike impression of an operational Army HQ, rather than the cleaned-up, stiff-lipped recollections of generals published long after. The comments on BBC and newspaper publicity were to be repeated in Normandy and are probably valid eternally. Material designed for the innocent home listener does tend to infuriate the actors in the drama.

Johnston took Pienaar's instructions to heart and parked for the night nearer to Cairo, to the sardonic amusement of his driver and technician who, being no longer green, knew when to be cautious and when not. In some other truck nearby somebody turned up the wireless. In calm and reassuring tones a spokesman for the Management assured his listeners that:

> ... however fluid the situation might be, there was no cause for alarm. Severe fighting was taking place about 15 miles west of Mersa Matruh and there was no reason to believe that Rommel had penetrated any closer to the Nile. In official circles a quiet note of confidence prevailed, although it would be foolish not to be prepared for all eventualities.

Men had gathered from the other trucks and sat around like birds on a wire, listening intently. When it came to the reference to the fighting being west of Matruh there was a sardonic chuckle. The unbeliever had been chased out of Matruh the day before yesterday, he said. Then he realised that he was talking to the BBC, which was in their midst. Then, horror of horrors, next on the air was a recording of Johnston himself describing his first impressions of Cairo, ignorant of the desert and in his mind anyway talking really to his mother and girlfriend. Fervently hoping that no one would associate him with that bland voice, Johnston listened to the laughter around him. This was his real audience, and he never forgot the lesson.

The unbeliever (late of Mersa Matruh) turned out to be a Signals officer who, as came to be the jargon later, 'put him in the picture'. The high-ups liked to call Rommel a 'damned Sergeant Major', but he was far from it. At high level there was some sort of feud between some of our generals and Rommel. Often the Germans took only officers prisoner; the rest they disarmed and let go, having no means of keeping them.

'Rommel and the Afrika Korps are all right. It's only the Ities who are swine. You want to avoid them if you're going to be taken prisoner. It's probably because they've always got the wind up.'

Just before ten o'clock, someone called out: 'What about our bedtime song?' A BBC man fiddled with the dials, then came the opening bars of a semi-military trumpet call with a rat-tat-tat background and the tones of a deep-voiced woman singing:

Vor der Kaserne, vor dem grossen Tor,
Stand eine Laterne, und steht die noch davor.
So wollen wir uns wiedersehn
Bei der Laterne woll'n wir stehn
Wie einst Lili Marlene
Wie einst Lili Marlene.

'Why can't the BBC give us something like that?' said one voice. 'How's that for a nice bedroom voice?' said another.

Apparently this record was played every night to a background of the sea stirring on the nearby beach, and the menacing rumble of the guns. Johnston, much moved by the thought of this German woman singing both armies to sleep, lay down on his bedroll and looked up at the desert stars, so much more brilliant than those of home, and listened to the irregular throb of German bombers passing overhead. Perhaps he might try this story at least on the censor?

For the war-buffs, sticklers for accuracy, I had better add that the song was by Schultze and Leip and recorded by Laie

Andersen in 1941. When broadcast on the German forces network from Belgrade it became an unexpected hit with both the warring armies; largely I suspect because it was NOT a war song (never popular with soldiers) but rather a song of farewell (always popular with Servicemen because wars and partings go together and the soldiers are thinking not of bravely dying for Winston Churchill or Adolf Hitler but of returning alive to their families, sweethearts and friends).

The less German you understand, the better it sounds, for the song is really no more profound than what I suppose were its British equivalents by Vera Lynn and Anne Shelton, which I recall without emotion. Two only had the effect Johnston records for 'Lili'. One, when I was a rifleman in the Gordon Highlanders in Second Army before the Second Front, was the deceptively titled 'We're *no* awa tae abide awa', which sung on the march with a hundred pairs of boots kicking up sparks in the night was perhaps a song of final farewell (as it was indeed for many in the battalion). And the second was 'The Holy City' sung in the Normandy night by young men who were almost certainly going to die in the next few days or weeks. And there too the rumble of the guns and the booming of the bombers above, and even the silent stars, were the essential background.

The revelation that the Eighth Army were singing a German song rather than some favoured patriotic trite rubbish infuriated the yellow press and through them England, until some glib person thought of claiming the tune as a British 'conquest', whereupon it became officially approved and thoroughly patriotic. But it did not take root in the home armies who would take on Rommel again. It was personal to the men of Alamein and Italy.

Aus dem stillen Raume, aus der Erde Grund
Hebt sich wie in Traume, dein verliebter Mund.

82

Wenn sich die spdten Nebel drehn
Werd' ich bei der Laterne stehn
Wie einst Lili Marlene
Wie einst Lili Marlene.

This was the situation at El Alamein as it appeared to a freshly arrived observer at the turning-point of the desert campaign. Without sanctioning the Prime Minister's unrealistic suggestions as to how his generals might win the war, one can see why he became impatient with the conduct of the campaign. And one can understand why Auchinleck did not even reply to letters from Churchill such as the one he received as early as 1941 suggesting that he force the German panzers to use up their 'scarce' ammunition by attacking them with Matildas, which had less than half their speed and none of their gunpower and range. Translated into warship terms, Churchill must instantly have seen the fallacy — the superior enemy would have stood safely out of range and sunk the lot.

The two were also at understandable loggerheads over the size of the forces Britain was maintaining in the Middle East, where the Western Desert was only one front. Auchinleck had already explained to Churchill that in the desert infantry armies were useless, even an encumbrance, requiring vast quantities of water and food even to stay alive, as the British victories over the Italians in 1940 had shown. The infantry had to be integrated with artillery and anti-tank guns, otherwise they were merely cattle to the enemy's armour, and all the British armour was already in Egypt. Nevertheless, the Prime Minister was still urging dramatically useless measures in June 1942:

> I hope this crisis will lead to all uniformed personnel in the Delta and all available loyal manpower being raised to the

highest fighting condition. You have over 700,000 men on your ration strength in the Middle East. Every fit male should be made to fight and die for victory.

It is easy to be unfair when appraising British military leaders at the beginning of a war. Although the nation is warlike it is rarely ready for war in all respects; so those holding high command rarely retain that position at the end. Of late a new hazard, a fresh field of appraisal, has been created: by how they used the information obtained by Ultra are they often judged. Most censorious of all are the most enthusiastic proponents of Ultra, some biased to the extent of absurdity in their claims for the new way of gathering information, not always giving credit to other methods of intelligence. But the commanders had to know better.

For instance, Ultra decrypts referring to a Mark III Special tank were not understood until an example had, with difficulty and danger, been captured and swarmed over by experts.[6] Then and only then did such references mean anything. Another means of first-hand reliable information came from the twice-daily reports of the Long Range Desert Group, who lay up in the enemy's back areas in hidden positions giving observation of roads and tracks, identifying and counting what they saw. There were also reports from (necessarily unidentified) diplomatic sources; and enemy disinformation (or spoof) attempts; aerial photography, and so on. Ultra was just one source among many, always provided that it arrived in time; occasionally delays were critical, even misleading. That

---

[6] As previously recorded in a footnote provided by Major Witherby, the Mark III was the German tank 'workhorse' of the desert. The 'Special' version had an uprated gun — a long-barrelled 50 mm. The example in question was captured by the Australians at Tel el Eisa on 10 July 1942.

the enemy had 67 tanks in the forward area four days ago did not mean that he had 67 runners now.

Eavesdroppers are traditionally supposed to hear no good of themselves, and so it was for Whitehall when a Hitler message was decrypted; the unspeakable fellow referred to British tanks as being 'tin'.

More important were insights into enemy tactical thinking. In June 1942 Rommel laid down three points: (a) fighting tanks with tanks was not economic and should be avoided if possible; (b) long-range artillery bombardment was a waste of ammunition and likewise to be avoided; (c) British tanks were to be allowed to advance until the anti-tank guns could be sure of killing them. These guns were the regular 50-mm PAK (Panzerabwehrkanone) plus the dual-purpose 88-mm FLAK (Flugabwehrkanone) used in a ground role. The 88 was to remain a significant factor on the battlefield until the end of the war. This decrypt might have changed Churchill's mind, about sending in Matildas to attack Rommel's tanks, for that tactic was just what Rommel wanted. It was one reason why he won his battles. The other was his feel for the battle and his habit of commanding in person at the crucial point, unlike the British chain-of-command system, slow and cumbersome, well suited to the 2 m.p.h. pace of a 1914-18 battle but not to fast-moving armour.

This was not quite the whole story, for the British armour, much of it recently converted from horses to machines, tended to begin with the nineteenth-century cavalry charge in mind, spurring the brutes forward into action. Churchill himself, as a young Lieutenant, had taken part in just such a charge himself, at Omdurman in the Sudan, where the natives knew how to deal with horsemen (they were beaten by the infantry and the guns, not cavalry). The Lancers were taught a lesson then, and

Rommel taught their descendants a lesson in the desert. And this lesson, when learned, had a depressing effect on the tank men and made them cautious, so much so that the infantry expected nothing from them and there was much bad feeling. Whoever the Army commander was, this was the Army he had to command. This, rather than his use of Ultra, was the crucial factor.

A subsidiary conflict was the current stage of the code-breaking battle, which waxed and waned as the enemy made things more difficult and then the Allied side achieved a new breakthrough — all too technical to follow here. However at this time, in June 1942, the people behind Ultra had a number of successes with breaking Army and Army-Air cooperation codes rapidly enough to be of real use in the battle. Some of the information concerned the enemy's logistics, some concerned the planned movement of divisions, their routes and a check on how far according to plan these moves were being carried out. That is mostly Order of Battle information — always the most valuable kind. If the enemy's dispositions are known exactly, his intentions maybe deduced. Better still if his tank strengths, ammunition states, reinforcements position, fuel states and so on are also known.

The term 'think-tank' had not then been coined, but a commander needed to be advised by a small group delegated to study and report on all forms of information received and, while doing so, make sure that the sources were not compromised. Such a group had been set up in late 1941, consisting of two RAF officers, two naval officers and an ex-infantryman who was also a Professor of Greek, Major Enoch Powell.

No system that the wit of man can devise would ever be able to cover every contingency, because war is the opposite of chess — chaotic rather than structured, the value of many pieces unknown, with chance playing a large part, and falsehood looming large. The best source of all in reading the enemy's mind would have been, for the British, the ability to open Rommel's letters to his wife, for although he habitually was less than frank with his German superiors, his Italian allies and even the Führer himself, he confided his real feelings to Frau Rommel; indeed, she was a great psychological support to him. And the same might be said of Brooke, Chief of the Imperial General Staff, whose letters to his wife would have been read with interest in Berlin and with shock and horror if published in Britain at the time.

Rommel's victories of early 1942 had led to his promotion to Generaloberst, with his force uprated from a Korps to 'Panzerarmee Afrika'. He had become a figure on the world stage and could write to Frau Rommel: 'World press opinion of me has greatly improved.' Surprisingly, in the house of Commons Churchill called him 'a great general'. This was not to the liking of Auchinleck, who had wider responsibilities than Africa; he found it necessary to circulate a message to all commanders and COs to warn them against talking about 'Rommel' instead of the enemy. He was not a superman.

> I am therefore begging you to dispel the idea in every way you can that Rommel is anything but an ordinary German general, and a pretty unpleasant one at that, as we know from the mouths of his own officers. I am not jealous of Rommel.

There seemed to be a curious parallel with the Elizabethan corsair Sir Francis Drake, for the Spaniards of his time never spoke of the English, but of 'Drake', so firm a hold did his reputation have upon them. Nor was it undeserved. At about this time, Flight Lieutenant Michael Foulis of the torpedo-dropping Wellington squadron wrote home to his mother (on 28 June):

> The RAF is out to stop Rommel (what a man!) and these boys have been working 100%. Nerves still good. All love. M.

At around his own level on the German side there was to be criticism of Rommel's habit of ignoring supply problems and leaving his HQ far too frequently to conduct the battle in person. But among the ordinary soldiers he was popular as a down-to-earth fellow without frills or vanities.

In England at that time, in an infantry battalion training for what two years later would be the last round against Rommel, we were under canvas, and in our camp was an enormous, formidable rat. Unanimously, the squaddies dubbed him 'Rommel', not as a derogatory gesture but one of admiration and also, I must admit, expressing our sentiments regarding the British Army at that time in a way which could not result in disciplinary action. A contemporary joke, not far from the truth, was that we ought all to contribute from our meagre pay towards Rommel's transfer fee to our team. When you expect, not without reason, that you will be going into battle, the matter of the man who leads you assumes considerable importance; and our generals did not impress us. Nor (although at the time we did not know this) did many of them impress the CIGS.

Further wisdom from the ranks, when eventually we did go over the water, was to toast 'Joe and the Royal Navy', as the people most likely to see us back safe. This also contained a semi-libellous truth. In a Continental country such as Germany or France, the Army assumes overriding prestige and importance as the main means of defence and security for every man and woman. In Britain naturally it is the Navy. Quite literally, before the war the Army came last. The most brilliant boy of a Service family would automatically be put in for the Navy. A bright but careless son might be entered for the RAF. A dim lad could be considered only for Sandhurst, and if he was not even up to that, then the Indian Army. The CIGS, Brooke, considered that the poor quality of senior commanders was due to the losses of subalterns in the 1914-18 affair; and perhaps it was in part — but had not the Germans suffered losses even heavier than ours?

Auchinleck did have the misfortune to be Indian Army; this was now a drawback because it made him more conscious of the Japanese drive through Burma to India, which was not held at Kohima and Imphal and then finally defeated until 1944. He would have preferred to give up all hopes of driving the Germans out of Africa if he could see the Japanese kept out of India. Churchill on the other hand was far more agitated about the fate of Malta, resting as all thought on a knife-edge.

At this moment the Prime Minister was in Washington, conferring with President Roosevelt. There were large decisions to be made about the overall world pattern of the war. If Germany was to be the Allied priority as had been agreed (although the US armed forces made sure that America's greatest effort was in the Pacific), where was the Wehrmacht to be engaged — across the Channel directly or the long way round in the Mediterranean? Consequently, the news of the success of Rommel's latest attack came as a staggering and for Churchill a personally humiliating shock. The news reaching the White House (undoubtedly including reports from Colonel Fellers) was that Tobruk had fallen to Rommel in one day with 25,000 (actually 32,000) Allied troops taken prisoner and great quantities of food, fuel, guns, vehicles and supplies of all kinds. Previously, Tobruk had held out well behind the German front as a stubbornly and successfully defended Australian fortress for half a year until relieved by a British offensive.

In the opinion of Colonel Fellers, US Military Attaché in Cairo, the British had now been decisively beaten and the time was ripe for Rommel to take Cairo and the Nile Delta. Almost as soon as Fellers sent this signal, the British knew from Sigint that the Germans had not only received it but could read it. That was on 24 June, three days following the fall of Tobruk. Within hours, a further decrypt told them that Hitler had ordered petrol to be sent to Tobruk 'with utmost despatch'. All information — by 'Y', by air reconnaissance, and by actual sightings on the ground — showed that the enemy's main striking force, consisting of two panzer divisions, the motorised infantry of the 90th Light, the Italian Ariete Armoured Division and recce units, were 50 miles west of Mersah Matruh and heading for the Nile at great speed.

On 25 June Auchinleck, who was in charge of the whole Middle East theatre of war, relieved General Ritchie, who was commanding in the desert, and took over direct control of the Eighth Army himself. He at once changed the plan, which had been to fight a decisive battle at Mersa Matruh; instead the army was only to delay the enemy and spare infantry units were to be sent back to the Alamein-Qattara gap, which could not be outflanked from the desert because the Qattara terrain was impassable for vehicles. The remaining infantry should be formed into small battle groups rather than divisions.

Cairo's estimates of enemy tank strength proved too high — 104 compared with 155 in Eighth Army on 26 June, whereas in truth Rommel had only 60 German tanks and 44 Italian. Nevertheless the British were in such chaos, and their signals communications so disrupted, that even if accurate advance information had been available from any source, it would have been worthless. Auchinleck was sending out signals (based on Ultra C38 decrypt) ordering certain units to beware of being trapped when in fact they had already been surrounded and were desperately trying to fight their way out of the net.

The American reaction to the news was splendid — in the long term. The US 1st Armored Division was ordered to release 300 Sherman tanks and 100 self-propelled (SP) guns for shipment to Africa. They would be too late for this battle of Alamein but would be vital in a later struggle fought over the same terrain. With this decided, bitter arguments began on the wisdom of opening a Second Front in 1943 with the cross-Channel invasion of France by British and American forces. For once, possibly sobered by Tobruk, Churchill urged caution, quite rightly. At home, trouble was indicated in Parliament. There always had been, and still was, an influential lobby who sincerely believed that the Prime Minister was an 'adventurer', ready to turn his Westminster coat as opportunity indicated and to conduct warfare for reasons of political and personal expediency. They were gravely concerned with the central direction of the war — not unreasonably — and would soon move a vote of censure which at the very least must seriously damage the position of the Prime Minister, even if it did not succeed in having him replaced.

7: WINNIE IN THE DESERT

ROMMEL handled his forces in exactly the same way that an Admiral handled his fleet, he personally led the Afrika Korps whilst keeping a firm grip on his forces to the west. As a result, if there was a pause in the fighting, Rommel, within minutes, could discuss the military situation with his Commanders, face to face, whilst he could almost see at a glance the fighting capability of his armoured units.

RITCHIE, on the other hand, controlled the 8th Army in exactly the same way as our Army Commanders controlled their forces in the First World War. Orders were passed to the Corps Commanders, who passed the orders to the Divisional Commanders, who passed the orders to the Brigade Commanders. Then if a Brigade Commander wanted a point clarified or wanted help, the details would be passed to Division and then to Corps and finally to Army. This was very time consuming and in the fast moving desert battles the information could be completely out of date, especially when it is remembered that often the messages were coded, decoded several times before they reached their final destination.

So, ROMMEL invariably knew the true military situation, whilst RITCHIE could only make a considered judgement or guess, and guessing in the desert was a very dangerous pastime.

Major David Parry, 57 Light A. A. Regt attd 50 Div

Major Parry's experiences that June confirmed the fallibility of stated figures. At a time when the total number of tanks possessed by the Afrika Korps was recorded as 12, a party he was with spent an innocent day stripping an abandoned artillery vehicle in full view of what turned out to be a much larger number of tanks — all of them German. The battered British artillery regiment concerned, with an authorised establishment of 36 guns, now counted 39, having by various devious Army means 'won' an extra three from somewhere or other.

He also noted that Anti-Aircraft Command in the Middle East were reluctant to release for anti-tank work any of the thousand or so 3.7-inch guns they had for the defence of the Delta, many of which never seemed to fire a shot, but could have been used as a Rommel-type anti-tank screen, the 3.7 being almost identical to the German FLAK 88. For that matter, if only they had realised what was really necessary the home government in Britain could have supplied the Desert Army with the many cast-off 3-inch A. A. guns which had now been replaced by the modern 3.7s, and been sent to Russia to help Stalin's war effort. In November of this year, the Eighth Army had the mortification of capturing one such gun from the Germans who had themselves captured it from the Russians on the Eastern Front.

On 2 July Major Parry spotted General Auchinleck driving around in his car, apparently delivering pep talks to the troops. Parry questioned some gunners to whom the Commander-in-Chief had spoken.

It was no pep talk. Auchinleck had explained that Rommel was now fully extended and that his advance troops were dangerously exposed. So it was essential that the 8th Army, seriously disorganised, was given a few days to re-organise and establish defence positions at Alamein. The answer — all the fighting troops which could be rallied would be formed into a striking force to bloody the enemy's nose within the next twenty-four hours.

Auchinleck knew that if such an attack was formally mounted through his Corps Commanders the delay could have been catastrophic. 10th Corps HQ had been destroyed whilst 13th and 30th Corps Headquarters were in a state of confusion.

So the Commander-in-Chief assumed the duties of Corps, Division, Brigade and even Battalion Commander, collected together a miscellaneous fighting force from the remnants of 8th Army, and gave orders direct to those involved to attack. Within hours the attack was launched, Rommel's advance troops were stopped dead in their tracks and 3,000 prisoners taken. On 4 July, just two days after Auchinleck's counter-attack, Rommel stopped his attacks and took up defensive positions. The first battle of Alamein had been won by the 8th Army.

That was one way of looking at it. Winston Churchill had a different view and, it seems, had made up his mind about Auchinleck while still in Washington, on learning of the fall of Tobruk on 21 June, although he had urged Auchinleck to take over the Eighth Army from his subordinate, General Ritchie. This had led the Commander-in-Chief to believe that the Prime Minister still had confidence in him, and he had promptly complied.

But the Prime Minister was determined to make a visit to the Middle East as soon as possible to sort out matters in person, having survived a vote in the House of Commons of 'no confidence' in the central direction of the war. And it was true that the war over which he had presided now for more than two years was not unfolding in Britain's favour — far from it. A great many people were worried about this, and some of them were in Parliament.

In the country there was probably still some feeling that Churchill satisfactorily conveyed the 'British Bulldog at Bay' stance of defiance which had been appropriate to the invasion scare period of 1940. The press certainly laid a great share of the blame for the failures in the desert on to the Army. *The Times* pointed to the deficiencies of British tanks, the *Manchester Guardian* highlighted the system or lack of it in co-ordinating design, choice and production of war weapons, the *Daily Mail* in the words of their war correspondent Alexander Clifford judged British generalship to be 'too slow, too cautious and too easily led into traps'.

The actual machinery behind the vote of confidence of 1 July 1942 is unknown. It was a little too convenient to take at face value. Sir John Wardlaw-Milne who was to move the motion offered on 30 June to withdraw, if that would help the war effort, but Churchill rejected this ominously the same day, warning that the War Cabinet

> desired me to inform you that in view of the challenge to the competence and authority of the Government, which has now for some days been spread throughout the world, it is imperative that the matter should go forward to an immediate issue, and for this all arrangements have been made.

The whole thing may of course have been fixed up behind the scenes, as such things so often are at Westminster (and elsewhere). Rumours of unrest in Britain had reached Washington even before Churchill had left America, and for some reason fathomable only by Parliamentarians, Churchill seems to have thought that a massive vote of confidence in himself might affect international opinion. It cannot ever cut much ice in Britain.

Even more curious was the process of debate. Sir John Wardlaw-Milne began by pointing out reasonably that the Prime Minister was trying to combine control of both the political and military fields and that this was too much for one man. In effect, a military overlord for defence should be appointed. And he suggested that this should be the Duke of Gloucester. Apart from the fact that it was astoundingly bad form to involve Royalty in political controversy, the idea seemed to have no practical value.

So, how seriously was it made? The *Daily Mirror* tartly judged that 'the strategy here seems decidedly better than that employed in Libya.' In the House, the government was roundly attacked but aspersions on the Prime Minister's leadership were soft-pedalled. However, Lord Winterton declared:

> No one dares to put the blame where it should be put constitutionally — on the Prime Minister. During the 37 years which I have been in the House I have never seen such attempts to absolve a Prime Minister from Ministerial responsibility as are going on at this moment.

On the second day of the debate Aneurin Bevan scored a hit by saying:

> The Prime Minister wins debate after debate, and loses battle after battle. The country is beginning to say that he fights debates like a war, and the war like a debate.

And this debate he won, by 475 votes to 25, speaking last and for one and a half hours, claiming that the criticisms of his government and of himself had 'been poured out by cable and radio to all parts of the world, to the distress of our friends and to the delight of our foes.' Alas, that is democracy, which we were supposed to be fighting for.

The suggestion that Churchill's opponents were unpatriotic was of course tactically adept if unfair, but what can one think of that part of his defence in which he spoke of the need for commanders in the field to feel they were free to take risks, free to fight their battles without over-frequent admonitions from Whitehall? Naturally it was just a lead-up to his demand for unconditional backing for his own war leadership, for it was exactly his own method, by virtue of reading Ultra, to seek to control by harassment his admittedly mediocre generals in the desert. Churchill had yet to meet a general who could take his measure, a prickly, awkward character, sharp and fox-like rather than straightforward. But he was going to, and not by his own choice.

It is clear, despite the usual politician's trickeries, that Churchill had been deeply shocked and ashamed to be closeted with Roosevelt in the White House on 21 June and handed silently the decoded message from the US Embassy in Cairo telling of the sudden capitulation of the Tobruk garrison. That the perimeter was no longer defensible, the Prime Minister had not known. He felt thereby devalued as a warlord.

The next rival warlord on his list was Stalin, whom he intended to see after visiting the Middle East and rearranging matters there. The Russian tyrant was nagging on about the necessity of practical aid, preferably in the form of an Anglo-American invasion of Europe (which if carried out in 1942 or 1943 must have been a disaster). The Prime Minister was hoping that an end to the enemy in Africa might be sufficient to soothe Stalin at this time, as it was intended to land an Anglo-American army in French North Africa, at the entrance to the Mediterranean, behind Rommel's back.

The background to his projected visit to Cairo was that as long ago as March he had suggested to Auchinleck that the C.-in-C. come and see him in London to discuss their differences over waging war in the Middle East, and Auchinleck had refused. Churchill was naturally furious, but Auchinleck's view can be understood too, for he found it difficult to leave the area at a critical time. He, and General Wavell before him, had already explained the practicalities. Auchinleck, a Scot, was dour and cautious; Churchill talked anachronistically in his speeches of 'cannon', evidently fighting his ancestor Marlborough's battles over again. As General Essame wrote, 'forthright, plain-spoken, without a trace of the politician, courtier or actor in his make-up, Auchinleck and Churchill were poles apart.'

But although Auchinleck had brought Rommel to a standstill at about the same time that Churchill had won that vote of confidence in Parliament, actually getting out to the Middle East was not then the simple matter it is today, and it was to be a month before the Prime Minister at length arrived. In the meantime the processing of Ultra traffic had been greatly improved and resulted in an important success for the newly arrived 9th Australian Division. By sheer determination General Pienaar's South Africans had, despite the general's sour witticisms to the BBC reporter Denis Johnston, held the 90th Light when they tried to march past him, aided by some Italians. Two dead Italians in a little car marked for later troops the furthest eastward point reached by the Axis forces.

One thing had led to the other. Just back from leave in Germany, Heinz Werner Schmidt, who had escaped from the Italian defeat in East Africa to join Rommel in Tripoli and ask him for a job, had got the command of a battalion in Special Group 288, operating with the 90th Light. They were stopped by the fire of the South Africans' 25-pounders just short of the wayside railway station of El Alamein. The German artillerymen found an observation point on a ridge called Tel el Eisa — the Hill of Jesus — perhaps a better name for the battleground. Rommel roared up in his armoured recce vehicle and ordered — what else? — an immediate attack, to take advantage of the setting sun, and hoping to drive right through a disorganised, demoralised and beaten enemy. The German infantry went forward, to be met by the distinctive sound of rifle and machine-gun fire. The battle which was to be called after the wayside station had begun.

Rommel now moved his forces southward for a right hook out of the desert. 90th Light was moved southward from near the coast in the north, together with 21st Panzer and the Italian Littorio Division. Enigma decodes brought Auchinleck the news together with similar information from Army 'Y', from prisoners and from captured documents. There began a race within the Intelligence community to beat Ultra, to be first with the news of Rommel's moves before the day's Ultra could arrive. The 'Y' data consisted of cryptanalysis, plain language intercepts, Direction Finding and radio traffic analysis. With practice, a team could read the enemy's moves from a combination of all these, together with growing familiarity with the way the enemy operated.

The 90th Light, Auchinleck knew, had been replaced on the hill of Tel el Eisa by two Italian infantry divisions; one of these, the Sabratha, was inexperienced, understrength and weak in artillery. The full story has not been told, nor is it likely to be; what is sure is the fact that on 8 July he planned an attack by an Australian infantry brigade to take the commanding height. Three battalions took part — the 2/24th, the 2/26th and the 2/48th. On 10 July, in the darkness an hour before first light, they put in a silent, unsupported infantry attack. It seems that it was the 2/24th which overran the 'Circus' — the collection of tents, radio vans and antennae which made up 621 W/T Intercept Company under Oberleutnant (captain) Alfred Seebohm, an important part of

56 Signals Unit, which was stationed on a height close to the attenuated gunline of the Italian division, within easy walking distance of the Australian positions.

Seebohm was a sensitive but extremely ambitious officer, intent on providing Rommel with a first-class monitoring system, the German equivalent of the British Y-service. The first requirement was a site giving good reception of wireless messages, with secondly, good connections to the direction-finding stations which would plot the sources of the British transmissions, and thirdly, constant wireless contact with Rommel's mobile forward headquarters. The site chosen was ideal. Often the British messages were with Rommel while the British units to which they were addressed were still querying their meaning because of poor reception. The messages being passed were from lower down the tree than the high-level information provided by Rommel's 'Good Source' — the intercepted and decoded reports of Colonel Bonner Frank Fellers to Washington; but that 'Good Source' had fallen silent on 29 June — the British having had their suspicions aroused by Ultra information from Luftwaffe and Panzer Army Enigma messages.

Now, in its turn, Seebohm's company was to fall silent too.

The Australian infantry came on casually, carrying their Bren LMGs on their shoulders until the first high-pitched irregular rattle of the German Spandaus began. The artillery supporting the Australians now opened fire with smoke shells, and mortar bombs came whistling down among the Germans. When tanks got forward under cover of the smoke, that was that. Some of the German vehicles got away, but most of the Intercept Company were killed or captured and Seebohm himself fatally wounded. Most of their irreplaceable files fell into Australian hands, providing proof positive of how much information the British had been giving away for free.

Apart from the obvious aim of efficiency, why did Seebohm risk putting his unique special unit so close to the enemy? Survivors on the German side recalled that a little earlier, during a previous Afrika Korps retreat, a burly, fire-eating colonel had threatened to court martial Seebohm for failing to stand and fight with the others. A saying in Germany before and during the war was that for success in the army a modicum of stupidity was essential — and here is an excellent example.

Within the space of a fortnight the Germans had lost two rounds in the radio war. Fellers, who had been in effect reporting to Rommel as well as to Roosevelt from a high-level position within the British command, had been cut off; and now the equally vital but lower-level work of the Seebohm company had been lost. This was to be a secret gain for the general who would eventually succeed Auchinleck in the command.

Elsewhere also the tide was on the turn, almost imperceptibly. On 7 July the German forces in south Russia driving for the Caucasus had reached Rostov on the Don, but not yet Stalingrad on the Volga. Offensives in the Pacific threatened Australia. On 21 June the Japanese had invaded New Guinea. Early in June the carrier fleets of Japan and the United States had clashed off Midway with results not at once apparent, although it soon became clear that the Imperial Navy of Japan had suffered its first defeat for 350 years and that the period of lightning expansion was over. One major factor in that result had been the ability of US Naval Intelligence to break the Japanese codes.

The overall cause of the final blunting of the German and the Japanese expansionist drives was that the aggressor nations, while initially better prepared for war, had both by political decisions ordered their armed forces to bite off a good deal more than they were able to chew. And although the Allied leadership could be muddled or inept, mistakes were not confined to one side only. Political and personal factors were present everywhere and often affected the course of events. The subordination of national interest to self-interest knows no patriotic frontiers. For instance, the US Navy claimed that the work of their Intelligence organisation in reading Japanese radio codes had been imperilled by a leak which could be traced to General MacArthur who, fighting to enlarge his own empire in the Pacific and lobbying the Australian government to get British aircraft carriers and British troops destined for the Middle East to be diverted to him, had spread a report about the forthcoming Japanese offensive in New Guinea. Fortunately for the Allied war effort, the Japanese apparently did not read the *Sydney Morning Herald*.

An example of the fact that this, unlike the 1914-18 affair, was truly a world war, where events at the far side of the earth could influence campaigns closer to home, was the journey of the 8th Armoured Division from Britain to Egypt, via Cape Town in South Africa, a passage of some 13,000 miles. The Germans were aware that convoy after convoy was rounding the Cape and heading up the Red Sea for Egypt, bringing reinforcements in men and material for the Eighth Army. The division expected to delay at Cape Town by mechanical trouble in the ship carrying 24 Armoured Brigade, but they sailed in haste without that Brigade and went at full speed for Australia because of the gravity of the situation there, and then, when the result of the American victory at Midway was realised, brought back on a course for Aden, which they reached on 1

July, a critical day at Alamein.

Lieutenant Tom Witherby of 46 Royal Tank Regiment in 23 Armoured Brigade was surprised to find no sense of urgency in Egypt. 'With a little drive and push we could have been at Alamein by 10 July,' he wrote. That was the day the Australians attacked Tel el Eisa and almost overran the HQ of the Afrika Korps. Colonel F. W. von Mellenthin was first alerted early that morning by the sound and sight of Italians rushing past the German HQ in 'panic and rout' but, using a machine-pistol, organised a defence soon reinforced by a regiment (equivalent to a British brigade) of 164 Infantry Division brought over from Crete. Had a complete new British armoured division joined the fray, the outcome would have been less satisfactory for the Germans, although the loss to their intelligence-gathering system was serious indeed. By then the old stagers of the Afrika Korps were totally exhausted, reduced almost to the state of zombies by continual fighting in the heat, lack of sleep, poor and inadequate rations, and the relentless driving of their commander. Their divisions were divisions in name only — 21 Panzer possessed 23 tanks and numbered 600 infantry; the 90th Light could count only 1,600 infantry — whereas the new British formations now arriving were up to strength in both men and machines.

As it turned out, 8 Armoured Division were not even reunited with their tanks until the 10th, let alone in the forward area. 'We were horrified by their state,' wrote Tom Witherby. 'They were also stowed with our personal kit. Nearly all the kit was looted and the tanks were in a terrible state after being "overhauled" in workshops.' Presumably the 'overhaul' was to prepare them for desert conditions, but the looting was normal British Army habit. In a unit, thieving was unheard of, but in anonymous places such as transit camps, Reinforcement

Holding Units, and so on, it was a case of 'watch your kit', for if anything was not actually chained down it would inevitably 'walk'. The Army reflected the society, of course.

More serious, thought Witherby, was the fact that although a few lectures had been given during the long sea voyage, they were not brought up to date with the realities of desert warfare.

> The British Army in Egypt seems to have had the strangest generals at this time. They cared little for training, paid no regard to the different characteristics of different units, made no allowance for inexperience, made no attempt to impart information and did not learn from their own experience. No one in Britain or the Middle East seems to have appreciated how good the Germans were. Although we saw regular pamphlets about the German Army these gave little idea of actuality. We were told nothing about their anti-tank guns. Until 22 July I had no idea that they had a gun that could pierce the armour of a Valentine!
>
> The bitterness between the New Zealanders and other infantry formations and the Armour seems to have stemmed from the old idea in the old Tank Corps that tanks could do everything and were independent of other Arms. (General Rommel, who seems to have liked making jokes about the Nazi Party, said of the British tanks that they were 'racially pure', meaning that they acted on their own, without the co-operation of the other Arms.) The Infantry for their part did not understand how difficult were the conditions for the Armour, most of all at night, where the tank crews could hardly see or hear anything. This tension was all part of the malaise of the time, with poor leadership, poor training, little liaison and the general lack of mutual understanding. Later the 23rd were to win the confidence of the Kiwis and the Australians.

While 23 Armoured Brigade were sorting out the muddle in the Suez Canal Zone, on 12 July there was a stormy meeting in the White House many thousands of miles away. President Roosevelt was arguing with his Chiefs of Staff about the future pattern of the war. He was urging that a major part of the three million American troops then mobilised should be sent to invade French North Africa, where vast numbers could be more easily deployed than on tiny Pacific islands; also it was necessary for his own re-election in November that the US forces should be seen to be taking a significant part in the war. This was a gamble of course. The reaction of the French to a largely American invasion (although the British whom they hated, not without reason, would also take part) could not be predicted with certainty; there was the Spanish reaction to be considered as well. This decision was to be vital. It involved sending a vast fleet of 650 large transports across the Atlantic direct to North Africa to create a 'second front' there behind the back of the tiny Afrika Korps.

On 18 July he sent General Marshall, Admiral King and the civilian adviser Harry Hopkins to London to do battle with Churchill for a Second Front in Europe for that year, 1942; but if the British proved obstinate, they were to settle for North Africa. Churchill did prove obstinate, arguing that a cross-Channel assault was bound to fail at this time; and he was undoubtedly right in this cautious estimate. The unbloodied Americans were as optimistic as the British had been formerly as to what could be achieved against the German Army. On 22 July the cross-Channel attack was shelved for the time being, to the bitter disappointment of the Americans. But Churchill agreed to resurrect the large-scale Canadian raid on Dieppe which until recently had been General Montgomery's pigeon.

In the desert, 22 July was also a significant day for the newly arrived 23 Armoured Brigade.

About 15 July, after two hard attacks on the German/Italian armies at Alamein, General Auchinleck seems to have decided that the enemy was in a bad way and one more hard push would finish him. Looking round, he must have noticed 23rd Armoured Brigade busily trying to recover from the muddles of the landing. A decision was made to use these new troops in one large attack. Brigadier Misa did not think we were ready for battle and he protested at our being sent straight into action, but he was over-ruled. This decision was made regardless of the fact that we were not acclimatised, were new to the Desert and had had no opportunity of learning about the situation. To make matters worse, instead of using the 23rd Brigade as a Unit, it was split up and 50 Royal Tanks were sent to the Australians for what was a raid near Tel el Eisa. To make up, a third regiment was added which at the time my friend Major Boyd Moss referred to as 'ALL-THE-TANKS-IN-EGYPT', composed of the remains of the renowned 22nd Armoured Brigade. The attack which followed must have been one of the most total disasters of the war.

By the evening of 21 July the two tank regiments of 23 Armoured Brigade together with the infantry of the 7th Battalion of the Rifle Brigade and the whole Support Group of 8 Armoured Division were in position along Ruweisat Ridge. Tom Witherby had charge of the forward group of supply vehicles.

At last light we came to two derelict Mark III tanks, standing on Ruweisat Ridge in a little minefield full of camel thorn. These were from 21st Panzer and must have represented the very furthest point of the enemy advance on the Ridge. When we reached the two derelicts we turned sharp right round them and descended to the bottom of the ridge where many of 23rd Armoured Brigade vehicles were already in position. It was dark by then and the battle to prepare for our advance next day had already begun. The red glow of fires lit the sky, coloured tracer arched across the horizon and the thunder of the bombardment was continuous. At 10 p.m. we received our orders.

They were confident and suggested that resistance would be light and so we were not to advance beyond el Daba [40 miles] without further instructions. But we were about to attack over ground that we had not seen, with no real idea of the enemy and without our third regiment, 50th Royal Tanks. Our Regiment, 46th Royal Tanks, was drawn up for the night in three lines quite close together, with Brigade HQ and 40th Royal Tanks not far away. There was no attempt at concealment and the enemy must have been well aware of our arrival.

The night attack to open a way for the tanks to break through did not go as planned. Strenuous but unsuccessful efforts were made to call off the attack. Auchinleck was the Army commander, with General 'Strafer' Gott next down the chain as the commander of XIII Corps, of which 8th Armoured Division was a part.

The long range 'jettison fuel tanks' which the Valentines had carried were dropped off and lay on the desert in three lines to mark the position occupied by our 52 Valentines and Matildas. Amid clouds of smoke we set off up the same slope to the top of the ridge. Beyond the two Mark IIIs there were the remains of an Italian battery standing in a breastwork of stones.

Being with the soft-skinned vehicles Tom Witherby did not advance beyond the ridge (which, as he remarks, is why he is still alive).

I saw great clouds of black smoke. Then the wreckage of the attack coming back. The tank wounded, half-naked. Mortar bombs falling. I took the supply vehicles back to try to form a defensive position. The attack is described in great detail by Mr Perrett in his *The Valentine in North Africa*, but he gives more of the experiences of 40th Royal Tanks. 46th R. Tanks had even heavier losses — only six Valentines and Matildas remaining afterwards, with comparable losses in personnel. Nearly all the British tanks were knocked out by German anti-tank guns, including the deadly 88-mm guns. One German Mark III was caught and destroyed at the beginning of the attack, but there were hardly any other engagements with German tanks. Captain Paddock in a Matilda fought with the only German Mark IV — an unequal contest because the Matilda only had a 3-inch mortar intended mainly to fire smoke. In the end, the Matilda was on fire and the crew escaped and were taken prisoner. Major Boyd Moss reached the objective, a point near a depression called el Mreir, and brought his Valentine back, an unusual achievement. The great mass of Valentines and Matildas were simply hurled across the minefield, regardless of the fact that in the confusion of the infantry attacks in the previous night it had not been cleared. The tanks that got across, manned of course by crews that were completely 'green' and had never been in action before, came under intense anti-tank gun fire and were almost all destroyed. This all happened between about 10 a.m. and 12 noon. This must have been the most ill prepared and disgraceful episode of the whole war. There must have been a kind of madness at the Army Command, a feeling that there was a once and for all chance to drive the Axis forces back and that all risks must be taken in the hope of success. The kindest thing that can be said is that tired men do make mistakes.

Certainly, as far as Gott at least was concerned, exhaustion seems to have been a factor. There was also the likely effect of the stream of nagging messages sent to the Middle East by the war leader in London, starting from when Wavell was in command and continuing after Auchinleck took over, demanding instant attack and the crushing defeat of Rommel in often abrupt and arbitrary terms.[7]

Behind the tanks when they set off on their Balaclava charge into the valley was the Support Group. Attached to each regiment was an armoured Observation Post riding in a Stuart tank, a lightly armoured American vehicle and quite distinctive. They were knocked out almost at once, so there was no one left to direct the fire of the guns. The anti-tank guns which went forward were still 2-pounders, which Witherby compared to stone axes, capable of stunning the Germans — with surprise.

Many of the German anti-tank gunners were in the el Mreir and el Shein depressions. These were features of the desert hollowed out by the endless wind. Not necessarily circular, they were often surrounded by small cliffs and contained sand, so that in mobile warfare they gave easy cover. It was not easy to get out of them in an attack, as the Italians found when they entered the Munassib depression during the battle of Alam el Haifa.

After the attack by 23 Armoured Brigade had been smashed, Major Offord of 46 R. Tanks cleared a gap in the minefield and six tanks from the 46th and eight from the 40th

---

[7] For examples see *Alanbrooke* by David Fraser (Collins 1982), *The War and Colonel Warden* by Gerald Pawle (Harrap 1963), *Auchinleck* by Philip Warner (Buchan & Enwright 1981).

came back through it. After them came tanks of 15th Panzer, one Mark IV and about a dozen Mark IIIs, moving slowly through the groups of derelict Valentines and Matildas.

But the Germans stopped at the minefield and the expected attack did not materialise.

Fourteen tanks, survivors from the Brigade, came back for the night. Each regiment had 52 tanks of which six were smoke Matildas, plus four in Brigade HQ, a total of 106. General Playfair (in the official history) says that of these 87 were lost or seriously damaged. I believe the number should be 90. Crew casualties were similar and there were many others, including the Brigade Ordnance Officer, who was severely wounded when his jeep struck a mine or was hit by a shot just as he drew up beside the Valentine of Colonel Dunbar of the 40th. The Colonel was killed and so was his driver, whose dead hands were left holding the brakes hard on. I do not know what were the casualties of the infantry of the Rifle Brigade or of the Gunners. We spent the night in a kind of shock. Round us were the lines of 'jettison' fuel tanks but only six actual Valentines with them. An enormous jar of rum, rations for all the tanks crews, came up — but there was no one to drink it! We, the remainder, felt strange. There were ghosts and reminders all round.

At morning Tom Witherby walked around the area. Clearly, this was an old battlefield. The hulks of some 20 German and Italian tanks lay around, many with their crews still inside them, marking the furthest Axis advance on Ruweisat Ridge during Rommel's last drive. In what was to be called 'Happy Valley' (or 'Tank Valley') there were graves everywhere, as well as the dead crewmen of all nationalities still in their tanks. From the newly wrecked British tanks the New Zealand infantry were later to 'win' many useful binoculars, at least from those in which the dead men were still recognisable. Flies rose from them in clouds and settled on the hands and faces of the living, and on the food they were trying to eat. When the morning and late afternoon winds blew, great dust clouds rolled steadily from the north-east.

> Our Brigade commander, Misa, was sacked, a most unfair and ignoble move. He had obeyed his absurd orders after protesting and was sacked for being proved right.

The remnants of the brigade were ordered to make several moves which seemed to be 'completely pointless', just a waste of fuel and a cause of unnecessary wear on the machinery, giving the 'impression that there was no plan and no one in command', and an attack which was 'a muddled failure'.

> The general waste was fantastic. I have seen a petrol lorry loaded with these disposable petrol cans with petrol running off the tail board as if a tap had been turned on. Danger of fire, particularly in shelling, was great. Usually there was a lorry to be seen somewhere on fire.

At about the end of July Tom was admitted, more or less unconscious, to a fever ward in a tented hospital in the Canal Zone, and was there for the first two weeks of August.

> The staff were a British Nursing Sister, a very efficient Sudanese medical orderly, a grave and statuesque ebony-black Egyptian, a very ugly girl from Palestine (she would now be called an Israeli) and a most beautiful South African Nursing Sister who drifted round with glasses of whisky. While I was recovering I talked to others who had been in the desert longer than I. I heard how bad morale was at this time. One story was that Rommel was to be allowed to advance right up to Cairo, but when he got to the Gezira Sporting Club on the

Nile the whole of GHQ was to spring to arms and overwhelm him by sheer weight of numbers. I remember one of the nurses saying 'There is a rumour Mr Churchill has been out here.'

The Prime Minister had indeed at last visited Egypt and was revelling in being near the action. He arrived in Cairo on 4 August, having come to the general who would not come to him. The visit was to have been made in strict secrecy, which the Prime Minister instantly violated by giving the V sign to any soldiers he passed on the drive to the Embassy. Middle East Command PR offered a further gift to Axis Intelligence by printing a photograph of a normally anonymous person with the caption: 'Commander C. R. Thompson, Personal Assistant to the Prime Minister, greets an Army officer at Cairo West', the officer being easily recognisable as General Alexander, secretly brought in to replace Auchinleck as C.-in-C. Middle East.

Brooke, as CIGS the professional head of the British Army, had flown out first on his own, leaving his political master, 'that old ruffian' the Prime Minister, at home. But a day later Churchill followed him, so that Brooke was not able to take the change of command decision after seeing Auchinleck alone. Auchinleck was a tall, fine-looking man and the Prime Minister was anxious to find him another appointment so as to soften the blow of dismissal. He dithered a great deal during these days, first saying that Auchinleck ought to come back from the front to GHQ and appointing General Gott to take over Eighth Army. Brooke noted that he was 'fretting' that first day in Cairo that no offensive was planned until 15 September. He then 'argued strongly' for Gott. When Brooke resisted (knowing Gott was very tired) Churchill then suggested that Brooke himself take over the Middle East, with

Montgomery as Eighth Army commander. This was an offer immensely tempting to make to a staff officer, no matter how senior, but Brooke resisted, feeling that his ability as CIGS to 'exercise a limited amount of control' on some of Churchill's more impulsive and romantic notions was far more important to the war effort. Montgomery was Brooke's own choice for Eighth Army, but next day Churchill visited 'Strafer' Gott, then commanding a corps in the desert (as we have seen), and was most impressed.

With Churchill pressing a reluctant Brooke, a 'package' for Middle East Command was prepared for War Cabinet approval: the genial, easy-going Guardsman Alexander for overall command, and Brooke's reluctant agreement with the Prime Minister's choice for the desert general to defeat Rommel — 'Strafer' Gott.

8: MONTY TAKES OVER

'I never interfere with Monty in tactical matters, he's generally right — and he doesn't let you forget it!'

General Brooke to a colleague

'Monty let you know who he was, what he wanted you to do, and had a feeling for casualties.'

Eighth Army veteran

The opponents on that fateful 7th of August were both NCOs. Warrant Officer Schneider of the Luftwaffe was with a group of fighters which spotted the target aircraft below him but still flying unusually high. It was a Bristol Bombay, a historic relic of air power theory left over from the 1930s. Twin radial engines, twin rudders, a gaunt, high-fixed undercarriage quite out of place now, and twin gun turrets, one in the nose, one in the tail. Supposedly capable, so the British air marshals had dreamed, of fighting its way to targets deep in enemy territory and fighting its way back. But now in 1942, not a striking eagle but a sitting duck. Which was why, converted to an aerial bus or transport van, Bombays were normally flown close to the ground to reduce the risk of being spotted by fighters. In this case the pilot, Flight Sergeant James, had been forced to gain a little height because one Pegasus engine was showing an oil temperature in the red. In case of a forced landing, James wanted time to select a good place to put down. And so Schneider saw him, flitting over the desert at 450 feet, and dived. As the German came in behind the big ex-bomber, James took the Bombay down for a crash-landing.

The passengers were not helpless non-combatants; they were military personnel, including a general going to Cairo from Alamein. It was Schneider's duty to kill them all, if he could. It seems that the general got clear, but ran back to rescue others trapped in the fuselage. The transport blew up, killing this brave man also. The would-be rescuer was General 'Strafer' Gott, Commander Eighth Army since yesterday.

There now ensued a further stage of 'general post' among the generals. Churchill's proposed splitting up of the Middle East to give Auchinleck a job was successfully resisted by everyone, including Auchinleck himself. Alexander, who had just returned from conducting a difficult retreat from the Japanese in Burma and was to have taken over the British First Army for Operation Torch, the invasion of French North Africa, was instead to replace Auchinleck as Commander Middle East, and he was in turn to be succeeded in the command of the British First Army by General Montgomery.

Churchill now appreciated that Auchinleck had been burdened with too many tasks in his vast Command and that beating Rommel required the undivided attentions of one purposeful, aggressive man. He proposed that this should be General 'Jumbo' Maitland Wilson, an imposingly bulky officer. There is universal agreement that Brooke and Smuts, the Boer commando leader now turned British imperialist, were right to talk the Prime Minister out of this idea. And, with both Churchill's nominees disposed of, one way or another, at last Brooke got his own way and Churchill not too enthusiastically agreed to accept Bernard Law Montgomery as the man who would actually fight the war in the desert, believing that he would be firmly controlled by the man who impressed him most, General Alexander. Montgomery was ordered to be flown out at once from England, where he commanded the South-Eastern Army and had just overseen two rehearsals for the Dieppe Raid of the Canadian Corps under his command during June.

The handover was supposed to take place officially on 15 August, but Montgomery jumped the gun: judging that Rommel would soon mount a full-scale attack and that there was no time to lose, he simply assumed command two days early on 13 August. On the way back from an unpleasant meeting with Stalin, where he had endured much sarcasm from the Soviet tyrant, including the jibe that Churchill would find war was not so bad, once he plucked up the courage to try it, the Prime Minister had made a brief visit to the Western Desert to see how Brooke's protégé Montgomery was shaping up. Denis Johnston, the white-kneed war correspondent for the BBC, had the same idea. The date was fateful — 19 August, the day the Dieppe Raid was actually carried out. The landings were counter-attacked, not by 2nd Battalion the London Scottish directed by Montgomery but by the German Army.

'... a fiasco, three-fifths of the Canadians — about 3,000 men — were either killed or taken prisoner...' wrote Churchill's doctor Sir Charles, later to be Lord, Moran when the news reached him in Cairo that day. Brooke simply grunted: 'It is a lesson to the people who were clamouring for the invasion of France!' Stalin, of course, was one of them; and he had many followers.

Denis Johnston was at XIII Corps when the Prime Minister arrived in boiler suit and topee and carrying a blue umbrella. This was the corps lately commanded by 'Strafer' Gott, who had now been succeeded by another white-kneed general straight out from Home Forces, Brian Horrocks. The Prime

Minister was not impressed. For the matter of that, the soldiers seemed to be in two minds about their Prime Minister. His route to Corps HQ was only thinly lined by phlegmatic soldiery. As Johnston had noted, for the officers generally it was their war and they were interested in it; for the common squaddies it was not their war, they were decidedly not interested, and they definitely did not intend to be killed in it, so far as that was possible. Few officers understood this; they assumed it was simply stupidity.

With the Prime Minister were Brooke and Alexander. They noticed already the change brought about by the new regime; the officers they spoke to were far more cheerful. Not so the squaddies. When Alexander's car with its pennant flying passed a group of lounging soldiery who took no notice of the arrival of a Commander-in-Chief, the ex-Guardsman Alexander told the driver to stop, said who he was, and snapped: '... and in future you will salute the union flag when you see it!' One would have loved to be a scorpion hiding under a stone to hear the squaddies' remarks when Alexander had gone in a cloud of dust.

The BBC team could see, when the Prime Minister arrived, that he was in an ill temper. We know from Brooke's diaries that he had been fretting during his previous visit that no one was apparently planning any offensive action until 15 September (that was when Auchinleck was still in charge); now under Montgomery there seemed to have been no change, and actually the situation was worse (from the Prime Minister's point of view) because the brash, opinionated Montgomery had no intention of being bounced into premature action which would ruin both the Eighth Army and his own hitherto successful career.

The BBC team were reluctant to approach the 'Old War Horse' in his present mood, so the problem was solved on truly Service lines. The most junior man would have to go over the top. There was a suggestion that Johnston might first approach the new Army Commander to approach Churchill for him. That put Johnston in the ticklish position of approaching Montgomery and saying in effect, I don't want you, matey, I just want your boss.

'That's an idea,' said Johnston. 'Where'll I find him?'

'He's over there, sitting in one of those staff cars.'

Johnston walked over, but the only occupant he could find was a man wearing an Australian slouch hat, turned up at the side.

'I say, where do I find the new Army Commander?'

'Who?'

'His name is Montgomery, I believe.'

'I'm the new Army Commander.'

'Oh, come. I know he's not an Australian.'

'Oh, don't go by my hat, I've just been trying it on. Rather good, don't you think?'

'I belong to the BBC, sir, and I was hoping we might get a short recording from you.'

'Not now. They've been photographing me all day. But I tell you what I'll do. The PM is somewhere around and I'll get him to do a piece for you instead.'

Monty, a characteristic of him, was as good as his word. With the press photographing the occasion, Johnston interviewed the 'War Horse' himself, with visions of the pictures being printed in the home papers. Alas, when the picture finally appeared in *GEN*, the Eighth Army's weekly illustrated, it had been drastically trimmed to show two pairs of legs only — one pair of thin, hairy legs with one stocking hanging down around the ankle, alongside another pair in the baggy trousers of a boiler suit and the end of a pale umbrella. The caption? 'Winnie in the Desert.'

Later, Montgomery was to take every opportunity of broadcasting in order to get himself known. There was vanity in it of course, but also necessity. In the eighteenth century it may have been possible to fight a battle in the space of half-a-dozen fields, with the commander riding along the tightly packed lines of squares of his men. Even with such a small army as the Eighth, this was no longer possible; men no longer had any conception of who their leader was, let alone his name. An almost exactly parallel case was to occur in French North Africa in a few months' time, when the Americans were to repeat the unwise Balaclava charges of the British in the bloodily mistaken belief that audacity is all; Rommel was to send them back in a rout (but as American soldiers in those days were never known to retreat, this sad affair is secret in the States). The man sent to take over the shaken formation was General Patton, who needed to impress on everyone that the corps was under new management. As well as riding in with a posse of command vehicles, pennants whipping in the breeze, and standing up like a six-gun conqueror, he also pondered on how to reach every soldier in his scattered command, and decided: Issue an order that they all wear their steel helmets at all times. That'll teach them that George S. Patton has taken command.

After the war the principle, that all should know who the Managing Director was and what he required of the staff, was universally accepted in business and the Company House Magazine flourished as a way of putting this across. Montgomery and Patton, in their very different ways, were simply acknowledging that war in the twentieth century had increased in scale from the small family business, where everyone knew the boss, to conflicts waged by mass organisations where the leaders and their ideas were remote — unless steps were taken to put them across. This explains the succession of hats worn by Monty until finally he fixed on what seemed the right image, the sharp, foxy, professional general.

Horrocks was later to become a famous television general, having led XXX Corps in the 'Brussels Swan' of 1944, the dash out of the Normandy beachhead and into Holland towards Arnhem. On this day he was not known in the desert; like his superior, Montgomery, he was just another white-kneed new boy fresh out from England and untried. Indeed, the only general (apart from Rommel) of whom the Old War Horse approved, it seems, was Alexander, and this apparently because in Churchill's eyes he looked the part. After the First World War and during the unknown campaigns in Eastern Europe which followed, he had commanded, among others, German troops — who greatly impressed him — and there is no doubt that he was a splendid leader at company and battalion level, and a cool Commander during the Dunkirk evacuation. But his prime quality in his new job, in Brooke's eyes, was that he was unlikely to interfere with Montgomery, who would have his own very clear ideas of what needed to be done and had on this occasion for the first time the advantage of Ultra. For Churchill, however, everybody except 'Alex' was on trial; to the old desert hands also, Horrocks was a doubtful new proposition — and although they knew he must have been briefed by Montgomery, the secrecy surrounding Ultra was properly such that they did not dream it existed.

The memoirs of the various generals are a trifle difficult to interpret at this stage, because they either did not know of the part played by Ultra or were forbidden by the Official Secrets Act to mention it. But Horrocks was well briefed by those junior to him, and firstly that the desert was a terrible place for infantry, for there was virtually no cover and the commanding hills were so rocky that the only way to dig in was by using explosives. They could attack only behind smokescreens fired by the artillery or at night. Consequently the tank was 'queen of the battlefield'; if you lost too many tanks, you'd lost the battle.

As for what Rommel was going to do, there seemed no doubt. He would make a right hook in the southern sector of the front, near the Qattara Depression, break through the 7th Armoured Division there, and then do one of two things: penetrate deeply and make a wide circle before turning north to cut the coast road and railway, or make a smaller circle which would save precious fuel, and attack the Alam el Haifa feature which overlooked his route. This latter option was the more likely. Most of these ridges were more or less parallel to the coast, and this one dominated any route chosen by Rommel. It was a perfect place to stage an ambush. And Montgomery had given Horrocks strict orders that the British tanks were not to be loosed in any wild charge or incur significant losses. It was to be a defensive battle, of the sort Rommel had so often carried out to the British ruin, letting the British armour rush to destruction on his screen of anti-tank guns. The Alam el Haifa ridge was a useful commanding height and the British Artillery were a notably efficient corps. In addition the Desert Air Force now outnumbered the Luftwaffe and were, under Montgomery, acting in close cooperation with the ground forces. To add sauce to the plot, a false 'going map' of the ground over which the Afrika Korps must pass was prepared. Very soft ground, likely to bog everything or at last drastically slow the vehicles, was marked as 'good' going, and the false map suitably stained with spilt tea and left in a wrecked jeep where the Germans were sure to find it.

The original plan had been for 22 Armoured Brigade to counterattack as soon as the Germans penetrated the positions of 7 Armoured Division; this was now cancelled. The Germans were to be allowed to drive right through until they were well inside the trap. Horrocks had only been in charge for a week when the Prime Minister paid his visit to XIII Corps under its new untried commander. Horrocks says he got the impression that the Prime Minister did not think much either of him or the new, defensive, policy (which was Montgomery's based on Ultra and a good look at the ground). Churchill became particularly impatient when Horrocks explained that the idea behind the new plan could best be explained as 'dog eat rabbit'. While the German armoured spearheads were being blunted on the British gunline and the dug in tanks, much of the artillery would strike at their 'rabbits', the soft-skinned supply vehicles upon which the panzers depended.

'That's no good!' snapped Churchill. 'Trouble with you generals is that you are defensive minded. Why don't you attack? That's the way to win battles, not by sitting down in defence.'

During the rest of the day the old man kept muttering 'Dog eat rabbit!' and before he turned to leave, he told Horrocks: 'You have a very big responsibility on your shoulders, young man.'

On the way back to Cairo he told Montgomery: 'He's no good, get rid of him.' Monty replied: 'Look here, sir, you stick to your sphere and I'll stick to mine.'

After the battle had been safely concluded, Horrocks begged permission to send the Prime Minister an informative message, 'Dog Ate Rabbit', but alas, permission was refused.

One more fact about the desert war Horrocks learned before the battle began. The Germans 'always fought cleanly... never has there been less hate between the opposing sides.'

Montgomery had arrived on 12 August in Cairo, and there he had been briefed by General de Guingand, whom he shortly made his Chief of Staff. Presumably he was told something of Auchinleck's plans and about Ultra, but can have had little time in which to absorb it, for the next day he toured Eighth Army in the desert, found the situation unsatisfactory and took over command immediately. It has been suggested that he probably never had time to read Auchinleck's plan for Alamein; and it seems doubtful that, even if he had had the time, he would have bothered. He was not a modest or retiring character. Addressing, or 'lecturing' (for he was an ex-Staff College lecturer), the Eighth Army's senior officers on the evening of his first day in the desert the 13th, he told them: 'I understand that Rommel is expected to attack at any moment. Excellent. Let him attack.' Clearly his information was good, for three hours later an order came from the Duce to the Axis desert HQ to make 'rapid preparations for a renewal of the offensive'. The date, added Mussolini, was to be decided by himself.

The signal was intercepted and decoded. Within 36 hours came a first indication of the date. Panzer Army HQ wirelessed the 'Q' office in Rome how much fuel, ammunition and food could be expected to arrive by 25 August. Montgomery had wanted 14 days to make his preparations, regroup, retrain, make defensive areas in the right places, and bring up a new infantry division, the 44th just out from UK, without allowing much time for the men and vehicles to be acclimatised. Ten days was a little too soon for all this to be done.

On 17 August two enemy signals were sent and intercepted. Taken together, they gave Montgomery Rommel's plan.

German reconnaissance near the Qattara Depression at the southern end of the Alamein 'line' furthest from the sea was forbidden, so that British suspicions of the point of attack were not roused. This point of attack was not unexpected, as it was so obvious. The second, more important signal, made by Rommel on 15 August and decrypted on the 17th, was the German commander's appreciation of the situation. Montgomery did not have to look at photographs of Rommel's face and guess; on the 17th of August, he knew. His opponent was not only telling the two German GHQs, OKH and OKW — respectively Army and Armed Forces GHQs — he was also telling the new British commander in the desert, who was foxy enough to make full use of it. In summary, under the usual headings, Rommel informed his superiors:

> *Own situation.* From being critical, was now better. The men more rested. Supplies would soon be adequate — provided that shipments of fuel and ammunition were maintained.

> *Enemy's situation.* An enemy convoy consisting of one armoured and one infantry division had just reached Suez; and in a fortnight would be followed by another. Eighth Army would be strong enough to attack by mid-September.

> *Balance of forces.* Until the end of August, the Axis would be slightly superior in armour and evens or better in other arms.

> *Intention.* Break through in the south where there are no fixed defences and only weak enemy forces at the moment (but which the British would begin to fortify in September). Enemy air superiority made it necessary to choose a moonlit night for the attack. There would be a full moon on 26 August. The next full moon period after that would be four weeks later.

After reading this appreciation by his opponent, Montgomery could be fairly certain that there would be no surprises, although he might spring some himself. But ranging far beyond the land battle was the indication of the Axis weak point — the absolute necessity for the continuing supply of fuel and ammunition. That was for the Navy and the RAF to interdict. This message made it plain that special measures needed to be taken to step up attacks on the convoys. These attacks, although taking place in many cases hundreds of miles from the desert battlefields, were inescapably part of the battle, although the soldiers might not be aware of them. The submarine that dived at dawn to stalk its prey, the torpedo bomber that went roaring in low over the water in the moonlight, these were just as much a part of the conflict as the tank man behind his armour plate or the infantryman advancing behind a smokescreen. All the Services were fighting the same war for the same ends, which was not always true back at home, where inter-Service ambitions could be serious.

This information, in its completeness and balance, had few true parallels in the war. In the previous year, General Student's plans for the invasion of Crete had been equally well known in advance — but the defence had lacked the force to make good use of the knowledge. Two years hence, Hitler's ill-advised counterattack against the Americans at Mortain during the Normandy campaign was also to be revealed by Ultra — and the Allies were strong enough to abort that offensive with heavy losses to the enemy armour. At the end of 1944 the few signs of the coming Hitler-sponsored attack into the Ardennes were not picked up and interpreted correctly — and a severe shock was delivered to the over-confident Americans and British (whose military commanders, Eisenhower and Montgomery, started fighting each other). At sea, Ultra played a vital part in the eventual defeat of the U-boats in the Battle of the Atlantic; and had played and was continuing to play an equally important role against Axis shipping in the Mediterranean.

But rarely can a new commander have had the enemy delivered into his hands as was Rommel to Montgomery in the summer of 1942. It was, combined with the promise of substantial reinforcements and tanks capable of meeting the Germans on not too unequal terms, the chance of a lifetime; and Montgomery was determined to seize it.

Tom Witherby, after being in hospital, returned to the front about 17 August, the day Rommel's intentions had been decrypted and less than a week since the 'new broom' had taken over. Yet the effect was immediately apparent.

> The aspect of the Desert was so different that I could not have recognised it. 'C' Track, once 200 yards wide and composed of fine dust, was now a smooth road running between fenced minefields. The road surface was a kind of tarmac made of a combination of sand and water. There were neat notices on the fences saying PLEASE KEEP OFF THE MINEFIELD. All over the Ruweisat Ridge there were neat slit trenches and other fortifications dug into the rock with neat parapets of sandbags. All these had been made with explosives and if one looked around one was sure to see a little puff of smoke as another hole was blasted out by the Sappers. At the top of the track down from the Ridge, the two Mark III tanks had gone and all the derelict Italian and German tanks had been cleared out of 'Happy Valley' and their crews buried. Even the stench was not quite so bad, but the flies were the same. They cared nothing for Monty.
>
> Everywhere there was a new spirit. One felt that there was at least someone in charge and someone who did not intend to be defeated. The intention was clear. All parts of the Army

were to be made as strong as possible. Every post was to have All Round Defence, with its own stores and supplied within itself. We were told that 8th Army had its post at Alamein and that it would fight there and, if necessary, be destroyed there. 'There will be no further retreat, none at all, none.'

Auchinleck, quite properly, had had 'last case' plans made for further retreat by stages; but clearly Montgomery had sniffed the air and felt that Dan Pienaar's sentiments expressed to Denis Johnston, the BBC newcomer, had force. The first target of his campaign must be in the sphere of morale; they'd had enough of retreat. But just to declare 'Here we are, and here we stay, alive or dead,' was not enough.

> In everything there were new ideas. There had been a prejudice, dating from December 1940 and the defeat of the Italians, against reliance on roads, which were said to reduce mobility. In a similar way, there was a dislike of fortifications. Montgomery rejected all this. His Army fought in a solid lump, with no flanks and so arranged that everyone was in a position to support someone else.

In England there had been developed the idea of concentrated artillery fire — the '800-gun battery' — thus making use of the British Army's excellent artillery. In Normandy it was to prove devastating, producing a legend among German soldiers of the 'belt-fed 25-pounder field gun'. Montgomery was busy organising on something like these lines, not for the coming battle of Alam el Haifa but for the one after that, of Alamein or Tel el Eisa, when he would not merely halt the German Army but start to drive it out of Africa. In the context of the long run of British defeats in the desert, this was almost inconceivable.

Montgomery was a totally different type of senior officer from the majority in the Middle East at that time. He was certainly not a 'nice chap', but he was good at winning battles. His casualty lists were shorter than those of other generals and his losses in weapons, guns, tanks and the like were low. Everything, both men and weapons, had to be used with the best advantage and with care. In the expenditure of human life, he was a miser.

That was Tom Witherby's opinion. Others echoed it. Sapper B. Easthope, son of a journalist and a journalist himself, later said: 'No one liked Monty but we respected his generalship.' He seems to have been extremely good at delegation (which the unfortunate Auchinleck certainly was not). To train his senior commanders, wrote Witherby:

Montgomery set an exercise in which he described what the Germans and Italians would do and what was the correct move against them. He actually used this exercise in the actual battle of Alam el Haifa, because after the first two days, when he wished to devote time to the preparation for the great battle of Alamein, he asked his Commanders not to trouble him if they could help it and to look up the exercise if they wished to see what the enemy would do next!

There was just time for 23 Armoured Brigade to rehearse how to get to five places by day or by night at the top speed of their Valentine tanks.

We were moved across the Ruweisat Ridge out of Happy Valley and were in fairly flat ground south of the Ridge. The whole Brigade was there, with 7 Rifle Brigade, and the Gunners. The days of complicated, obscure plans, of constant pointless movements and of the splitting up of formations were gone forever. The battle of Alam el Haifa began on the evening of 30 August and Montgomery had taken command on 13 August. In that time he had created quite a new spirit in 8th Army, settled any disputes or mistrust that had existed between the RAF and the Army, joined their HQs together, instituted a programme of fortification, created a new 'turned back' front on the Alam el Haifa Ridge and moved 44 Division on to the Ridge as a garrison. He also found time to reorganise the Army into three Army Corps, to teach what appeared to be new ideas about the need for tanks and artillery to be used in mass, as well as going round visiting units. The army that he took over on 13 August could not possibly have stopped Rommel's German/Italian attack. Gott was a brave man but he was tired and did not have the intellectual stature for the Command.

After much study Witherby came to the conclusion that the virtually non-stop run of German success up to that period of the war was due, not merely to their being good soldiers equipped with good weapons, well organised and well trained, but also to the fact that usually their weapons outranged those of their opponents. Their 'Special' tanks for instance outranged any of the British tanks or even the American-built Grants, and in addition their anti-tank guns outranged all those set against them, so there was a kind of double outranging. What Montgomery did was to turn matters round the other way. Firstly, by fortification he gave protection to his tanks and anti-tank guns, making that contest more even; and then by massive use of his artillery and air power he outranged the enemy. German tanks had thick frontal armour, but were weaker at the sides and on top, so were vulnerable to artillery and bombing, as of course were infantry in the open and the mass of soft-skinned supply vehicles. In the Alam el Haifa battle, the defenders were so positioned that the Germans were constantly under artillery fire, often from several directions at once, and this fire was directed from higher ground, from the air or on pre-arranged targets; whereas the German and Italian OP officers were on lower ground and under fire themselves.

Although the British official history stressed Rommel's poor health at that time (after being long in the desert) and supply difficulties (which were partly of his own making), Witherby felt that insufficient weight was given to the British Commander's methods and the result he achieved.

> The truth is that this battle was altogether astounding. It was unbelievable. In the whole of the 1914 to 1918 War and up to 1942 in the 1939 to 1945 War, an 'all out' German attack had never been stopped at once. Even the great 'Crusader' battle of 1941 had only been fought to a draw. In August 1942 hardly anyone could conceive of the idea of simply stopping the Panzers in their tracks! This was regarded as impossible.

In fairness to the Germans it should be stressed that a number of senior officers believed that Rommel was reckless, particularly with his supplies. The more reinforcements he demanded, the worse the strain on his supply system; the further he advanced, the greater the demand for fuel. Africa should be a sideshow, just a prop to the Italians; the splendid scheme of driving for the Middle East oilfields and joining up with an offensive launched by von Kleist from the Caucasus into Iran was an ambitious dream, beyond the power of the Third Reich while the Soviet was still in the war.

The battle began with feints and demonstrations in the north near the coast, and in the centre, intended to cause the maximum noise and confusion. It was preceded by a call to surrender, possibly intended only for the Indian division. Two German soldiers came forward with a white flag and were immediately taken prisoner; although later, after second thoughts, the British sent them back to Germany via Turkey. But the main attack, as Ultra had indicated, was in the south, carried out by the two German panzer divisions and the motorised infantry and mobile anti-tank gun screen of 90th Light, plus the Italian Ariete Armoured Division with its inferior equipment. The British defences here had been kept deliberately weak, to tempt Rommel to put his head right into the sack. Nevertheless, the Germans had trouble with the elaborate British minefields, through which their engineers had to clear routes under heavy observed fire. There was no lack of push at command level. No less than three out of the four German generals were killed or wounded in the opening stages. When Rommel arrived in the morning, his famous sixth sense may have warned him of the trap, for he wished to abandon the attack, no surprise having been achieved, but General Fritz Bayerlein, who had taken over the Afrika Korps when General Nehring was wounded during the night, persuaded him to attempt the Ridge. Witherby naturally did not know of Bayerlein's urging but pointed out:

> Rommel's solution to a difficulty was always to 'bash on'. He had supply problems, but he must have hoped to capture ample supplies at the top of Alam el Haifa. His health was a problem but his Army was so well trained that its action was almost automatic.

By this time Rommel, a First World War veteran, had been in the desert for a year and half, with that nervous strain peculiar to command as well as the normal climatic trials. German Army diet was even more unsuitable than that of the British (who ought to have known better): on both sides desert sores which would not heal were common; and that form of dysentery peculiar to armies gathered in almost any climate (see

Agincourt 1415 for an earlier example) and which, in spite of modern medical science, was still paralysingly severe even as late as Normandy in 1944 — and here I write from doleful experience. A sufferer could hardly crawl, let alone march.

When Montgomery was awoken during the night of 30/31 August and told that the Germans and Italians were passing through the minefields in the south, he exclaimed 'Excellent, excellent!' and turned over and went to sleep again. Tom Witherby's unit, which was almost in the centre of the old front line, was stood to, then stood down until dawn. Then 'C' Squadron moved off to support the Indians in clouds of diesel smoke as they drove off along the south side of Ruweisat Ridge. Tom was with the rest of the regiment when it moved off to the south and was posted on a low ridge about five miles away.

> I remember passing a number of field batteries dug-in in deep pits with camouflage nets over them. Probably these were the guns supporting the Indians. When we arrived our guns were already in position on our left and began to fire soon after. They were properly dug-in and the pits must have been prepared in advance. About this time, about one p.m., four Mark III tanks came onto a low ridge about a mile away. Instantly, heavy artillery fire came down on them and one was hit and began to burn. The others withdrew. These tanks would have been looking for a gap, and if they had not been fired on would have tried to come on towards Ruweisat Ridge. At this time also, some German guns began to fire at us — or at least where they thought we were. Four shells would explode together in the valley just below us. These tanks and guns must have been from 90th Light, who were moving up slowly, delayed by the going, by the bombing and by the constant artillery fire from the New Zealand Box, from 7th Armoured and from our Ridge. The smoke from the

burning Mark III rose in a column a mile away. Our own artillery were all around and were firing continuously, sending off one dozen shells for every German one.

Tom got into conversation with a South African officer who had been observing from an armoured car. He asked what he thought unusually unwelcome in the *Penelope* because her bridge had just previous battles he had seen, the Germans would come on all together and get on to Alam el Haifa, then they would break up into smaller parties and tear about doing as much damage as they could, and finally they would all join together and smash us. Tom noted that this was more or less what had happened at Gazala. But this time, it didn't happen.

The two panzer divisions moved east and north for their attack on Alam el Haifa. Tom followed the battle by listening to Brigade HQ wireless traffic on the regimental rear link. The activities of the Germans were being continuously reported. They seemed to have halted in the Deir er Ragil depression to take on ammunition and fuel after their forward march and the fighting in the morning. Then they issued from the depression and advanced to the attack. Messages came in all the time.

'Column of 80 approx. tanks moving north-east from Ragil Depression.'

This was 21 Panzer Div, moving across the front of Tom's regiment towards the higher ground — rather like the Bournemouth cliffs and chines without the houses — which was Alam el Haifa. They would have to ascend these low cliffs to reach the British positions. The German column included captured Valentines, heavily sandbagged and with their tool boxes and ammo cases filled with concrete as additional protection.

'Second column of 80 approx. tanks moving north-east from Deir er Ragil. They seem to be following the line of telegraph poles.'

This was 15th Panzer Div. Both columns contained a high proportion of 'Specials' fitted with a more powerful gun. With the battle at its height about twenty Junkers 88s approached over the New Zealand Box, which belched up heavy fire at them, and were received in the same way when they flew over Tom's brigade. Still over the New Zealand Box, a tiny pin of light showed on one of the Ju 88s — engine on fire. The fire grew steadily, but the burning bomber flew on and made its attack with the others. As they turned away the stricken bomber was just a ball of fire. Finally, as the aircraft reached friendly territory, parachutes appeared. Their bombs had fallen on the transport of Tom's brigade, the Junkers diving low over the cliffs on their return. Some of the Bofors followed them down and a shell shot off the top of the Brigadier's wireless aerial.

As the light faded a mist arose which largely frustrated RAF attempts to bomb the concentration of German armour and supply vehicles in the lower ground overlooked by the ridge of Alam el Haifa. On 1 September the Germans made a number of attempts to get up the cliffs and reached the 100-metre contour about 200 metres from the British infantry posts. 40 Royal Tanks and part of 46 Royal Tanks of 23 Armoured Brigade were moved south to support them and from 'hull down' positions engaged the Germans at advantage.

> This was the effective end of the first part of the battle. As the light faded, flares appeared in the sky over the German camp. Soon the ground began to shake as heavy bombs were dropped. The last thing I remember before going to sleep was the sight of the flares hanging in the sky and the ground heaving and vibrating.

The British had now received a number of 6-pounder anti-tank guns and more of the American Grant tanks which were not all that inferior to most of the Germans. And of course they were properly dug in and positioned on the heights all along the flank of the German advance. That concentration of guns and armour could not simply be ignored in a wild dash for the coast road and the Suez Canal over the temptingly empty desert ahead. Alam el Haifa Ridge had to be taken first. It is clear now, as it was not to those who witnessed it at the time, that German knowledge of the British defences and their intentions was inadequate. This was because they had lost the ability to read the reports of Colonel Fellers, their unsuspecting 'fly on the wall' inside British GHQ conferences, and because of deliberate British action (almost the last action of Auchinleck) to capture or destroy Captain Alfred Seebohm's wireless interception unit on Tel el Eisa. By contrast, British ability to read the German messages had vastly improved, not only in balanced information but in speed of transcription.

The Germans were in fact in considerable trouble, pounded from the air and by artillery, facing solid, effective defences on the high ground above them. They did still have a superiority of force, except in the air, but insufficient knowledge of their enemy's dispositions. Tom Witherby assumed that both generals may have been confident on the evening of 1 September, Montgomery because for the first time in the war anywhere (including the Russian front) an all-out German attack had been stopped literally in its tracks, and Rommel because he appeared to have broken through the British defences between the Ridge and the Qattara Depression and passed his attacking force into open country, had inflicted significant losses on the British and had reached almost to the top of Alam el Haifa.

Rommel had been fighting British generals for eighteen months. He knew exactly what the next move would be. At first light on 2 September he could be certain that the whole of the British armour would descend from the Alam el Haifa Ridge and would endeavour to drive the two panzer divisions back whence they came. There would be a confused battle lasting two or three days in which most of the British armour would be destroyed. On 5th or 6th September after the Luftwaffe had made a series of heavy attacks on 44th Division, the panzer divisions would again attack the Ridge, gain the top and would begin the process of destroying the 44th Divisional positions, while 90th Light and the Italians moved to attack the New Zealanders and to roll up the old British front line. Captured petrol would be there in plenty.

Recalling how his own brigade under Auchinleck and Gott had lost 93 per cent of its tank crews in their first battle, Tom's guess seems reasonable. But he knew, as Rommel almost certainly did not, that there was a general on the British side who had forbidden any counter-attack and had also ruled that no petrol dumps should be held anywhere near the enemy, so as to prevent possible captures.

British staff officers, men of experience, on the Ridge on 3 September, could not understand what the Germans appeared to be doing. The British simply did not believe that the Germans were pulling back and retreating after a severe defeat. Up to that time all German attacks, like those of Napoleon up to the battle of Busaco in the Peninsular War, had ended in victory for the Germans. They had never retreated.

At last light on 2 September the British still expected a renewal of the attack. The infantry of 7 Rifle Brigade brought in a German doctor as a prisoner, who was in a shocked condition 'from the appalling shelling and bombing' the Afrika Korps had had to endure below the Ridge. During that night the Luftwaffe flew low overhead trying to draw A.A. fire, but the British units had been ordered not to give away their positions. It was probably next day, 3 September, that the Luftwaffe made a desperate, sacrificial attempt to save the situation.

> Eight stukas appeared to try to silence some guns that were firing near the New Zealand Box. They were flying in a storm of anti-aircraft fire. At least ten Bofors guns were engaging them at the same time, plus numerous Besa machine-guns from tanks and the infantry Brens. At one time, five of the stukas were on fire in the air simultaneously. We like to think we got one of them from our tank. Just above us two men baled out and floated down nearby. Bernard Heath, our technical adjutant, rushed out in a truck and made them prisoner. They came back past us on their way to Brigade HQ, standing up in the back of the truck and looking scornfully at us, but they must have been impressed by the long line of Valentines that stretched along the ridge for two miles to Brigade HQ.

The Desert Air Force was flying nearly three sorties more over the Germans than the Luftwaffe was putting up over the British. In the air, the conditions of 1940 were now almost exactly reversed. But although the Germans were retiring, it was carried out in a soldierly and dangerous fashion. It was anything but a rout. Montgomery did not intend to push the Germans too hard, knowing that many of his troops simply were not up to the job, nor were they present yet in sufficient numbers. The British advance was not very well conducted, and Witherby guessed that Montgomery had left it to his subordinate commanders so that he could concentrate on planning for the final battle of Alamein which should decide the war in Africa.

> Not unexpectedly, there was strong opposition and the attack was a failure with heavy loss. 44th Division were inexperienced for a night attack of this kind. Our Squadron was left out on a ridge all day under heavy fire. One officer, who was killed, had his tank surrounded by Italians who were calling on him to surrender. This was not at all the copybook fighting of the earlier part of the Battle. But on the 6th or 7th of September it was almost over. The slow Axis withdrawal had taken Rommel to a line close to the January and February minefields. Montgomery decided that it would be a costly matter to push him back further and so, with some finesse, Montgomery left Rommel there in possession of the twin peaks of Himeimat, 600 feet high, where he had excellent observation of the southern part of the British lines. This allowed him to watch the dummy preparations that were soon to begin there for the dummy Battle of Alamein that appeared to be timed to start about 10th November 1942.

Montgomery was late (in Churchill's eyes — and in those of senior RAF figures). Auchinleck had been dismissed for saying among other things that no offensive could be mounted until mid-September. But there was a great deal to do, not least in the field of elaborate deception measures, as well as training and acclimatising the new divisions, if this last offensive was to be not only successful but final. Montgomery was planning to attack in the north in the last week of October, and therefore wished the Germans to believe that he would strike in the south several weeks later.

> For our part, we of the 23rd Armoured Brigade moved east to the far end of Alam el Haifa Ridge. The air was cooler. There was a feeling of autumn. Under the camelthorn, beautiful lilies

appeared briefly in the sand, brought out by the morning dew. The snails seemed to move less slowly and the chameleons were quite sprightly as they made their way through the camelthorn. At dawn we heard the bagpipes. Another prime infantry formation, the 51st Highland Division, had arrived. All possibility of a further Axis attack was removed. Our battle was over.

9: HECATOMB OF THE TANKERS

Because of the revival of Malta as an air base and the numerous sinkings in the Mediterranean, supplies for the First Panzer Army have fallen far below normal requirements. Unless Malta is weakened or paralysed once more, this situation cannot be remedied.

Count Ciano, 14 September 1942

In all, we have little more than a million tons [of merchant shipping] left. At this rate the African problem will automatically end in six months, since we shall have no more ships with which to supply Libya.

Count Ciano, 29 September 1942

Rommel's message listing his casualties for the battle of Alam el Haifa, which was intercepted, gave them as approximately 3,000 dead, wounded and missing (killed being 369 Germans and 167 Italians); the Axis tank losses had been 36 German tanks destroyed and about a dozen Italian, plus 55 guns and 400 vehicles. Personnel casualties had been due mainly to the continuous attacks by day and by night carried out by the RAF, according to this report. The Axis had destroyed, according to British records, 67 tanks, which was greater than the Axis total. But Rommel had been stopped for good. And the build-up of men and equipment for the final battle had begun.

That was on both sides, of course. In August the Axis fighting strength in North Africa was 42,000 Germans and 82,000 Italians, with fuel for eight days' fighting and ammunition for a fortnight (an improvement on the situation at the time of Alam el Haifa). The prime importance of Ultra was to point to the main Axis weaknesses and enable the British to select for destruction the particular shipments which would damage their enemy most. The Ultra decodes, mainly of Italian material, frequently revealed port of loading, cargo, and date of sailing (but not necessarily route and port of discharge). As the often unknown factors had relatively few practical solutions, guesswork as to route and destination could be usefully employed. In sum, the use of Ultra was before the battle took place; when action began its uses became limited.

At first glance, the greatest anti-shipping measures seem to have been taken by the Malta submarines. The official history which includes Sigint (Signals Intelligence)[8] prints as an appendix an 11-page list of Axis shipping losses in which an unnamed 'Submarine' is given as the cause of the sinking. Also listed are a fair number of losses by 'aircraft torpedo' or 'bombs', but when these losses of named ships are compared to air crews' records, a large discrepancy occurs. To give but the first two examples I had access to, there was a navigator/observer from 39 Squadron which flew torpedo-carrying Beauforts, Terence McGarry. He flew on antishipping strikes with Beaufighter escort on 17, 20, 21, 24, 26, and 30 August, 6 and 23 September and 2 November 1942. Three of his targets, the tankers *Rosalino Pilo*, *San Andrea* and *Zara*, featured in the Sigint list; the remaining six did not, although there were photographs to back up the log entries, for these were daylight strikes. McGarry cautioned me not to forget the work of the Malta-based PRU (Photographic Reconnaissance Unit) of which Adrian Warburton was the star, and clearly this

---

[8] *British Intelligence in the Second World War* by F. H. Hinsley, E. E. Thomas, C. F. G. Ransom and R. C. Knight, Vols 1 & 2 (HMSO, 1979 and 1981). See also *Ultra and Mediterranean Strategy 1941-1945* by Ralph Bennett (Hamish Hamilton, 1989).

was one answer. A large number of air strikes on shipping were the result of air reconnaissance, not Ultra.

There were other means of locating ships, apart from decoded wireless transmissions on the one hand and accurate aerial photographs on the other. The subject divides conveniently into night and day. For instance 38 Squadron operated by night, flying Wellingtons adapted to carry two torpedoes. Mike Foulis, who died as a Squadron Leader over the Mediterranean in 1943, and cannot be questioned, was one of the first half-dozen pilots to perfect the technique of torpedo-bombing by night. In support of 38, another Wellington squadron, 221, developed a technique of search by highly specialised radars, coupled with a method of marking a moving target at night by flares so that the torpedo bombers could attack with best results.

By day, 39 Squadron, flying the faster Beauforts adapted to carry one torpedo and escorted by even faster Beaufighters and occasionally Spitfires, sought out prey indicated most often by PRU aircraft from Malta, frequently stripped-down Spitfires, and occasionally by Ultra decodes. The Beaus, like the submarines, were usually based on Malta, whereas the longer-range Wellingtons usually flew from fields in Egypt or Libya (depending on the positions of the rival armies at the time). The task of the Beaufighters was primarily flak-suppression, their targets the destroyers that escorted the tankers, and occasionally the German or Italian aircraft which also accompanied these dreadfully inflammable vessels. Anyone who disparages the courage of Italians generally should consider the merchant seamen who for many months sailed in the expectation of a fifty-fifty chance of being burnt to death in a red-hot ship or in a flaming sea. Truly, the Italian navy historians dubbed this period as 'the hecatomb of the tankers'.

Similarly, many of the attackers were doomed. Strike squadron losses averaged 33 per cent. In three months, Mike Foulis won the DFC and bar before going on to do a second tour which he did not survive. His second DFC was gained by a night attack on a convoy sighted on 28 August 1942 steaming west of Crete with a strong destroyer escort. In the evening Wellingtons and Liberators found the convoy and sank one of the two main fuel-carrying storeships. To supplement the purpose-built tankers, some merchant ships carried fuel for tanks or aircraft in barrels or other containers. Next day, 29 August, a second wave of Wellington torpedo bombers also found the convoy. Afterwards Foulis reported:

We sighted the ships at 0015 in the moonpath. There was no cloud and a bright moon. We could see the ship clearly, a vessel of about 8,000 tons or perhaps a little less. There was one destroyer about two miles ahead of her, another about a mile on her port bow, and a third close in to her starboard quarter. I spent about twenty minutes flying across the moonpath on the west side to work out my line of attack. Eventually I made up my mind on the best approach and we commenced a long run-up on the ship's starboard bow. She was not fully in the moonpath but she was clearly visible. I could see no white wake astern of her, but the track in the sea along which she travelled could be seen. I dropped my first torpedo at a range of 700 yards, and the second at 400 yards. We flew ahead of one destroyer but were not fired upon until after the torpedoes had been released. As soon as the second torpedo was gone, I pulled the aircraft up and we passed over between the centre and the stern of the ship.

The torpedoes were on their way but had not yet reached her. The destroyer closed in and the ship herself opened fire, the latter at point blank range. My rear gunner could not fire at the ship because he could not depress his guns sufficiently. I took violent evasive action and we escaped damage. The navigator, who was in the astrodome, reported two bright orange flashes on the vessel, astern and amidships. I swung the aircraft round and we could all see two great columns of water going above her masts. It was clear that both torpedoes had hit.

We ran up and down on the west side watching developments. Very quickly thick grey smoke began to come out of the ship. The destroyers closed in to her, and within five minutes a heavy smoke pall lay all over the ships. We could plainly smell this smoke in the aircraft; it smelt oily and acrid. We sent out our first target report: 'Two hits on tanker, stationary, smoking.' About ten minutes later the smoke cleared and a large oil patch was all that remained of the merchant ship. The destroyers were there but nothing else. We sent another signal: 'Tanker believed sunk, large oil patch seen.'

Fred Oldfield, a W/T operator, radar operator and air gunner of 221 Squadron, whose Wellingtons developed into a pathfinder force for 38 Squadron's torpedo bombers, lost his logbook in a December 1942 ditching but was able to reconstruct the record during the period they changed from bombing ships themselves to finding convoys for 38's Wellingtons to torpedo and lighting them up by a new flare-dropping technique. Of the nine operations Oldfield listed between 2 July and 3 November 1942, one — just possibly, but doubtfully — might have been Ultra-inspired. The other eight most definitely were not. 221's Wellingtons had very special radars for ship search by night; and only a limited number of sailing route options were open to the Axis ships. The search aircraft usually operated from various airfields in Egypt or Libya.

We carried special aerials — Sterba curtain arrays on the spine and sides of the Wellingtons and a Yagi beam aerial under each wing. When the Sterba arrays were connected to the radar they gave a very narrow cone of detection with a range of some 70 miles on each side of the aircraft. When the forward-facing Yagi aerials were connected they gave a large cone of detection in front of the aircraft and the facility to steer directly towards the source of the echoes. During normal sweep search the Sterba arrays would be connected and the operator would have to keep a constant watch because any echoes would only be present for a very short time due to the narrow beam on each side. When an echo was detected it showed up on the radar screen to either port or starboard with an indication of its range; the aircraft would then turn 90 degrees and the Yagi antennae would then be connected, giving a steering indication on the display, again with an indication of range. This system worked very well in detecting submarines and shipping, and during the summer of 1942 a pathfinder operation was developed by 221 in conjunction with 38 Squadron's torpedo aircraft for attacking convoys supplying Rommel's Africa Corps. Previously 221's crews had dropped parachute flares singly down the flare chute, but now the flares were stored in the bomb bay and dropped in sticks.

The method of pathfinding at sea was for three Wellingtons of 221 Squadron, bomb bays loaded with parachute flares, to take off and fly in parallel westwards along the Mediterranean, spaced some 50 miles apart, so that their combined side-search radars covered an enormous area of water. Some time later, 20 or more Wellington torpedo bombers of 38 Squadron would take off and follow the screen of search aircraft. When one of the searchers detected echoes on its beam aerials, it would turn 90 degrees towards the source of the echoes and switch to the forward-looking aerials. If the source turned out to be a single ship or a convoy, a sighting and position report would be transmitted, the search aircraft circling the target and sending out continuous signals for the other aircraft to home on. This successful aircraft would then become the 'Master of Ceremonies' to co-ordinate the attack. The next search aircraft to arrive would fly to a position some 10 miles east of the convoy and lay and maintain a flare path of flame floats. The third and last of the search aircraft would circle the convoy and stay in reserve.

Homing in on the signals made by the Master of Ceremonies, the torpedo bombers would sight the flare path of the flame floats and circle them at stepped up heights, each one reporting its arrival. When the Master of Ceremonies considered that enough torpedo planes had arrived to launch an attack, he would send an attack signal and drop a single flame float at a point where, if the torpedo bombers aimed for it, they would arrive at the convoy. He would then fly behind the convoy and drop a stick of parachute flares, and would be followed by the second and third search aircraft who would maintain the illumination with further sticks of flares until all the 38 Squadron Wellingtons had dropped their torpedoes.

The development of this technique from the simple bombing of ships in North African harbours is recorded in Oldfield's log, reconstructed after his ditching. On 2 July 1942 the Axis-held ports of Tobruk and Derna were bombed, the targets being a destroyer and a merchant vessel. A week later, on 9 July, Oldfield's aircraft flown by F/Sergeant Gay, carried out a torpedo recce, found a convoy, homed the torpedo aircraft onto it and dropped flares. Two ships were hit and set on fire, and Oldfield's aircraft was pursued by a night fighter equipped with a searchlight. On 21 July they found a convoy off Crete but the torpedo bombers did not arrive. 15 August was memorable. They found a convoy, homed the torpedo bombers in and dropped flares — by the old method, down a flare chute, instead of held in the bomb racks. As they turned away, a smell of burning was reported, and then the sound of something bumping under the rear turret. Search revealed the alarming cause — the last flare put down the chute had got its parachute caught on the radar aerial with just enough length to swing and bump under the rear turret. It had not fully ignited but might do so at any moment. They were three hours away from base and so the three air gunners took turns of one hour each on watch in the rear turret. Oldfield says that he had his knees up to his chin and was 'thinking about moths in candle flames'.

On 7 September everything went as planned. A convoy was found off Derna, they homed in the torpedo planes and dropped flares. The convoy consisted of one merchant vessel with a strong escort of three destroyers and a motor torpedo boat. One destroyer was hit but not the obviously important merchant ship. On 1 October there was another successful interception and attack on a merchant vessel and a tanker escorted by three destroyers. The tanker was set on fire. Two more convoys were found during October — on the 6th, off Derna, no results reported; on the 18th, north of Benghazi, the attack was spoiled by cloud.

On 3 November, with the last Alamein battle in its final stages, Oldfield's pilot went wild with excitement during an attack on a convoy off Benghazi — two merchant vessels and a tanker escorted by no less than five destroyers. The tanker burned so furiously that the pilot kept on circling and had the crew dropping flame floats and even empty bottles — anything that was loose — until long after all the other aircraft had left for base, and they were so low on fuel that they had to divert to Malta. That probably was Rommel's last tanker in the Alamein position.

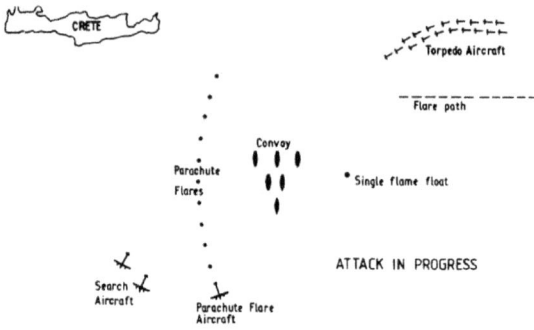

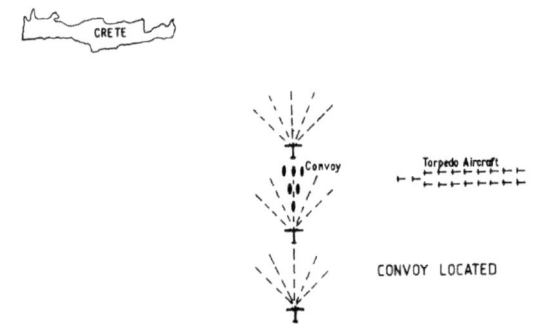

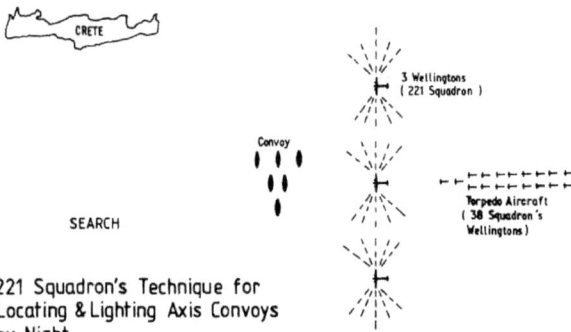

CRETE

Torpedo Aircraft

Flare path

Convoy

Parachute Flares

Single flame float

ATTACK IN PROGRESS

Search Aircraft

Parachute Flare Aircraft

CRETE

Convoy

Torpedo Aircraft

CONVOY LOCATED

CRETE

3 Wellingtons (221 Squadron)

Convoy

Torpedo Aircraft (38 Squadron's Wellingtons)

SEARCH

221 Squadron's Technique for Locating & Lighting Axis Convoys by Night

The pilot's exhilaration at their success in this risky game contrasted strongly with H. A. Taylor's experience with a very different pilot back in June. Taylor's first operation had been as second pilot to Mike Foulis of 38 Squadron attacking an Italian battleship, when Mike had demonstrated his dictum 'Get in as low as you can'. His next operation was as second pilot to an officer who had best be nameless but whose behaviour is puzzling. The idea was to mine Tobruk harbour from 70 feet, now that it had been captured by Rommel, to the unconcealed rage of Winston Churchill. Instead of coming in low down as Mike Foulis had done when faced by a battleship, this pilot approached the flak-defended port at 2,000 feet, flying right over it, as if to give the Germans due warning; then he flew out to sea and started a steady descent from 2,000 feet pointing to the middle of the harbour, with flak pouring up from both sides at him. They were down to 300 feet when Taylor saw with horror that the pilot was screaming and, while trying to take over from him, discovered that he was holding the control column with so fierce a grip that Taylor could hardly move it. Then their burly Australian navigator joined in, punched the pilot and dragged him out of his seat while Taylor held on to the stick. His logbook entry read:

> Grabbed stick at 50 feet to stop us going in beneath the flak. Brought [pilot] back strapped to bed. Left Squadron. LOMF. (Lack of Moral Fibre).

Taylor was sure that if this had been his first operation instead of that with the brilliant Foulis, he would have lacked the wit and experience to realise that the pilot was incapable and that he had to take over. Yet what the frightened airman had done was deadly dangerous, really asking for trouble. The Foulis way was not merely more effective, it was safer.

39 Squadron, equipped with Beaufort torpedo bombers, flew daylight attacks, mainly from Malta, escorted by flak-suppression Beaufighters also based on the tiny beleaguered island. Sometimes the Beaufighters were stationed on the same airstrip, widely dispersed; in any case the distance between airstrips was small. On some occasions the surrender of Malta was only a week or two away, if the next convoy did not get through, but by July Malta was recovering from the incessant Luftwaffe attacks which had almost knocked it out, and in mid-August the fateful 'Pedestal' convoy brought some relief at heavy cost, for the Axis anti-shipping forces were most effective, employing dive bombers, torpedo bombers and E-boats. Submarines were also effective. On 12 August, for instance, the Italian boat *Axum* sank the old light cruiser *Cairo* now converted to fleet flak ship.

PRU played a greater part in target-finding for the Beauforts of 39 Squadron than did Ultra. In summer Mediterranean skies are usually clear and virtually cloudless, and for the pilot of a highflying aircraft visibility is virtually unlimited — the curve of the earth can be seen. Just as the complex of code-breakers and their machines at Bletchley were by familiarisation and constant study enabled to acquire great skills in reading the mind of the enemy, so too did the complex at Medmenham devoted to continuous interpretation of aerial photographs achieve a matching but more reliable efficiency, depending on weather rather than enemy cunning; and both UK complexes eventually spawned sub-units working abroad rather closer to the enemy than country complexes to the west of London.

When Air Vice-Marshal Lloyd arrived in Malta in May 1941 he had been briefed that his main task was to help cut Rommel's supply routes; with a flight of Maryland twin-motor light bombers and no staff skilled in interpretation, he had to start from scratch. Most headquarters were in underground tunnels at that time, but Lloyd chose a deep ravine which runs through the city of Valletta and is (or was in 1925-8 when I was first there) served by a lift built against the cliff face. When the interpreters arrived, they were installed in a small room opening off Lloyd's own office, so that Lloyd was the first to get the results, long before they could be transmitted to Cairo or wherever. What he wanted to know immediately were the key facts — where ships were loading, when and what they were loading, when they were going to sail, and after what course and speed.

That sounded impossible, and indeed from a single photograph would be impossible; but not to continuous photo coverage intensely studied day by day by staff who soon got to know not only the enemy's habits but every part of every Italian port in the south. Naples was by far the most important port for loading and it was not long before it was realised that ships for North African destinations were loaded at the same spot — soon to be called 'Rommel's Quay'. Open hatches meant loading not completed, closed hatches meant ready to sail as soon as deck cargo is on. The nature of the deck cargoes could be seen — tanks, armoured cars, drums of oil. Once the ship had sailed another Maryland would be sent out to find it — and that gave course, obviously, and also speed, less obviously. During the war, indeed spurred by the war, a great deal of scientific experiment into wave heights and patterns had been undertaken. Apart from explaining why anglers tend to be swept off rocks by exceptionally huge waves just rising out of the deep, it was discovered that measurement of the wave patterns behind a ship could give you its speed. The unfortunate Italians assumed that enemy agents were passing on information which was in fact obtained largely by aerial photography and less frequently by Ultra. This natural desire for the direct, dramatic explanation over the technical and complicated also helped to camouflage Ultra itself, for the existence of the aerial recce planes was clear.

39 Squadron was posted to Malta in June 1942 still in Northern waters camouflage. Terence McGarry recalled:

> The Air Officer Commanding called the crews together and informed them that they were at Malta to prevent the Italian fleet getting at an August convoy — with the usual padding about King and Country. When the four surviving vessels of the convoy made Malta the Squadron went on the offensive.

That was the 'Pedestal' operation in mid-August. McGarry's first operation from Malta was on 17 August. Unknown to him, this was the result of several Ultra intercepts and decodes. The first decode was made on the 14th, stating that the ship was the *Rosalino Pilo*, 8,326 tons, ready to sail on the 12th with a cargo of (in tons) 431 diesel, 591 ammunition, 233 motor transport and tank spare parts, 917 rations, plus guns and vehicles including three Mark III tanks. A later decode on the 16th stated that the ship, escorted by the destroyers *Maestrale* and *Gioberti*, was to leave Trapani in western Sicily at 0400 on 17 August, estimated time of arrival at Tripoli in North Africa 1030 on the 18th. Referring to his log, McGarry recalled:

> Six Beauforts and six Beaufighters with the luxury of an escort of Spits attacked a 9,000-ton motor vessel, escorted by two destroyers and Me 109s, west of Lampedusa. The Spits mixed it with the fighters and gave the Beaus a clear run at the target.

The official 1944 booklet *The Air Battle of Malta*, a surprisingly sober publication for wartime, actually underestimates the size of the MV at 6,000 tons, saying that it was left well down in the water with smoke pouring out of it.

McGarry's next operation was on 20 August against a 10,000-ton tanker off southern Italy escorted by four destroyers and aircraft. Nine Beauforts accompanied by Beaufighters made the attack. Next day a similar tanker escorted by five destroyers was attacked near Corfu by the usual mixed bag of Beauforts and Beaufighters. The tanker stopped and began emitting steam. Next day she was found beached, with a large patch of oil on the sea.

Charles Grant, a sergeant navigator of 39 Squadron, also took part in the 20 August attack, and his recollections are more vivid than those of the 1944 HMSO pamphlet. His first op from Malta had been a month earlier on 21 July, soon after they had arrived in Malta during the hottest period and while still unacclimatised; that target had been a merchant ship off the Greek island of Cephalonia. On 20 August it was even hotter. (During my boyhood in Valletta, I recall how everyone who could got out of Malta during July and August — far too hot even for those who lived there — and we holidayed somewhere cooler, like Italy, travelling in Italian ships because they were cheaper.)

Take-off for this 20 August op was 2.15 in the afternoon. Hellish hot and the metal inside the aircraft could burn your skin if you touched it. The strike force was 12 Beauforts in four vics of 3 and escort of 12 Beaufighters. Our target was two merchant vessels escorted by four destroyers five miles south of a position just inside the toe of Italy. The depth settings of our torpedoes had been set too deep and a number of 'tin fish' were seen to pass under and out the other side of the target ship. As far as I know the attack was completely unsuccessful, the tragedy of it was that we lost two Beauforts and two Beaufighters — 12 aircrew! Despite this, my logbook records that for me there was a brief moment of humour during the attack. I assume that it was an Italian sailor who was rowing himself from one ship to another on a quiet sunny Mediterranean afternoon when the RAF arrived to spoil his short idyllic sojourn! When I looked out of my side of the Beaufort, he was about two or three hundred yards away and about 100 feet below us — his forearms going like pistons at the oars! In addition, there were Me 109s, Macchi 200s and 202s as aerial cover and they hit into us — so there was quite a rammy in the sky above the poor wee 'eyeties'.

Perhaps it was the appalling heat back at base which led the technicians to put the wrong depth-setting on the torpedoes. This was not an Ultra-directed strike and most probably was the result of a PRU report, the usual source of intelligence for the Malta squadrons. McGarry recalled:

The crews at immediate readiness would generally be sitting in the open, reading and whathaveyou. If the PRU Spit had found anything it did not break R/T silence but on making the Island would shoot up the Squadron hut. The stand-by crews would then gather their kit and make their way to the building which served as HQ. The Strike Leader and his navigator would decide on the best way to intercept and from that the best way to attack, the navigator working out times for Take Off, Set Course, and Attack. This information together with other details would be passed to the Beaufighters who were stationed at Takali (although one squadron of them was stationed with us at Luqa). Briefings usually took place in the open. Strike Leader would outline and then detail attack — usually along the line of the convoy's advance, either from front or rear. It was very early on in the Malta strikes that 'fluid pairs' were introduced as opposed to the old method of Vics of three. The navigator would give out tracks, distances, turning points, and also the compass course to steer after the attack. The aircraft would start up, taxi out from the widely dispersed areas and take off after the leader, who would make a wide circuit and fire off a white cartridge to assist identification.

The adoption of 'fluid pairs' instead of the pre-war Hendon Air Display style 'Vic' formations considered professional seems more than merely a move towards tactical common sense, but rather evidence of the fact that some elements in Britain were taking war seriously, as the Germans always did. Most Fighter Command squadrons during the Battle of Britain had flown conspicuously in Hendon-style Vics and suffered for it; you could always tell a German fighter formation from a British one because instead of neat regimented segments of threes, it looked a great droning gaggle, spread out and irregular — but in fact formed of loose pairs with the pilots able to scan the sky for prey or enemies instead of watching their wingtips against imminent collision. The Germans had learned the hard way in Spain, but the British — far more formal and disciplined than their tough opponents — took long to learn.

Notoriously, the British Army pre-war discouraged 'shop' talk in the mess; the proper business of the British Army was not war but 'Fuss and Feathers', Royal Birthday Parades and so on, with glossy-coated horses and bearskins and tossing plumes, and the task of the ordinary soldier was to be a male ballet dancer in a piece of military choreography, his rifle not a weapon but a theatrical prop to be ceremonially wielded. The War Office regarded with horror — and at first resisted — the introduction of machine carbines and automatic rifles because they could not be properly 'sloped' or 'presented' or 'ordered' in truly 'Regimental' fashion. Much thought and ingenuity was given to this key subject. The Navy had the same habit of clinging to traditions which had once been valid tactical methods at the time of Blenheim, or even as late as Waterloo; but my friends who were in the Navy at the time of the Spanish Civil War in the 1930s did lament the fact that while their potential enemies, Italy and Germany, were able to gain valuable operational experience by joining in, they themselves were compelled just to look on and not truly profit from history being made.

Similarly, all the old ideas of aerial reconnaissance and photography had had to be destroyed and buried; and now indeed had been. The 1914-18 conflict had encouraged the use of slow, stable, low-flying aeroplanes from which to map trench lines and back areas; the idea of sending out very high-speed, very high-flying stripped-down fighters with better photo equipment (that of 1939 proved useless) to photograph say Naples docks at dawn and then again that evening, and so on day after day to build up a comparative archive on the enemy's supply position, had now been adopted and was normal. An Italian admiral was to lament that his Navy had in effect to play chess blindfolded. 'We never knew where the Allied Navy was, but the Allies knew the exact position of every unit of our fleet at all times.'

Men like Adrian Warburton of Malta PRU never achieved either the official recognition nor the public fame of Douglas Bader or Guy Gibson, partly of course because no books were written about him nor films made. Arguably however his contribution was greater than theirs. Bader's real achievement was in the example he set of determination to succeed despite obstacles, but his part in the Battle of Britain (contrary to general belief) was in 12 Group on the fringes of the battle and not in Keith Park's 11 Group which bore the brunt of the fighting that summer. Similarly Gibson's dam-busting exploits made good propaganda in giving us all the impression that a dramatic blow had been struck at German industry and titanic effects caused (but as immediately after the war I spent three years in the area of the Möhne-See I at least was forced to face reality).

In many other areas this year was to be the turning-point of the war. In the land fighting effective techniques of air cooperation with ground forces were being worked out, just as the photographic methods had been, and too the techniques of attacking ships. At long last the British were learning how to make war — which is not the same thing as fighting, a purely animal act, as has been pointed out.

When the gaggle of Beauforts and Beaufighters had got more or less into position after take-off, they would set course from the south-east tip of Malta and then came down to 50 to 100 feet above the waves to avoid detection from the enemy radar scanners and kept radio silence. McGarry explained:

> The mixed formation would usually turn onto the convoy's track about 30 miles ahead of them, which gave time to settle down after the turn.
>
> When the convoy was sighted the aircraft hugged the sea to avoid detection. The signal for attack would be the R/T Yellow-yellow and a cartridge of two yellows fired at the same time. The top cover Beaus would then climb while the Beaus detailed to shoot up the destroyers with cannon would surge ahead. Then the Beauforts would deploy to attack the chosen target. The attack on the destroyers was to draw their fire and give the torpedo aircraft a clear run. They were usually successful. Success or failure depended upon the accuracy of the interception, for without it the element of surprise was lost and the carefully-briefed attack plan would be useless. A good interception also cut down our own losses, for a bad one meant that the aircraft would be out of position, thus giving the enemy time to deploy. All depended therefore on a

good recce (Wing Commander Warburton was the kingpin) and accurate navigation by the strike leader. The method was track crawling with constant checking and re-checking for drift, windlanes and relating the results to the tactical plot. It also meant that after every strike, when a new torpedo was put on, the leader's navigator's first job was to swing the compass to correct the deviation error. An often forgotten factor was the wonderful ground crews who under difficult conditions and on siege rations did an excellent job to keep the aircraft flying. At one period the petrol shortage was so severe that after an aircraft had been repaired, a flight test was not possible.

There were two more strikes in August in which McGarry took part and which were down to PRU not Ultra. On 24 August nine Beauforts went out with nine Beaufighters to strike at dusk a 7,000-ton tanker escorted by two destroyers and aircraft. It was hit and later beached. On this occasion too the attack signal was a yellow Verey cartridge. Immediately a Ju 88 which was carrying out antisubmarine escort also fired flares to warn the ships and jettisoned its depth charge — which may have been taken by the Italians for a splashing torpedo; anyway the Italian destroyers shot down the German aircraft instantly.

On 26 August nine Beauforts attacked a 6,000-ton merchant vessel escorted by a destroyer off Benghazi. One torpedo broke the ship's back and subsequent hits left her ablaze from stem to stern. An escorting Cant floatplane was shot down by a Beaufighter.

The next attack was Ultra-inspired. A message sent early in the morning of 28 August revealed that the tanker *San Andrea*, 5,077 tons, was loading at Taranto with fuel for the German and Italian armies. Loading was to cease by the afternoon of the next day, whereupon the ship was to sail for Tobruk to arrive on 3 September. The next intercepted message was timed 2139 hours 30 August. The *San Andrea* had been torpedoed and was on fire. Her cargo had included 3,000 tons of Otto fuel for Panzer Army Africa. As well as McGarry, Charles Grant took part in this attack.

> There were 8 Beauforts and 8 Beaufighters on this strike and we took off from Luqa at 1145 a.m. Our target was a tanker which we located ten miles offshore west of Cape Santa Maria di Leuca on the heel of Italy near Taranto. I have no record of it having a naval escort but it did have aerial support. My logbook says our pilot, Hugh Watlington, fired 400 rounds from our two wing-mounted Browning machine-guns at a Dornier 18 flying boat and Leslie Tester our air gunner damaged a Macchi 200 fighter which attacked us. Our torpedo was seen to run OK and we claimed an almost certain hit. I know that one if not more of the 'tin fish' launched by the Vic in front of us did hit the target as the bridge of the tanker seemed to erupt in front of us and our skipper had to take violent avoiding action from bits of debris almost immediately after we had dropped.

McGarry mentioned that one pilot's prized moustache was endangered as he performed a 'fly through fire' act at 250 feet when passing over the burning ship. An unfortunate Cant 501 seaplane was savaged by all the Beaufighters and most of the Beauforts' gunners as they passed, shooting one float completely off.

The 6 September affair was memorable for 39 Squadron, although not given in the list of Ultra-directed targets. McGarry thought there was something odd about it and believed the fortunate interception must have been made 'as a result of information from agents'. Who knows? That side of Intelligence work is still secret (except where politicians write books about some of it), although the wireless and code-cracking side of Intelligence now have their official histories, albeit discreet ones. The target was two convoys joined sailing southbound from Taranto along the Greek coast with a heavy destroyer escort — some reports say 10, some 11. Charles Grant recalled:

> There were 9 Beauforts and 10 Beaufighters on this strike with take-off at 1230 p.m. This was the biggest convoy we ever attacked and was made up of four merchant vessels and ten destroyers; we located it just off the southern tip of the island of Corfu. The enemy sighted us almost as we sighted them; and their destroyer escort immediately laid down a 'black barrage' of ack-ack fire through which we had to run the gauntlet on our way into the attack. My logbook says: one MV sunk, one damaged, and we claimed a hit with our 'fish'. The enemy had quite a strong aerial escort and we had a running fight all over the sky for approx 15 minutes with Me 109s, Macchis and a Ju 88. Tester, our gunner, was wounded and I tried to get him out of the turret but it was jammed and so was he. I tied a tourniquet on his leg wound and then manned a Vickers gun on the side of the aircraft, but it jammed on me after I fired a couple of bursts. McIllaney, the wireless op, was also wounded at the wireless set, and when we did get back to Malta we found our dear old Beaufort looked like a sieve from the cannon and machine-gun hits. We lost 2 Beauforts. I see from my logbook entry that Air Vice-Marshal Park watched us return.

Park had been the commander of 11 Group in the Battle of Britain. Like his Fighter Command chief Dowding he had been unjustly removed after victory had been won as a result of some unsavoury bumping-and-boring at higher levels, but now he commanded the RAF in Malta and was superbly qualified to do so. Grant's Beaufort had come back to Malta in company with a PRU Maryland which was lost and had attached itself believing that the torpedo bomber (which would have set the return course before the attack) would be headed in the direction of Malta, and Grant busy with his charts assumed that because the better equipped PRU plane was flying in the same direction, he had got it right. In the chaotic air fighting around the convoy results were not accurately observed, but later reconnaissance indicated that one 10,000-tonner had been sunk and another MV of 6,000 tons damaged and beached.

On 23 September 39 Squadron with six Beauforts accompanied by six Beaufighters attacked a 6,000-ton tanker off the Greek island of Paxos at dusk. It was escorted by six destroyers but hits were obtained. On 1 October half the squadron left Malta for Egypt, and it was from an Egyptian base that on 2 November they carried out an Ultra-directed strike in the final stages of the Battle of El Alamein. The previous day a message had been intercepted giving the route to be taken by the small merchantman *Zara*, 1,976 tons. The next message, timed at 0014 on 3 November, detailed the steps to be taken at Tobruk to tow in the *Zara*, which had been torpedoed; and the message after that stated that she had sunk 27 miles from Tobruk. This ship had been part of a convoy which had been temporarily 'lost' — a dusk search by Beaus and a night search by Wellingtons had failed to find it. But Air Marshal Tedder, commanding the Middle East RAF, had given them a pep talk, stressing the importance of impairing Rommel's supply position, and demanding maximum effort during the next few critical days, while the result of Montgomery's great land battle hung in the balance. 'Maximum effort' for 39 Squadron in Egypt amounted to six worn Beaufort II torpedo bombers with time-expired crews escorted by the same number of Beaufighters. At that time, the chance of a strike air crew surviving one tour was 17½ per cent; of a second tour only 3 per cent, the highest losses of all airmen.[9]

For this 'maximum effort' the six torpedo bombers were moved to a strip at Gianiclis, just behind the battle zone. At 0625 on 2 November they took off in search of the disappearing convoy, reasoning that as it had been reported spotted by a Liberator a few days earlier the ships had turned westward, thus avoiding the search made on the line

---

[9] On 16 November 1942, the Air Member for Training, Air Marshal Sir Guy Garrod, sent a table of RAF casualties to the Air Member for Personnel, Air Marshal Sir Bertine E. Sutton. Rearranging this table in decreasing percentage of danger to the flying crew, it reads:

1. Torpedo bomber, Percentage chance of survival one tour: 17½, Percentage chance of survival two tours: 3

2. Light bomber, Percentage chance of survival one tour: 25½, Percentage chance of survival two tours: 6½

3. Fighter reconnaissance, Percentage chance of survival one tour: 31, Percentage chance of survival two tours: 9½

4. Night fighter, Percentage chance of survival one tour: 39, Percentage chance of survival two tours: 15

5. Bomber reconnaissance, Percentage chance of survival one tour: 42, Percentage chance of survival two tours: 17½

6. Day fighter, Percentage chance of survival one tour: 43, Percentage chance of survival two tours: 18½

7. Heavy and medium bombers, Percentage chance of survival one tour: 44, Percentage chance of survival two tours: 19½

8. Light general reconnaissance landplane, Percentage chance of survival one tour: 45, Percentage chance of survival two tours: 20

9. Medium general reconnaissance landplane, Percentage chance of survival one tour: 56, Percentage chance of survival two tours: 31½

10. Long-range fighter, Percentage chance of survival one tour: 59½, Percentage chance of survival two tours: 35½

11. Sunderland flying boat, Percentage chance of survival one tour: 66, Percentage chance of survival two tours: 43½

12. Heavy general reconnaissance landplane, Percentage chance of survival one tour: 66, Percentage chance of survival two tours: 43½

13. Catalina flying boat, Percentage chance of survival one tour: 77½, Percentage chance of survival two tours: 60

connecting their reported position and the port of Tobruk, and so would approach the port from the west, not the east, and as near to land as possible along the shallow North African coastline.

The six Beauforts flew north from Gianiclis over the sea until they were out of sight of land, then turned west, intending to turn inwards towards Tobruk when a few miles past it, to avoid being picked up.

> We flew in loose formation of fluid pairs, just above the sea, with the sun fairly low and behind us it was not too difficult. The leading pairs had been allocated targets and the third pair to help themselves to whatever was presented. If we found the targets in the right place and the aircraft were in the right pattern for attack, our leading pair would take the leading vessel, the pair on the port side to take the second ship, with the third pair hopefully to clear up. Two Beaufighters were to look after the destroyer and the remaining four to give fighter cover.
>
> We had guessed right, we found the ships where we had hoped and in the right position, our 'turn in' position had been bang on and we were able to get between the ships and the shore and dive to the attack from an unexpected quarter and drop the torpedoes before the defences were fully alert. Then we were on our way out to sea — but nevertheless we lost two Beauforts in the ensuing melee.

That is, one-third of the torpedo bombers lost in a single morning, casualties that mounted up and extinguished a squadron in a short time. And the loss might well have been 50 per cent that day.

> The air gunner reported that one of the ships appeared to have blown up and the other was on fire.... and then we had problems. We had lost our number 2 and were turning on the

predetermined course for home — we always gave that out, hoping to join up with others, the principle of safety in numbers — when we found we had a couple of Ju 88s for company. They attacked in turn — one got a bit too near and we managed to get some good bursts into him and he disappeared with an engine on fire and losing height, but help was on hand, a Beaufighter coming back on the given course was able to get in undetected and shoot the other Ju 88 down. We were lucky, the rudder and tail suffered a lot of damage, but nothing vital. We landed five-and-a-quarter hours after take-off. One Ju 88 confirmed and 2 damaged for the loss of 2 Beauforts and as far as I can remember no loss of Beaufighters.

The *Zara* certainly went down. A similar ship, the *Brioni* of 1,987 tons, with a cargo of Otto fuel for tanks and aviation spirit for the Luftwaffe and Regia Aeronautica, was reported by Ultra intercept to have blown up in Tobruk harbour during an air raid.

The small size of these vessels — even by the standards of the 1940s — indicated that Italy was running out of ships. There was a further problem. By the coastal road rather than by the flight of the Messerschmitt the small port of Tobruk was some 300 miles from the Alamein positions; to Benghazi by the same route the distance was nearly as much again; and to the better port of Tripoli was another 600 miles. Call it in round figures 1,200 miles. These are not great distances on modern motorways for modern tourists travelling light. But as Army supply lines over indifferent surfaces they were formidable. In our 1944 advance out of the Normandy bridgehead the British-Canadian 21st Army Group under Montgomery began to feel the effect after some 250 miles; and we were close to UK industry and bases. Clearly, it paid the Axis to land their supplies as close to the fighting area as

164

possible, to Tobruk rather than Benghazi and to Benghazi rather than Tripoli. But Tobruk's capacity was very limited. Therefore the Germans and Italians did what we were to do later in Normandy, run supplies ashore by means of landing craft over open beaches or into pokey little places like Mersa Matruh, 100 miles from Alamein. Quite possible, provided that the sea state was kind and that landing craft were actually available.

The Axis organised a sea ferry service by landing craft to run from Tobruk to Mersa Matruh, starting in August 1942. Krupp of Essen supplied prefabricated parts and some 30 'L-Craft' were assembled at the Riuniti works in Palermo, Sicily. Arnold Bongartz sailed with the first convoy of new landing craft. Four of them were German-manned, and nine Italian. With them in the convoy were a tanker and a torpedo boat. They arrived in Tobruk on 6 August and spent most of their time taking reinforcements from Tobruk to Mersa Matruh, much nearer the fighting. On the afternoon of 14 August, 12 L-Craft left in convoy for Mersa Matruh and next day were bombed by a four-engined flying boat (probably a British Sunderland).

> It flew over the convoy at 50 to 100 metres, but permission to fire on it was not granted. Then it started to bomb the leading boat, three bombs falling ahead of it and three ahead of the following boat. I was manning a 2-cm automatic weapon on the next boat and I was able to make out the British pilot in his cabin. The boat next to us had four men severely wounded and five lightly, hit by the gunners of the plane. We landed the wounded at Bardia and left again that evening for Mersa Matruh.
>
> A little later a convoy arrived in Tobruk. One of the transport ships had been sunk at sea. Another transport was hit by bombs as it tried to moor at the pier. Several hundred men were killed, some of them from the ship's crew but also

those labourers (mostly black POWs) who unloaded the ships. I myself was some 300-400 metres away from that ship at the food reception depot and I was buried under boxes but was unhurt.

The Battle of Alamein began on 23 October, a murderous dogfight in the sand dignified later as a typical Monty 'set piece' battle. Two weeks later, Bongartz saw the end.

On 5 November we sailed to Mersa Matruh with 3 German and 3 Italian L-boats; five of them were empty, but our boat had 50 tons of petrol in 200-litre barrels aboard, intended for the tanks. On 6 November the entire coastal road was crowded with vehicles — tanks, lorries, etc — and enemy planes were shooting at this retreating column of the Afrika Korps. In the distance we could make out the shapes of British tanks which were firing at German soldiers. When we attempted to enter the port of Mersa Matruh a small motorboat came towards us. It was the harbourmaster, who immediately ordered us to turn back. So on 7 November we were obliged to unload the petrol ourselves at Bardia. We were bombed as we left that evening for Tobruk. And from there next day we sailed with about 10 boats for Palermo.

Susanna Agnelli, aged 20, was the daughter of the man who owned Fiat. Rather than be idle in wartime she became a nurse serving in hospital ships sailing between Naples and North Africa that summer of 1942. The Italian Navy, as she remarked, always had better equipment and a superior style to the other services; the nurses were smartly turned out and strictly chaperoned, a relic of the nineteenth-century attitude (which Florence Nightingale met in the Crimea) that nurses were essentially menials and necessarily 'fast'. As with most people of around that age, in Italy as elsewhere, peacetime groupings had been broken up by war — so-and-so had died in

Russia; while this young man had become an air hero, of another there was no news but perhaps he was a prisoner. On her first trip, long before the African beach of Mersa Matruh became visible but when the hot wind blowing out of Africa could be felt, she was on deck.

As the white-painted ship with its vivid red crosses closed the shore, there came out to it what she described as 'large rafts'. Probably these were some of the L-Craft at work. On them the torn and mutilated men lay on stretchers, their bloodied bandages as red as the crosses painted on the side of the ship. The stretcher cases were swung up in large nets and all the casualties were lined up on the hot, windy deck to be categorised by rank, status, nature and severity of wounds.

The men were of all sorts, enemies, allies, fellow countrymen. You could recognise the Italians, she was to write, by the darker colour of their skin; the Germans blond and proud, often with their red, white and black medal ribbons pinned to their chests; the English laughing but very white, creamy and vulnerable-looking (probably just out from home); and some of them were 'black' (probably brown-skinned Indians). One 'child', really too young, tugged at the elegant young lady's skirt, saying with a trembling voice that he was an officer, a French officer. She told the doctor, who snarled back: 'If he is French, he is only a traitor.' In wartime, things are very simple.

Apart from air raids, this was Susanna Agnelli's first direct look at the war:

Flesh torn up, despair, pain, missing limbs, young eyes questioning, utter nonsense, medals, pride, adventure.

Next day she discovered some wounded British officers making gentle fun of a small Italian guard who did not understand English. She told them to get back into bed.

'Where did you learn English?' they called out.

'From my governess,' she replied.

A little later they began to ask her: 'Are you really Miss Fiat?'

The German officers made trouble. They threatened to go on hunger strike unless the NCOs and ordinary soldiers were given exactly the same food as they were. This was the rule in the German Army and more or less the rule in the British Army also, give or take a little class distinction. The Italians refused to obey the German officers' trade union, pointing out that the different ration scales were laid down in regulations.

When the hospital ship reached Naples the wounded were not allowed to be disembarked immediately because a gracious VIP from the Italian Red Cross was to visit them first and give out sweets and oranges. 'Miss Fiat' was mildly critical (but recalling a similar visit by high-born Belgian ladies to a British military hospital in Antwerp, I submit it does a lot for morale just to be spoken to by beautiful, sympathetic women). When it came to Susanna's turn to be presented to the Princess of Piedmont she curtsied and the Princess whispered: 'How tall she is.' In fact the high-born lady was really very shy and so got completely muddled. 'She managed to speak German to the Italians, Italian to the English, and English, to their horror, to the Germans.'

The hospital ship ran like a liner from Naples that summer to Benghazi, Tobruk, Mersa Matruh. Once, as the bombs whistled down into Naples docks around them, Susanna felt like a rat inside a metal trap; once, approaching an African port, the hospital ship was mined but did not sink; several other hospital ships were torpedoed and did sink; once the ship she was in sailed on a secret mission searching for survivors, but all they found was a yellow RAF rubber dinghy, only half inflated, with three bodies lying on it burned almost black by exposure to the sun. The nurses leaned over the rail as a launch was lowered into the sea. The officer in the boat signalled to their captain: Enemy airmen, two alive, one dead. When the captain replied: Pick up the live ones, leave the dead man, there was a burst of indignation, particularly from the chaplain, as the corpse, held up by its life-jacket, drifted away over the Mediterranean.

Helmut Heimberg belonged until the summer of 1942 to the signal company on the staff of Field Marshal Albert Kesselring, first in Belgium, then in Russia and now in Italy, where Kesselring was in effect Rommel's superior. In reply to Rommel's repeated requests for reinforcements, volunteers were asked for to go to Africa as part of a so-called Luftwaffe Feldbataillon O.B.S. That was in July. They trained at Foggia on the types of anti-tank guns they would be using in the desert. He recalled:

> Because the African supply routes became steadily more difficult and more and more vessels were attacked and sunk by aircraft and submarines we flew over during September in Ju 52 transport planes, first to Maleme in Crete and then on to Tobruk in a bulk formation of 30 aircraft, escorted by only two Me 110s. We flew close to the sea both in order to prevent attacks in the blind areas below the fuselage and because, if we were shot down, then there was some chance of escape from the aircraft; we all had life-jackets. From 1,000 metres there would have been no escape from a crash. After arriving safely at Tobruk we had to wait for more than a week before learning that our anti-tank guns had gone down in a ship torpedoed by a submarine, although the guns of the other companies got through.

Heimberg survived the sea crossings in Ju 52s in time to go into action in the Alamein battle a month later, with unpleasant results; but Kesselring's airlift to Africa became an RAF target also, although less vulnerable than the ships because faster. Speed was also a factor in beating Ultra and other forms of intelligence-gathering.

Jack Trotman was a navigator with 272 Squadron's Beaufighters, which operated from a strip adjacent to that of their sister squadron 252 some 20 miles east of Alexandria. The primary objectives of both squadrons were the ships and air convoys bringing supplies and reinforcements to Rommel, combined with long-range intruder operations. 272 Squadron was made up of two flights each of eight crews and aircraft. Normally the flights stood down on alternate days, unless there was something special planned. On 17 October two flights carried out an offensive sweep south of Crete. One flight intercepted an aerial convoy of 32 tri-motor Ju 52 transports towing gliders and escorted by Me 110s. They claimed two Ju 52s destroyed. Trotman, on his first operation, was with the other flight, which found a schooner and set it on fire; he remembers seeing one of the crew jumping overboard. This too might have been a supply vessel, although the Italians also used sailing vessels, fitted with modern anti-submarine gear, to protect shipping convoys and to search for unwary submarine commanders.

On 22 October, the day before the great battle of Alamein was due to begin, Trotman's flight carried out intruder sweeps along the coast road behind the German-Italian positions. Frequently these were made both in the morning and in the afternoon.

> We flew usually in pairs well out to sea at very low level to avoid detection and then split up to cross the coast at

different points before returning independently. On this occasion we attacked a convoy of six lorries causing considerable damage and encountering only light flak somewhere between Sidi Barrani and Matruh.

On 25 October, with the battle entering its third day, eight Beaufighters from the squadron intercepted a bulk formation of 35 Ju 52s escorted by 6 Me 109s north of Tobruk. Jack Trotman was in one of the four Beaus given the role of top cover while the rest engaged the transport aircraft. In a dogfight between the four top cover Beaus and the six Messerschmitt two-seaters Trotman had the task of reloading the cannons. In the Mark I Beaufighter the cannon shells were fed from drums, so the empty drum had first to be removed, and then replaced by a full one. Trying to do this while the Beau was being thrown about causing violent 'G' forces was not without its difficulties. Apart from getting a lungful of cordite and barking his knuckles, Trotman recalled little of the dogfight apart from seeing a great sheet of tracer passing just underneath. Four of the Ju 52s were destroyed and one Me 110 damaged; the squadron lost a Beaufighter.

Rommel's fuel situation was now critical, his ability to manoeuvre strictly limited, and he was forced into a slugging match with a much more powerful enemy instead of being able to use the superior skills of the Afrika Korps in a fluid battle. It was imperative to get tank fuel to him — and equally important for the British to stop it. From 0442 on 24 October a series of intercepted signals told the story. The tanker *Proserpina*, 4,869 tons, was loading with a fuel cargo — 888 tons of B4 for the Luftwaffe, 2,500 tons of Otto fuel for the German tanks, 1,165 tons of Otto fuel for the Italians. The *Tergestea*, 5,890 tons, was also sailed, cargo not stated. The convoy was due in Tobruk at 1500 on 26 October at a speed of nine knots, or earlier if no stop was made.

> With Beaufighters of 252 Squadron we joined up with 6 Beauforts and 6 or 8 Bisleys [Blenheim Vs] from a South African Squadron (No. 15). Great stress was laid upon the importance of success, especially in getting the tanker. The strike was to be led by the Beauforts with the Beaufighters providing top cover and I believe one section going in first as a diversion. Because of the relatively slow speed of the Beauforts the Beaufighters had to take station to the rear of the formation flying figures of eight. We went well out to sea at very low level and our object was to come in at an angle direct to the target. In the event we made a landfall well to the east and had to turn and fly parallel to the coast, attracting flak from various shore batteries.
>
> Eventually reaching the convoy we climbed to act as top cover and engage the enemy equivalent. In the ensuing skirmish we broke up the fighter cover — at one point my pilot said that he had nearly shot down a Beaufighter when he thought he was attacking a Ju 88 but pulled away in time, for in combat it was extremely difficult to differentiate the aircraft from some views.
>
> As the attack proceeded two convoys of 30 or 40 Ju 52s and Me 110s crossed the coast, one inwards and the other outward bound.... Then there was a flight of Macchi 202s in the fray although I only saw them flying in close formation some way off. There was pretty intensive flak and although a number of our strike were lost — 5 or 6 I think — we left the convoy with great clouds of black smoke enveloping the tanker and rising high in the sky.

Trotman's Beaufighter had engine trouble, R/T failure and a madly spinning compass after the hectic flying of the dogfight, and the crew were very very glad to see Alexandria to starboard and know they were almost home. They had of course seen only part of the action, and even if they had seen it all, the human brain is not designed to cope with much more than one-to-one single combat; and certainly there is no great all-seeing, all-knowing, stupendous almighty computer in the sky to which the historian can plug in and automatically be offered the truth. Even the other side suffers from the same tendency to ignorance and error, and of course the Ultra decodes were subject to human fallibility at all stages.

The Ultra decodes for 26 October recorded that the tanker *Prosperina* was set on fire by bombs (presumably from the South African Bisleys) and sunk off Tobruk, while the *Tergestea* went down after being torpedoed by an aircraft near Tobruk. The Sigint list of civilian ship casualties due to wireless intercepts and where appropriate code-breaking lists between 2 June and 6 November 1942 a baker's dozen sunk by submarine alone, plus several where an already stricken ship was finished off. Because of the submarine's slow surface speed and even slower gait when submerged, interception was more difficult and a lot depended on the skill of the commander of the 10th Flotilla, 'Shrimp' Simpson at Malta, in pre-positioning patrol lines in the most likely places. It was a different way of dying, spaced out and lonely. Only the captain saw the enemy. The rest waited blind in a steel cylinder when they were themselves hunted, as was virtually inevitable after an attack.

The submarine *Unbroken* under Alistair Mars was off the coast of North Africa near Khoms and in dangerously shallow waters had just missed the *Amsterdam*, a beached merchant ship surrounded by a buzzing swarm of escorting vessels, when a petty officer brought him a pink signal slip. Orders from Malta were to intercept an important convoy which was passing along the north coast of Sicily and was expected to be off

Lampedusa during the night. *Unbroken* was to proceed to a position off Lampedusa. Further messages came in. Convoy consisted of one large tanker, four supply ships, seven modern destroyers, and heavy air escort.[10] Their course would take them past Pantelleria and Lampedusa to Tripoli. Further messages detailed the other submarines which were also being ordered to converge on the spot. *United* was also closing from the North African coast, *Safari* under the famous Ben Bryant had left Malta in a hurry. *Utmost* and *Unbending* returning to Malta had been diverted to give them a hand. When because of their low submerged speed or because the ships zigzagged, submarines were unable to close the convoy, nevertheless they were able to pass on sighting reports to other submarines in the patrol line.

Bryant in *Safari* (P 211) sighted the masts of a ship which was never identified but was probably unconnected with the convoy, and also two aircraft which may have been the escort. A submarine's main search periscope is in effect only a pole some five or six feet high sticking out of the water and does not give a far-reaching view. The much smaller attack periscope gives even less. On the other hand, as the submerged hull and conning tower are moving, a periscope throws up a foamy wake conspicuous on a calm sea as clear as champagne. Great cunning and caution are required to succeed and survive.

During the night of 18/19 October the convoy was reported by aircraft to be 40 miles south of Pantelleria. The sighting was at 0100 on the 19th and at 0840 Lt Coombe's *Utmost* sighted the enemy at long range, fired but probably without result. Nevertheless, the sighting report she got off was critical. P 37

---

[10] An official history lists one large tanker, three supply ships, eight destroyers. (Naval Staff History of the Second World War: Submarines, Vol. II.).

under Lt Winter was 21 miles further south than *Utmost* and at 1050 found herself dead ahead of the approaching Axis ships. At 1115 the convoy altered course, which was fortunate, for this put P 35 between the convoy and the port wing destroyers; that is, she was now inside the screen of escort vessels, undetected. Winter fired a salvo at 1,000 yards range, sinking the 4,859-ton troopship *Beppe* and the 1,917-ton destroyer *Da Verazzano*. Possibly because Winter's escape method was to dive under the convoy, the counter-attack was light. When it came to his turn, Lt Mars was not so lucky. Heavily depth-charged, his boat limped back to Malta where it was suggested that her name should be altered from *Unbroken* to *Badly Bent*.

At 1540 a reconnaissance aircraft reported the convoy to be in confusion, with one ship and an escorting destroyer making for Lampedusa. That night at 2200 Lt Barlow in P 44 was approaching from a position far to the south when he sighted flares dropped by aircraft during a successful attack. An hour after midnight the previously damaged tanker *Petrarca*, 3,329 tons, was further damaged by a torpedo from P 44. Meanwhile Commander Bryant, travelling south through the night at high speed, sighted a stopped ship with two destroyers guarding her. This proved to be the *Titania* of 5,397 tons, which Bryant sank with two torpedoes. Like the *Beppe*, she was a troopship and had been damaged the previous day. The more valuable tanker got away, being seen by aircraft near Tripoli, out of reach of the submarines. Finally, on 23 October, the day the battle of El Alamein began, the crippled supply ship *Amsterdam*, 8,670 tons, which was still aground in Khoms roads (after being torpedoed by P 35), fell victim to the same submarine when she was sent back to finish her off. The target was hit again and further damaged, but was not written off as beyond salvage for another three months. At the same time, P 35 sank a tug attending the damaged supply ship, the 182-ton *Pronte*.

The Naval Staff history, which gives exact times, does not mesh precisely with the Sigint list of sinkings given in the Intelligence history, probably because the action stretched over the three days 18-20 October, some of it took place at night, and it is not clear whether Allied or Axis time is being used, but Sigint does give decodes regarding the *Beppe*, the *Titania* and the *Amsterdam*. The *Petrarca* is omitted, presumably because not an Ultra-directed target, and also the destroyer because a warship. Quite the most illuminating document is the description by Lt Mars in his book *Unbroken* of the stream of Ultra-derived messages which he received during these operations.

This suggests a good explanation for a gross breach of security by the Malta submarine base commander the previous year when, as the British Intelligence history points out, the CO sent virtually the exact (translated) text of an intercepted and decoded message to one of the submarines regarding the details of an Italian convoy for North Africa. With a stream of messages and orders being transmitted from Malta, some overstressed individual would have found it easier to stick to the original rather than carefully reword so as not to give a clue to any Axis personnel who might intercept, decode and ponder the Malta messages. But apparently no one on the Axis side made the necessary correlation. It is possible that their people, like ours, were occasionally distracted from the severe demands of duty by thoughts of their next leave or the urge simply to have a break and go for a cup of char and a wad.

Histories such as this and worse, post-war films and TV, suggest that everyone at all times thought of nothing else except the war. Some did, it is true, but a reading of letters home and especially the productions of the Service war poets will kill any such idea stone-dead. The story of the war would be incomplete without considering the personal feelings of millions of unknown participants few of whom had actually willed the war to take place, and whose strongest desire was just to return to their families, preferably in one piece. For all too many, that was not to be their fate.

10: CASUALTIES

I met Heinz Pechmann in Germany after the war, when I was still serving in the British Army. I was interested to find that he had been a gunner in a battery of 88s in North Africa, for even at the end of the war that weapon still had a formidable reputation — this at a time when the standard RA anti-tank gun was the 17-pounder and the infantry had their own 6-pounders and the little pop-gun 2-pounders had been consigned to the nursery where they had always belonged (the very first British tanks of the First World War had had 6-pounders — two of them)! But, as usual, the other side know their own weaknesses far better than you do. Heinz said that the drawback to the 88 was its height (necessary because it was originally an anti-aircraft gun). That made it a target difficult to conceal.

Heinz had naturally been in the Luftwaffe, which controlled the FLAK, and he had done a great deal of gliding and sailplaning before the war; another mutual topic, for I had done the same after the war at a former NSFK[11] gliding club requisitioned by our brigadier during 1945/46. This experience did not save Heinz's leg but it possibly saved his life in the desert in January 1942 when his battery was attacked at Agedabia by RAF Blenheims. The low-flying bombers came so suddenly that he had time only to throw himself down under the heavy towing vehicle for the gun. Bomb splinters were flying everywhere; one hit his left leg and severed it just below

---

[11] National Socialist Flieger Korps, a grand title for an organisation designed to train youngsters in motorless flight.

the knee, another went right through the calf-muscle of his right leg.

> At first I felt no pain, but when I tried to stand up and run I found that my left leg was held together only by the laced-up army desert boot I was wearing. I looked back towards my leg and saw the blood but did not pass out. I lay quiet until the orderlies came with a stretcher, lifted me into a lorry and took me to the nearest field hospital, which was just several large tents. A Ju 52 was expected to arrive shortly to collect all the wounded and fly them back to Germany for proper treatment. But this plane left without me and so I was just left lying there on my stretcher outside the hospital tent. I had given up hope of being moved when a pilot who was walking past thought he recognised me from somewhere. It turned out that we had met several years before while taking a gliding course at Lauchna on the Unstrut. This man was now the pilot of a Ju 52 and was about to fly to Rome, so he had me taken on board and at Rome handed me over to the Red Cross. They put me onto a fast train to Munich. It was an ordinary passenger train and I lay there on my stretcher, completely unattended, with no food and no drink and by now in considerable pain. Here, as in Rome, passersby insulted me and some spat at me, and that was almost worse than the original experience of being wounded. I spent a year in a Luftwaffe hospital in Unterföhring and was not allowed home until August 1943.

Heinz had arrived in Africa early, on 11 February 1941, and had won an Iron Cross and reached the rank of sergeant when he was cut down. The wounds ended his career as a sportsman and he died early in the Russian Zone of Germany.

'Ginger' Ware was a Cockney rear gunner in a Wellington bomber of 40 Squadron based on Shallufa in Egypt. On 7 August 1942 they were to carry out a raid on the port of

179

Tobruk. Ginger woke up that morning with a peculiar feeling; he was downright uneasy for no good reason. He sipped his morning tea quietly, which was most unusual — Cockneys have the fastest and funniest repartee in the UK and Ginger was no exception. Mail arrived from home that morning — but none for him. He went out to the aircraft, checked the guns and the turret — everything OK. The pilot asked Ginger if he felt all right, and he replied shortly that he was. They'd been to Tobruk before and knew what to expect.

They experienced a lot of flak and were coned in the searchlights, but got away and bombed the target. As they set course for home Ginger was feeling more like his usual self and thinking what a fool he had been for feeling so moody. He was taking a drift sight for the navigator when he saw death approaching. Another Wellington was almost on top of them, coming in on the port quarter. There was no time even to shout a warning before the impact, which sent the other Wellington down in flames. Ginger was stunned by the collision, then saw the warning light flashing, which meant bale out. But the turret was now jammed and he had to go into the fuselage to find an escape hatch. He kicked out at the hatch with his left leg and this leg was indeed through the hatch when the aircraft hit the ground and slid along on its belly.

Ginger knew he'd been hurt pretty badly but that the pilot had made a good crash-landing. He was given first aid, injected with morphine, lit a cigarette and dozed off.

> Next morning we had a good look at my leg — and it frightened the life out of me! There wasn't much of my foot left, and the lower part was smashed right up; all we could see were pieces of bone. There was little we could do about it except rip a parachute up and put a rough bandage round it. At least this hid the grisly mess from us.

The two pilots, who had survived, brought in the wireless operator, who had a broken leg and a badly burnt face, and laid him beside Ginger. They had found the body of the navigator, who had bailed out too low. The two pilots, F/Lt Robin Grant and Sgt 'Jock' Whyte, calculated that they could not reach British positions but might be able to contact the Germans. So they made the two injured men as comfortable as possible and set off to walk over the desert about midday on Saturday the 8th.

When they had gone, Ginger felt miserable and alone. The combined effects of shock and morphine had worn off and his leg — or what was left of it — hurt damnably. 'Arfer' Dunn, the W/T op, was also in great pain. But they were helpless, could only wait — and think. Ginger's train of thought led from wondering how the walking pilots were getting on, to his parents, and to realisation that the day of the crash had also been his young sister's birthday... That brought him up short and he decided not to think any more or he would go crazy. The rest of Saturday passed, and then all of Sunday, and then it was Monday; and it was clear that if help did not soon arrive, they would both die. This was not frightening, indeed the pain was now so terrible that death might even be welcomed. Only the thought of Robin and Jock, walking through the desert to get help, allowed him to hang on.

Around noon on the Monday I heard what I thought was the sound of aircraft engines, but I felt I must be imagining them. As I searched the sky I saw them, two of them, Fieseler Storch light aircraft. They landed near us and I could see they were German Red Cross planes. A doctor was with them, and they told us that this was their third search for us that day — and would have been the last. They had been picked up the evening before by an aeroplane, and I was told later by a

181

German officer that Robin and Jock had walked through two German minefields and never knew it! The Germans tried to bury Johnny Hull, then put 'Arfer' in one aircraft and me in the other. They took us first to Mersa Matruh, but kept us apart, then after a few days I was flown to Athens, where I had my leg amputated.

One of the last casualties of Alamein was Helmut Heimberg, who had been flown to Africa with an anti-tank unit destined to reinforce the Ramcke parachute brigade originally intended for the capture of Malta.

When the retreat from El Alamein started I was seriously wounded on 6 November near El Daba. Six days and six nights lay ahead of me while I was transported from El Daba to Tobruk. Here in the main dressing station I received my first medical attention. Those six days were hell. But I would like to pay my respects to the British fighters which attacked us by day and by night. Several times they came flying straight towards where I was lying helpless in a Red Cross car, but when they saw the Red Cross they turned aside. I arrived in Tobruk on 12 November, the same day the British entered. Marked with a big Red Cross flag our lorry drove eastward to the harbour. When they saw us the British immediately ceased fire and we were loaded on to a hospital ship lying in the port. The harbour was continuously bombed by the RAF but no bomb hit our last hope — the hospital ship. We left Tobruk that evening. The ship was full of wounded soldiers, some of them British officers. As I was lying on the lower deck I knew only that the ship had stopped for half an hour next morning; we were told that a British submarine had stopped us to check that we carried only wounded men. On 14 November we arrived at the Piraeus and finally felt safe again when we reached a hospital in Athens.

Helmut eventually recovered and went back to duty with the Luftwaffe; towards the end of the war he was serving with 6 Parachute Division in the Rhine-Maas area against formations of the First Canadian Army and was captured near Arnhem. Oddly, I was serving with the Canadian Army in that area at that time. The Parachutists fought wonderfully well with very little — their medical services were down to using paper bandages. But the campaign as a whole, particularly in Normandy, had at times been vicious, with no prisoners taken on either side, especially when Canadian and Waffen-SS troops fought each other.[12] Clearly, North Africa was different. With a few exceptions of course, the opposing British and Germans respected each other, there were no political undertones, and the old-fashioned decencies uncommon in this dreadful age largely ruled, to the dismay often of the people whom Denis Johnston was to call the 'civilian promoters of the war'. Even Montgomery, after victory, was widely criticised by the yellow press in England because his attitude to the enemy was insufficiently stern and politically motivated. Kitchener in the Sudan had had the right idea about the media, even though his war correspondents were more or less gentlemen. 'Out of my way you drunken scum!' he is reported to have addressed them, while his orders to the media sarcastically allowed them to proceed in front of the troops into battle, if they wished. But they were not to talk to the staff, who had better things to do.

Still, it is pleasant to be able to report that the desert war was conducted generally without hate or notable atrocity.

One pattern of the war where the change was most marked was in the fight for air superiority. In a very short time domination of the skies passed from the Germans to the

---

[12] See Alexander McKee, *Caen: Anvil of Victory*

British, although the Luftwaffe had a technically superior fighter in the latest type of Me 109. The sheer numbers of aircraft, plus greatly improved cooperation with the Army under Montgomery, was responsible.

Hans Drescher had begun his tour of duty in Africa as the leader of a Staffel of Ju 87Ds, dive-bombing mainly Free French targets, such as Bir Hacheim, where he even attacked an old-style desert fort of Foreign Legion type. Then in July 1942 his logbook records dive-bombing of British tanks at the southern end of the Alamein position as a daily occupation.

> In situations where the enemy had air superiority, if possible we were given a fighter escort. Generally the German Me 109s used 'free hunt' tactics, flying high above us. We began by flying in close formation at between 3,000 and 5,000 metres — representing a tempting target for the enemy fighters who in their turn were pounced on by the ME 109s flying higher still. If Italian fighters provided our escort they usually stuck closely to the German bomber units and became a much easier prey for the English fighters. In all fairness, I must admit that I personally preferred this close escort of our Stuka group because in this way a direct attack on our planes was the exception.

The single-engined Stukas — the JU 87s — were much slower than the twin-engined JU 88s and were frighteningly vulnerable to the fighters of Western air forces (the Russians with their primitive aeroplanes were a good deal less formidable). Consequently, when Drescher's unit was withdrawn from North Africa in October to renew the attacks on Malta, defended by Spitfires and Hurricanes as well as by massively efficient gun batteries, Drescher on arriving in Sicily for the attack put his doubts to Field Marshal Kesselring.

I suggested that for this purpose my Staffel should at once be reequipped with Me 109s carrying bombs, which would require retraining but give a better chance of success. This was accepted and it was decided to include young fighter pilots also and thus form a Jabo [*Jagdbomber*: fighter-bomber] Group.

The Me 109 fighters would escort the bomb-carrying 109s, attacking so high and fast that successful interception should be difficult; it would certainly reduce the terrible losses suffered by the slow JU 87s. On 2 November the new fast group made their first attack on Malta, bombing Luqa airfield. But it was also their last attack against the defiant island, because a few days later the battle of El Alamein had been lost. The unit flew via Greece to North Africa to find a desperate situation:

> Everyone was in full retreat. Because petrol was so short we couldn't use the planes much, were forced to retreat ourselves and were completely choked off by the RAF bombers and fighters. During a low-flying attack by Beaufighters on our airfield at El Magrun, south of Benghazi, I was severely wounded (with the loss of my right arm). But I was lucky, because on the day after I was flown to Lecce in the heel of Italy in an He 111 which had ferried petrol in barrels from Italy and would otherwise have been returning empty. I was then taken by Red Cross train to Germany via Naples. After a long stay in a Munich hospital I returned to my unit, which was now in Greece and flying sorties against the Italian forces of Marshal Badoglio.

The former allies were now fighting each other, as indeed the British had fought the French in 1940 after the surrender. Even more tragic incidents occurred, when British aircraft or submarines sank enemy ships carrying British or Dominion prisoners of war. As far as the submarines were concerned there was a general order not to attack northbound merchant vessels, precisely because of that possibility, but sometimes this rule was broken.

When submarines could be spared from covering the Allied landings in North Africa, they were sent to prey on ships, vessels and landing craft supplying the retreating Axis forces coming back from the lost Alamein position. One of the unusual targets was the *Hans Arp*, 2,645 tons, the German depot ship for L-Craft. *Safari* (P 211) under Commander Ben Bryant sank her in mid-November 1942, along with a number of landing craft, schooners and other small vessels.

On 14 November *Sahib* (P 212) under Lieutenant J. H. Bromage sighted a darkened ship heading west towards Tunis. *Sahib* attacked on the surface with her gun and scored hits, which resulted in the enemy steamer, which was the *Scillin*, 1,580 tons, sending out an SOS to summon help. As the calls were likely to be answered by warships, *Sahib* had to finish the job quickly, so fired a torpedo which struck by the forward hold. The submarine moved in on the surface to pick up selected survivors. Out of the night they heard voices shouting at them in English. The ship they had sunk had been bound from Tripoli for Trapani in Sicily with 810 British prisoners and 200 Italian soldiers.

Sahib cruised around slowly looking for British survivors, now they knew what they had done. To a call of 'Are there any more Englishmen in the water?' the surly reply came back 'No — but there's a Scotsman.' The submarine was able to pick up 61 men, 26 of them British and 35 Italian. The submarine commander's report stated that although weak from wounds and lack of food, the British survivors patiently took their turn to be rescued. Rescue had to stop when a ship was reported coming up from astern, and *Sahib* returned to Malta to land her passengers.

In this case there was no doubt in anyone's mind what had happened. With undersea warfare in general it is not always possible, even when the witness is on deck, to tell the difference between the explosion of a mine and that of a torpedo warhead; and the mine may have been laid by an aircraft, a surface ship, or by a submarine. Even if a guess of 'torpedo' proved correct, to identify the submarine may not be easy.

Tom Beel, a mortarman of the 20th Battalion of the Second New Zealand Expeditionary Force, experienced the sinking of a prisoner of war ship in late 1941 after being captured at the battle for Sidi Rezegh near Tobruk during the period of unfortunate British generalship. They had been promised support by British Matildas and South African tanks, but only the German tanks turned up, concealing the advance of their infantry by towing brushwood bundles to raise immense clouds of dust. The New Zealand mortar barrels became red-hot from firing, the baseplates buckled on the rocky ground; the crews' eardrums were almost split by the two batteries of 25-pounder guns supporting them. The panzers took heavy losses but when all the guns were knocked out the German tanks were free to roam among the New Zealand infantry positions — shallow pits with rock piled around the edges — into which the Germans could now fire by depressing their turret guns. When they had run out of mortar bombs to fire and had only their rifles, the New Zealanders surrendered.

Once out of the forward area, their captors had to hand them over to the Italians, who were fond of watches and rings but not free with water for the thirsty men. On 8 December 1941 they were marched down to Benghazi harbour and embarked with other British and Commonwealth prisoners totalling some 2,000 men in a ship they called the *Jason*, which was Dutch-built and named *Sebastiano Vener*, of 6,310 tons.[13] They were penned in the holds with guards at the head of the ladders. The latrine was a crude structure fastened to the side of the ship. Beel had just used this when he heard a lot of excited shouting in Italian.

> This gave me the impression they were in a state of panic. The guard screamed to me to get below, hastening me with a prod in the back with his rifle. My companions in the hold enquired what all the commotion was in aid of. I replied that perhaps an RAF plane or a Royal Navy ship had put in an appearance. There was a deep muffled boom that made the whole ship shudder. A great cheer went up.
>
> Minutes later we heard the clatter of the hatch covers being thrown off and daylight appearing above our heads. Instead of a guard we were greeted by a 'Kiwi' voice shouting for us to get out of the hold. 'What's happened?' we shouted, as we scrambled up. 'We've been torpedoed by the Royal Navy! No. 1 Hold is a shambles, we need help to get the survivors and wounded out.'
>
> The water in that hold was red with blood — scores of bodies in the swirling water and many more hanging from torn and jagged plates... severed limbs were everywhere. Ropes were quickly found and man after man was hauled out. Some went down that twisted ladder to assist the wounded. I saw men terribly maimed, with arms and legs dangling by sinews. Hasty crude operations were carried out, limbs being

---

[13] During research, this proved confusing as none of the official histories I consulted mentioned the *Jason*; but when I discovered her Italian name it was possible to check. The Naval Staff history describes her as a supply ship, the date 8 December 1941, with no mention that she was carrying prisoners.

hacked off with Army service knives. Keeping one's feet was difficult with so much blood on the metal deck plates.

Other men were throwing hatch covers, or anything that would float, overboard and then leaping into the sea; but as there were already men in the water these objects could kill or wound. Most of the prisoners were calm but there were those who believed the ship was going down. Not being a swimmer, Tom Beel decided to take the chance of remaining with the ship.

> Not one of the Italian crew was in evidence, apparently all had taken to the lifeboats, leaving us to our fate. In all this confusion, a number of shots rang out, clearly heard above the screams of the wounded, the shouting and the howling of the wind. The weather had deteriorated, the rising wind whipping up the sea to a fury. The ship wallowed in the deep swells with the bow almost submerged. We were curious to know the reason for the gunshots. We heard a guttural voice, raised to a shout, and saw a lone figure standing on the raised hatch cover, holding a revolver. His voice was unmistakably German and his cap badge confirmed this. One of our men called out that the German was asking for an interpreter, and a big South African stepped forward and after a few minutes' talk with the German turned to the crowd.

The South African told them that the German was the ship's engineer, that the ship was in no danger of sinking and that they should stop throwing themselves overboard, where they would certainly perish. His message was: Remain on the ship, do as I ask, and I will take you to safety. Then he explained the plan. As the propellers were almost out of the water, he wanted all fit men to go to the stern, where the weight would bring the propellers into the water. The ship's engines were undamaged, the Greek coast was only a few miles away, and he intended to run it aground.

In the darkness some time later, with a terrific grinding of metal over rock, we struck the coastline. The storm was at its height, heavy seas dashing over us, the wind screaming. Somehow a thick rope was secured from ship to shore and dozens of men swarmed down the rope using arms and legs to propel them. A lot must have made it but many did not. What they did not take into account was the great drunken roll of the ship as it was buffeted by the huge seas boiling all around. This resulted in the rope being loose and sagging one minute, the next as taut as piano wire. Men were catapulted into the boiling sea, there to drown or perish on the rocks. Several of us took shelter in what turned out to be the ship's medical officer's quarters. Foraging through lockers and cupboards, a large bottle of brandy was found. Passed from man to man the fiery liquid restored some warmth to our chilled bodies. We lay down to sleep, to await daylight. When we emerged next morning the sea was calm and the ship almost high and dry.

In Greece there is virtually no tide — if the sea rises or falls six inches overnight, it's sensational! But nevertheless, the prison ship was virtually high and dry, so Tom could walk ashore and survey the damage to the bow area. Clearly, an onshore gale had raised sea level a good many feet at its height.

I made my way forward. I was horrified: bodies still lay in the tangled wreckage of metal and wood, with pathetic belongings floating about. The bow looked as though a giant fist had punched its way through. The jagged hole was large enough to drive a three-ton truck through. I walked to the port side of the ship, which was the shoreward side, only to be met with an equally horrifying spectacle of hundreds of bodies laid out in rows where the Italian soldiers had dragged them from the water.

Eventually all the prisoners, some 1,500 of whom were still alive, were taken off the wreck and put aboard the hospital ship *Toscana*. But before they left the German engineer appeared again and some POW called out for three cheers. There was a roar of approval and as it died away, a New Zealander was heard to say: 'I never thought I would live to see the day I would cheer a bloody Jerry, but that man deserves the VC.'

The submarine which torpedoed her was the *Porpoise*, under Lt Cdr E. F. Pizey, who had just completed a run to Malta with supplies for the garrison (the boat was a capacious minelayer) and was allowed to patrol the west coast of Greece on his return. The German engineer's judgement of the seaworthiness of his ship was confirmed by the Royal Navy, for even hard aground as she was, on 15 December the submarine *Torbay* put another torpedo into her. No effort was to be spared to sink Rommel's supply ships.

Some 500 POWs had died in the 6,310-ton *Sebastiano Venier*. Just around the time of Montgomery's arrival in the desert in August 1942 Ultra was tracking the *Nino Bixio*, 7,137 tons, which was to carry 2,921 British and Dominion prisoners. A decoded message originated at 1822 hours on 15 August gave her estimated time of departure from Benghazi as 0500 the next day, with estimated time of arrival at Brindisi on the Adriatic coast of southern Italy as 0100 on 18 August, with details of route and air escort. The submarine most favourably placed to intercept was the *Turbulent* (Cdr J. W. Linton), which was patrolling the Anti-Kithera channel after taking off an agent from Crete and landing two others near Navarino. When sighted the convoy was seen to consist of two large ships escorted by destroyers and aeroplanes. *Turbulent* put two torpedoes into what proved to be the *Nino Bixio*, killing 434 prisoners of whom 117 were New Zealanders. But the ship remained afloat and was towed into Navarino roads, in southwest Greece, the site of a famous sea battle which brought Greece freedom from Turkish rule in the nineteenth century. That did not save her. It was essential to deprive the Axis of its supply ships and the RAF torpedoed her on 1 October, so that she played no part in building up the Afrika Korps for Alamein.

British submarine losses in the Second World War totalled 74, the last of them being *Porpoise* off Penang in 1945. *Turbulent* was lost with all hands off Sardinia in May 1943. *Sahib* was also sunk, but some men survived to become prisoners.

11: THE HILL OF JESUS

By the third week of October Montgomery's forces amounted to some 230,000 men organised in 11 divisions, four of them armoured. Four of the infantry divisions were veterans of the desert — the Australians, the New Zealanders, the South Africans and the Indians. The new infantry, recently arrived from the UK, made the composition of the force more British than Commonwealth. Rommel had some 100,000 men organised in 12 divisions, four of them armoured. Four were German, the remainder Italian. In the air, the British had a five to three superiority. In armour they had over 1,000 tanks to the 500 Rommel commanded. 250 of Montgomery's tanks were the new American-built Shermans; only 218 of Rommel's tanks were German. The British artillery numbered 1,460 guns (including 850 6-pounders as against Rommel's 500 field pieces and 850 anti-tank guns. The British supply position in fuel, ammunition and food was ample, their ports and depots being close behind them. Rommel's supply position was tenuous, his forces being at the end of long supply lines with mostly inadequate ports.

Nevertheless, the defence has considerable advantages over an attacker. In brutally simplified terms, the defender is usually lying down behind some sort of cover; whereas the attacker must get up and go forward, exposing human skin to bullets travelling at over 2,000 feet a second. In normal circumstances the attacking force must suffer far more casualties in dead and wounded than the defending army, which will tend to lose more in prisoners than in dead, hurt or missing, if the battle should go against them. At the end of the war, the advantage is theirs.

Montgomery's problem was more serious than it appears. The Alamein position had a frontage of only 35 to 40 miles between the obstacles of the Mediterranean Sea in the north and the impassable Qattara Depression in the south. The enemy position could not be outflanked, and it seemed hard to achieve surprise with an attack which the enemy expected and against which he had built up defences in great depth interlaced between layers of minefields covered by fire, the mines being mixed anti-personnel and antitank, many of them undetectable by electronic means.

So how was it to be done?

The first difference from normal was that this was to be a night attack. But not black night, instead a bright moonlit night. This was to become a Montgomery trademark in Africa and also in Normandy where the Mediterranean moon not being available, 'artificial moonlight' created by searchlights trained on the almost inevitable clouds, haze or mist would take its place.

The second difference was a reversion to First World War practice — a heavy preliminary bombardment from massed artillery. Now that 6-pounder anti-tank guns were available in numbers, the medium and field artillery were freed for their proper tasks.

Thirdly, not as planned but as developed during the battle, what was to become a Montgomery habit — all your forces concentrated at one place, heavy bomber and artillery bombardment, and bash on. In this case the principle could not be fully applied because Montgomery was aiming to achieve the impossible — surprise — by obvious preparations for the attack to take place in the south, in the form of a build-up readily apparent from the German-held Himeimat feature and proceeding at a pace indicating a later date for the attack than was actually intended. The south was of course where Rommel had attempted to break through at Alam el Haifa, carrying out his usual right hook from the desert and turning north towards the sea as soon as a breakthrough had been achieved. Even without Ultra, that had been fairly predictable on grounds of previous experience and the layout of the geographical features. For the British to make their main effort here was perfectly believable, and everything was done to encourage the belief, from the construction of dummy dumps of petrol and ammunition to increased radio traffic.

In the north however all the real preparations had to be concealed. Tanks were brought up by night and camouflaged as lorries. The medical arrangements to deal with the thousands of torn and maimed men would be a complete giveaway and therefore casualty clearing stations and surgical units for instance did not mark themselves out with the Red Cross. All this is very easy to list, much more difficult to do. But it was done. Montgomery, not Rommel, was to be the real Fox of the Desert. And, as Montgomery intended that Rommel should dance to *his* tune, Ultra became of minor importance.

What was planned for the north was a two-pronged attack on parallel lines in the area of Tel el Eisa and Miteiriya Ridge. The distinction is vital. The planned break-in was to be in the north near Tel el Eisa — the Hill of Jesus — while the diversionary attack which nevertheless had to be pressed to be believable and impress the enemy was in the south, by the impassable depression.

At the same time, Montgomery intended to put on a bullfighter's display of capes and drapes to take the bull's eyes away from the coming decisive blow. A naval convoy of landing craft with escort was to sail along the coast as though threatening the rear of the enemy's positions. This was also believable because of an operation which had been planned for mid-September and which because it failed has tactfully been forgotten except by the Germans and the LRDG, for it cost them the life of their leader, John Haselden. To the survivors, it will always be 'The Tobruk Massacre Raid'. Actually there were four such operations, which were to involve a great deal more than the Long Range Desert Group. All were designed to hit Rommel's communications, already under great stress from air and submarine attack. Tobruk was to be assaulted and captured — and British prisoners freed — by attacks both from out of the desert and out of the sea. Perhaps it was too complicated, but if successful it would have been well worth while. It was run at the highest level in the Middle East by a combined staff. The Royal Marines and the Navy suffered severely when it was defeated.

The plan to take Benghazi was more of a wrecking raid of brief duration; the raiders were to be commanded by David Stirling of the SAS. Another party was to appear out of the desert wastes by going south of the Qattara Depression and emerging to wreck the aerodrome at Benina. The fourth operation was for the Sudan Defence Force to take Jalo as a base for Stirling and for further raids from the wastes. These were to be carried out by small, very light forces accustomed to travelling long distances through the desert; no army could go this way.

Apart from these attempts to worsen Rommel's supply problems, there were plans for tactical interference with his tank radios carried out by special jamming aircraft at critical moments during the battle, and a programme of intensive air operations to first obtain air superiority and then maintain it. This was another Montgomery preliminary which was to become standard, and which was now possible in fact rather than theory firstly because of the forces now available and secondly because the RAF wished to cooperate to the fullest extent in the battle — which was not true of the RAF in England, for some of its senior commanders there believed that they could win the war single-handed. At Alamein, everyone — every Service — was fighting the same war wholeheartedly.

And when the actual time arrived Montgomery played an old First World War trick — the previous night the infantry left their positions and lay out in front all day in the blazing heat without significant movement, so they would rise to attack unexpectedly far forward and away from the most likely areas for enemy harassing fire. For this was to be an infantry battle, once the massed artillery had ceased, and they would have to clear lanes through the minefields through which the armour could pass, and destroy the enemy's tanks which would hurry to the point of any threatened break-in. This was a weak point: the Dominion infantry generals, when told by Montgomery of this plan for the armour to help them, had stood up and declared firmly: 'They won't!' In the past, they felt that they had been let down, perhaps not realising quite how blind are the crew of a tank, particularly in dust clouds and at night. In some, there was real hatred of the armour — the British armour, not the German.

There have been many books written about Alamein, especially by generals, and in very great detail. These may be consulted, although it must be admitted that no full, detailed history is possible. As Montgomery himself remarked, there comes a time when the battle is out of the generals' hands — it all depends on the soldiers and the junior leaders.

The battle was due to begin after nightfall on 23 October, but some opening moves were made in the afternoon. At that time Rommel was under medical care in Germany, having made precise preparations to fight a battle which he felt he was unlikely to win. In particular, defences to a depth of five miles constructed like a web, but getting stronger and more concentrated as the enemy advanced; this foreshadowed the method he and others were to use during the Normandy campaign, as the only possible answer to the by now overwhelming air power of the Allies. The German commander in the desert was General Stumme, an expert on armoured warfare imported from the Russian front, with General von Thoma as second-in-command. Rommel still stood high in Hitler's estimation, although the Führer would not grant him the forces he felt he really needed. On the Allied side Winston Churchill was still sending restive, irritant, prodding notes to Cairo, where they were now dealt with by the languid General Alexander, who simply neglected to answer them, thus shielding Montgomery's back during this critical time.

L. J. Sheppard of 260 Squadron flew two operations that afternoon. The squadron, equipped with Kittyhawks, had been developing the fighter-bomber technique to do the same job for the British as the Stuka did for the Germans; this too was to reach a peak of effectiveness in Normandy with the Typhoons controlled by the 'Cab Rank' system. But this day they were doing bomber escort jobs.

> 260 Squadron were flying top cover in three flights of four, the leading flight being 'Red', the middle flight (which I was

leading) 'Yellow' and the top flight 'Blue'. The target for the bombers was I think a concentration of Jerries between El Alamein and El Daba. The usual procedure for the bombers was to turn in from the north-east towards the south-west; after their bombing run, they would turn south-east into the desert, thereby flying away from any ack-ack and of course away from Jerry aerodromes and fighters. Fighter cover in the afternoon was invariably to the right of the bomber formation and above, thus enabling the fighter cover to detect any attack on the bombers which might be made out of the sun. On the afternoon of the 23rd we were airborne about 3 p.m. and in the target area about half an hour later. A gaggle of 109s attacked and were engaged by 'Blue' flight. As soon as the attack began I gave instructions to 'Yellow' flight to turn about and immediately the flight was engaged by 109s that had broken through. From my point of view there was nothing very clever about the fight — we engaged at once, endeavoured to sort a 109 out, and I suppose I was fortunate, that as I pulled around I came upon a 109, lined him up and shot him down. When I turned the flight into the fight, I had been checking that there was nothing on our tails to surprise us, and now I looked for the remainder of 'Yellow' flight, but it just wasn't possible to sort them out — there were aircraft dicing everywhere, and in the distance I could see the bomber formation getting well away, having done their job. Our job was to keep the 109s from following them.

Sheppard then saw a 109 beginning to chase a Kittyhawk and turned towards the German, firing a little out of range, which made him break off and dive to the deck seawards.

The Kittyhawk was a much heavier aircraft than the 109 and by cutting the turn I was able to get close enough to have another go at him. By now he knew he was in trouble, and all I needed was to get a little closer for a final burst to finish him off. The 109 realised what I was after and knowing that a 109 could outclimb a Kittyhawk pulled up to do just that. In a determined effort not to lose him, I pulled up under him and fired a final burst that I knew couldn't miss, but the firing of the guns caused me to stall, and I was then too busy to know whether I had eventually got the 109 or not.

After sorting himself out after the stall Sheppard found he was over the German lines and totally on his own — most unhealthy. Worse, oil began seeping back over the engine cowling, obviously a stray hit from a 109 or even ground fire during the stall.

> I made straight out to sea to fly along the coast, thinking I may have a chance in the water as against being put in the bag, and when I calculated I was back on our side I came in to the water's edge, and finally when the engine packed up, put it down on the beach. By good fortune I had managed to prang alongside a casualty clearing station. At the Squadron the doctor insisted that I stand down the next day, but I flew again on the 25th.

That proved to be an almost identical affair, much the same target, again flying top cover, again a brush with 109s — fewer of them this time, and they called it a day; but a group of three Italian Macchi 202s were not so quick. Sheppard tried to join them, hoping to shoot down all three, but when he got the first one, the others speeded up so rapidly they left him behind. Even so, he felt he evened things up a bit — two definite and one probable in those two days.

From time to time his squadron had been working with South African squadrons flying Kittyhawks or Tomahawks; the latest to arrive were a significant reinforcement from the United States, joining in the desert air war with three Pursuit squadrons equipped with Kitty ha wks. What it was like to be with the bombers on these operations is described by 'Dickie' Richards, a radio operator and air gunner with 223 Squadron flying Baltimores.

A mobile gong alerted all those taking part in the sortie. We then assembled for the briefing on the target which had been selected by Eighth Army HQ with whom we were cooperating in close support. There were four members to each crew. We circled the airfield gradually getting in the correct formation — a box of 6 leading followed by two boxes of 6 port and starboard. 18 in all in arrowhead formation. We set course climbing to 15,000 feet, soon to be joined by the fighter escort. We crossed the coast and flew a short distance out to sea and then turned parallel to the coast; recrossing the coast we gradually dropped height on the approach to the target area. At the same time the entire formation would spread out and adopt the familiar weaving tactics to fox the predictors below who would be calculating our heights and speeds. Over the target area all the weaving would cease, each plane flying straight and level, the bomb aimer waiting for the target to appear on his equipment. This was the real danger time, as the gunners below would be getting an uninterrupted fix on us. The wireless operator (myself) would have left his cabin and gone down to the lower fuselage, opened up the winding hatch and pulled out a pair of Vickers guns in readiness for any planes coming up to attack from below. The top gunner immediately above me would be rotating 4 Brownings in readiness. When all guns were firing the row in the cabin was horrendous! Over the intercom the observer would announce the release of all the bombs in succession. Then I would have to poke my head out of the hatch and confirm the release of each bomb, until all 6 were off. I had a perfect ringside view of what was coming up at us, seeing the flashes of all the guns firing below. I was not very keen on this part of the operation! As each plane left the target area it did a steep diving turn and we all tried to regain quickly our formation back to home. Meanwhile the ack-ack was exploding around us and frequently our flight was interrupted by Messerschmitt 109s who had marked us out for attention and there would be a running dogfight until we got clear and continued for home, at which point the next lot of 18 would be ready in waiting to take over the same operation.

For F. Goldsmith, an ERA in HMS *Belvoir*, a Hunt-class destroyer based at Alexandria, the morning of 23 October was just like any other. Around midday orders were received to raise steam and proceed to sea late that afternoon. Still nothing out of the ordinary, probably a run down the coast to bombard Mersa Matruh.

When the ship was slowly making for the entrance to Alexandria harbour, four or five landing craft followed us in line ahead, turning to port when outside. This was a different operation to the norm and interest was aroused. Were we to invade some small port or take some soldiers from the beach? The latter seemed more likely when it was realised that the landing craft were empty. But there was something strange, as there was no urgency and we were in sight of the shore for all to see. Later that night one of the ERAs came into the mess and said: 'There is a hell of a battle going on ashore.' We all went to the upper deck and saw what proved to be the barrage at El Alamein. It reminded me of electric storms we had seen at Freetown on the way to South Africa with a large troop convoy — some of them were now probably firing the guns ashore. How anyone survived that onslaught I really don't know. We returned to Alexandria with our dummy invasion fleet and were given to understand that this small exercise kept a German division on the coast. Come to think of it, if by this they evaded the awesome bombardment it also did them a good turn.

Martin Ranft, in peacetime a machine textile knitter from Chemnitz (later to be renamed Karl-Marx-Stadt in the DDR), was serving in an artillery battery equipped with French guns positioned between the sea and the main coastal road. At 8.45 p.m. their time he was looking out, when suddenly the sky lit up. He shouted: 'Look at that!' There was a wait of six or seven seconds, then came the sound.

> Fantastic. Never experienced anything like it. We were on the receiving end of artillery concentrated on a half-mile square. Next morning when we looked out of our holes, all was different.

Bombardier Louis Challoner was serving a 25-pounder gun in 2 RHA of 1 Armoured Division in the north near the sea, their task counter-battery fire on the German artillery.

> Men stood at their stations, strained and silent, as they waited for the two words which would trigger off the holocaust — 'Take Post!' — and then a further three minutes of quivering tension had to elapse before the synchronised command rapped from a thousand throats — 'Fire!'
> The roar from the massed guns defied any description. No fury of sound had ever assailed our ears like that before, it cuffed, shattered and distorted the senses, and loosened the bowels alarmingly. I was more than startled, I was shocked, and needed to know that everyone else was there. When I could focus, the faces I saw at first looked blanched and then flushed brightly in a kaleidoscope of passionately flickering hues as every line and detail was etched into relief by the flashes from the muzzles of the guns. It was bad enough to withstand without wavering the crack of our own piece, and

the concerted roar of the four guns in the troop firing together worse still, but now, with hundreds of guns almost hub to hub, all bucking, recoiling, spitting fire and snapping like a pack of vicious terriers, all at once, it was sheer horror. More thunder rolled and reverberated across the front as the heavier guns behind us added their base tones to the discord of the mighty orchestra. But no orchestra in this world ever made a clamour like that; the inmates of Hell must have taken over to demonstrate how their music compared with that of the human species — and how well they demonstrated their malice! The very ground trembled and winced, the noise eddied and roared out fanwise in all directions, massive waves of blast swept the air and smoke into tremendous currents and the moaning undertones of echo from the smoke-cloud and the whine of the departing missiles sounded as if even the spirits of the underworld were adding their voices to the tumult.

The constant drill by which our army life had been ruled was now our saving grace, and even before the initial shock had been fully absorbed we fell into the routine of performing all our tasks automatically. Gradually our minds took over their responsibilities again. Our gun team had a sort of communal pride in our speed and efficiency, we knew that we were good but each of us appreciated the other's contribution to the task and was determined to maintain the standard. I felt myself different from the rest in that for the life of me I could not see the sense in grown men hurling chunks of red hot metal at each other, the only direct object being to mangle and maim. I remember Len Chandler alluding to one conscientious objector who had volunteered to become a medical orderly and who had seen more action, danger and death, than most of us. 'I wish I'd had the guts to do what he has done,' said Len, 'but I'm not that kind of conchie. With all my conscience, I object to Hitler and all his brood; I object to his ways and I object to his means, but just objecting, however conscientious we are about it, is not enough. We have to do something about it, and this is what we can do.' A long speech, even for Len, who was not usually tongue-tied like the rest of us when serious matters were under discussion.

The thunderous action continued throughout the night, each gun being rested periodically for ten minutes so that the barrel could cool. Our targets had been enemy artillery between four and five miles away and we had received very little answering fire, but in the early hours of the morning our range was shortened in order to subdue the Axis machine-gunners and so that our infantry, who were just ahead of us, could advance under cover of our creeping barrage. We had to shout at the tops of our voices to make ourselves heard for our heads were beginning to feel numb right through and ordinary tones of voice failed to get to us. Those who had refused to accept earplugs were now regretting their bravado.

The infantry opposite the guns which Martin Ranft helped to serve were New Zealanders, and they broke through the Italian infantry opposite them. From the way the gun barrels were trained round on their unseen targets as the direction altered, the German gunners could see that the advance was flowing round their battery.

On Sunday morning early, a lovely morning as usual in Africa, we were near a slight hill. We smelled something funny (later, I learned it was whisky). It was the New Zealanders very close — and there was a fire fight. We held them, they had to withdraw. Three or four of them were killed and also our CO. He looked out of his hole, shouted, 'Fire, boys, fire, we're not lost yet!' Then his hands went to his face and he fell. A New Zealander sergeant got to within a metre of one of our guns, when he was shot in the temple. We had to continue firing our guns and the muzzle blast of this one blew his body into the air. Two New Zealanders waved something white. Our sergeant said: 'Come on, boys.' We searched them for weapons and I had the pleasure of escorting them back. We passed a German field kitchen. The cook asked them if they were hungry, and gave each of them a tin of Compo and they sat down and ate there; but the cook didn't give me anything! I suppose 80 per cent of us believed the propaganda in the papers and on the radio, all the stories about the Poles and how the war started, but we never hated the English, we were more like friends with English POWs!

The battery withdrew a mile or so to avoid being cut off by the slow British advance and were five days in this position, where they were harassed by the RAF. Gunner Ranft, who now lives in Sussex, referred admiringly to what he called the 'stubborn eighteens', the bomber formations in three flights of six 'flying as if on parade for the Queen'. His opposite number, Bombardier Challoner, was impressed by the slow, methodical advance.

> Each day, and with infinite caution, we pressed forward a little further. There was no attempt this time to sweep exultantly through the enemy lines and go fanning out over wide stretches of sand. The line remained solid and just moved forward with the inexorable steadiness of a steam roller.

The RAF were developing methods of close co-operation with the army, in which the use of fighter-bombers was combined with the high-level parade bombing of the twin-engined aircraft, as Gunner Ranft found.

> We were also attacked in this position by low-flying fighters, who I think were a bit over-confident. Beside our big gun was a light four-barrelled flak gun. In a split second this gun shot down the fighter leader — he had a red nose — who crashed 30 metres from me, and burst into flames. Two others were shot down further away. I suppose they had thought there

were no Germans there, that we had all retreated. I also saw a plane in a 'stubborn eighteen' formation get a direct hit on a wing, which fell off, and the plane went into a spin. At this time we saw only two or three of our planes in a week. In general, the enemy artillery was terrible. The bombers didn't worry us so much at Alamein but the gunfire was a hell of an experience.

Charles Philbrick was with 44 Royal Tank Regiment in the 1st Army Tank Brigade and had the job of helping to clear a lane through the minefield for the New Zealand Division. Opposite them were the Italians of the Trento Division corseted by Germans of the 164th Division. Philbrick had been a motor driver in civilian life, and this time the Army had put the square peg into the square hole; he was commanding a Scorpion tank — basically a Matilda designed for European conditions and now modified at the suggestion of a South African engineer called Du Toit. Two diesel engines drove the tank, but attached to it on the outside was a Ford V8 lorry engine and transmission driving a drum to which were attached long chains. It was the first of the 'flail' tanks and this was the first time it was to be used in action. Its flailing speed was 1½ m.p.h. and the flails struck the ground every seven inches. What the flails were supposed to detonate was the Teller anti-tank mine (which required a heavy pressure), the wooden Schuhmine, undetectable by metal detectors, and the diabolical Schutzenmine, the 'S' or 'jumping' mine which had three prongs — if you stood on just one of them the contraption would leap out of the ground and explode about the level of your midriff, considerably impairing your chances of fatherhood or digesting food by a shower of ball bearings.

The Scorpions came up at night, and were camouflaged as a pile of boxes under tarpaulins. The crews lay out there for some days, with no movement possible in daylight, and had to live in the heat under the stifling tarpaulins.

We were briefed that the attack was to be at night and we were to follow a line of tiny lights — Ever-Ready cycle lamps on posts. The barrage started on time. It was unbelievable, I think there was one gun every 25 yards. A terrific noise and it went on for a long time. We followed the tiny lamps until we came to our start line into the minefield marked out by white tapes. We couldn't see much for the dust we were kicking up with the flails, but it seemed a long way. It was like driving around in a steel box, when closed down, learning to feel if you were going uphill or down. There was a periscope but the German anti-tank gunners knew all about them. But we were successful and reached our stage point, but the noise was still terrific. All we could see were the gun flashes lighting up the troops and tanks and a rush of Bren carriers coming through where we'd cleared. We stopped, having done our job, but in front of the other divisions they were still working. Two days later we were able to visit our area. Terrific devastation in the German positions. Blown up bodies, millions of flies — how they got there so quickly I don't know — and wrecked guns and vehicles.

Reginald Vine was with an LAD (Light Aid Detachment REME) for the repair of tanks in action in the 9th Armoured Brigade which was in effect the 'cavalry' of the New Zealand Division.

We moved up in rear of the Alamein line at night and were put under cover by some so-called wrecks littering the desert, about 50 tanks for each for the three regiments. Finally, we were in German artillery range. As we approached I saw a number of 5.5s and 25-pounders — and beside the 25-pounders were stacked 1,000 rounds. A gunner shouted to me: 'We'll be shooting these over your head tonight!' We had been told that in the past the tanks had let the New Zealanders down, and there were problems in the New Zealand Parliament because their troops in the field were not getting a square deal. Our orders were on no account to let the New Zealand infantry down. New Zealand is a small country but they came and fought for us; they were good and conscientious soldiers and had heavy casualties. We took Miteiriya Ridge, and were then pulled back because Monty wouldn't risk his armour in the open. The Germans stood and fought us bravely; and they always praised a good fight. The Italians were not as bad as they were painted, because in the early days the Matilda was unstoppable by anything they had. It was only after the Germans landed that I saw the first hole in a Matilda.

The armoured brigade had had fairly heavy casualties when after a few days they were pulled back into reserve. Rommel's defence scheme and the stubbornness of his soldiers was tending to blunt the British attacks — they could break in but not break through. Montgomery, in spite of what he was to claim later, was forced to change his plan — thus showing in fact commendable initiative and flexibility. This was also the moment when the restless Churchill lost faith in his new commanders and feared yet another desert disaster, in spite of all the men and material he had managed to send out at great cost to the Middle East. Nevertheless, by making his main effort in the north Montgomery had obtained a measure of surprise. This was to have its drawbacks.

Bernard L. Williams spent five and a half years in operational areas, and with the exception of the 1940 retreat to Dunkirk, found himself at the base during retreats and up forward during the advances. At Alamein he commanded No. 6 Field

Surgical Unit, which was behind the northern part of the position.

> War is interesting if you're winning, horrible if you're not. Generally it is a hateful, dirty and dangerous business. Many of the best young men of all the nations concerned are trained and motivated to kill and maim their fellows. In this they are usually controlled and directed by older men further back in comparative safety. In some it brings out the worst, but in many it brings out the best, revealing unsuspected capacity for bravery and heroism. A certain chivalry existed in the desert war, both sides respecting each other as fighting men who were doing their job under conditions of great natural difficulty, far from home. Both sides listened on the radio to 'Lili Marlene', a song full of nostalgia and yearning for normality. The Red Cross was honoured by both sides. To our dismay orders came through that this emblem was to be removed in the build-up to battle for security reasons. We were machine-gunned from the air on a couple of occasions but no one was hurt though the QM's store took a pasting. One bullet went through five tins of Elastoplast but came to rest in the sixth tin.

The fighting formations had their own regimental MOs; behind them were the field ambulances whose prime task was the evacuation of casualties to surgical centres, usually located in Casualty Clearing Stations (CCSs) where emergency surgery to render the wounded fit for travel back to base hospitals in the Nile Delta was undertaken. Alexandria was some forty miles away and Cairo about 120. From desert experience Field Surgical Units (FSUs) had been evolved. There were two officers (a surgeon and an anaesthetist) and seven other ranks, including a theatre assistant, a clerk and two drivers. A three-ton lorry and a staff car took all personnel and tented theatre equipment. The units were highly mobile and designed for attachment to a CCS or Field Ambulance, larger units which provided services and beds. Bernard Williams was the surgeon of No. 6 FSU, positioned behind the two-pronged main thrust near Burg el Arab.

> On the evening of 23 October I was visited by a friend who commanded a Field Ambulance. He told me the battle plan, and together we climbed on to nearby high ground. There was a full moon. The silence was suddenly rent by the simultaneous firing of a thousand guns. Their first objectives were the enemy artillery emplacements, the positions of which had been plotted during the previous weeks, without returning their fire. This tactic was effective and was followed by a creeping barrage behind which the infantry advanced. It was a few hours before the first casualties reached us, and they soon became a flood. Much of the work was 'life and limb' surgery which meant dealing with chest and abdominal wounds, amputating hopelessly mangled limbs and trying to preserve others. Our facilities were limited. There was surprisingly little sepsis, no doubt because the desert was a clean and comparatively sterile place, and we had ample supplies of the newly discovered sulphonamide powder which was mixed with flavine antiseptic. Wounds were left open after trimming and removal of dead and contaminated flesh, and powdering. We enjoyed an excellent transfusion service. Troops were bled back at the base, each donor being given a pint of beer in exchange for his blood. But for ten days we were overwhelmed. Many were pretty seriously smashed up. Young men shattered, legs, eyes, arms gone. One never gets over seeing this. It gave me a tremendous admiration for our soldiers — they were tough, resilient and brave.

Albert Freeman was in 2 Cheshires, a machine-gun battalion whose guns were farmed out to support various battalions in the area of 50 Div. He was one of those who, in training for the battle, went out on patrols and dug in 600 yards to their front, practically in the German lines. When it came to the battle the German mortars fired at where they should have been. But to lie out in the sun all day in the heat and the gradually accumulating stink was a trial. The only entertainment was watching the aerial activity. A 109 fighter-bomber coming down in flames, South African Kittyhawks tearing into a Stuka formation and ripping them down. Groups of RAF bombers going over in their formations of 18, Stukas bombing what turned out to be a German position. At first light, three figures walking towards them through the minefield. A short warning burst and up went their hands — three British airmen unaware of their danger.

> We were never far from the enemy. After a sandstorm you could see the Jerries shaking out their blankets less than a mile away. It was a gentleman's war in the desert; only later, in Europe, did it get vicious. What mainly worried us, particularly with mines, was the possible loss of our wedding tackle. We knew the time it was to start — 9.40 p.m. And we were out already, due to Monty's skill. But we never realised how powerful the barrage would be. Our trenches just collapsed in on us. Later, we crossed the old battlefield of Bir Hacheim. The jackals had been at the bodies — eyes and faces gone. We saw that hair and nails also continue growing after death. We buried them.

Albert Freeman was a regular soldier, joining up under age before the war; he had been in France in 1940, where it was hard for them; then after North Africa he went to Italy, missed Normandy but went to Arnhem with the airborne and was taken prisoner.

J. E. Drew was a private soldier with HQ Company of 18th Durham Light Infantry (DLI). He had to write a letter home describing what happened to him and his brother Joe (who were teamed together on a Bren) on the first night of Alamein. Whereas the Vickers MG used by the Cheshires was a heavy, belt-fed gun requiring to be broken down into three separate loads for carrying by three soldiers, the Bren was an LMG using 30-round magazines and was carried and could be operated by one man, but a number two was provided to reload the emptied magazines (he also had to carry spare magazines and ammunition, and of course his rifle). The idea that soldiers leap lightly, Rambo-like, at the enemy and fire off 10,000 rounds in one tremendous burst is romantic for the young enthusiast to contemplate, but not factual. I write with feeling, having been both a number one and a number two on a Bren, and also operated one on my own. They were awkward to carry, with too many bumps, protuberances and hard angles, hence the two brothers took it in turns for a mile or so at a time.

When they first heard that there was to be a 'push' soon, Drew wrote that he could not put into words the excitement felt in the company that night. They were taken up in trucks originally. British Army trucks are not designed for comfort even on tarmac roads; after bumping and pitching across the desert in the dark they were glad of a breakfast stop at dawn.

It was after breakfast that we were informed of the job that was before us, and I must admit that the officer spared us no details of what we were to expect and what was expected of us, and by then we were beginning to shake a little in our shoes, not without reason. Then we were told about the barrage which I am sure helped us through the next few hours. Now comes the part of my letter that has kept me so long from writing to you.

We were now dressed ready to move up to a forward position and from where we were to have what was to prove our last meal together. Actually it was Bully Beef and Biscuits with jam, which we ate sitting together behind a mound of earth at about four in the afternoon.

After only a short rest they put on their webbing — belt and ammo pouches, water-bottle, entrenching tool, small pack — and the final stage of their march 'into the blue' began, one carrying the Bren, the other a rifle and the spare mags and ammo for the LMG.

At last we halted and were formed up ready for the big push which we knew would be the turning-point of the war. We lay there quite a while and after the sweat of the march we were beginning to shiver as we only had khaki drill on, so we cuddled up together to keep warm, sardines had nothing on us. We had an issue of rum and nothing was ever more welcome; in fact we felt ten times better. The order came to take up positions and everybody was keyed up, and it was a surprise when we were told to fix bayonets. We moved up a few yards and the next thing we heard was a crescendo of guns which shook us at first. Now we were off and although we had to keep spread out Joe and I kept in touch with one another till we were held down by machine-gun fire.

Things were looking pretty grim here and it was only the audacity of an NCO that got us out of it, which cost him an arm. Joe and I had got our gun going again and we began to advance with the section. The next thing I knew was a tremendous crash behind us and as I fell forward I caught a glimpse of Joe going down. Picking myself up, I discovered that except for a few scratches I was OK. I then walked over to Joe and found that there was nothing I could do for him.

Looking around, I found what had been the cause of it all. One of the Jerry panzers had feigned dead and was just going to move off. I picked up the gun and because I must admit I was pretty mad by this time I let him have a full magazine and I am pretty certain he never lived to tell the tale.

Drew did not see his brother buried, nor did he have the opportunity to see the grave, because the attack here had been so successful that his battalion was brought back. In the south, the diversionary attack did not go well.

South of 50 Div was the 44th Infantry Division and 7th Armoured, overlooked by the Germans on the Himeimat feature. The 44th was to force a corridor through the minefields, Rommel's 'Devil's Gardens'. But in front to clear the way went the Royal Engineers. Sapper B. Easthope, son of the editor of a Portsmouth paper, was with 577 Field Company RE.

We used bayonets. Mine detectors were not satisfactory. Besides there were wooden mines. You probed lightly — if you struck something solid you explored gently around it with your hands. If a wire, where did it lead? Don't cut it, don't lift it. Expose it and find where it goes to. You had to take your chance when clearing mines. One chap from an 'S' mine got a pellet in the jaw which came out by his neck behind the ear. There were 348 ball bearings in an 'S' mine, which would jump three feet out of the ground before exploding. Occasionally a mine would go off by itself, causing a 100-ft-high column of smoke which you saw before you heard the bang. Minefields were not small, more the size of Southsea Common. We lifted mines, yes, but we laid them as well.

The flies were terrible, we tried squirting petrol at them with fire extinguishers. You had two gallons of water a day for everything. So you didn't throw any away. Water in which you had washed your teeth you might then use to wash your socks. Even if the water was dirty, you had a use for it. We had more petrol than water, so we made little slow fires with petrol and sand to boil clothes. No water for rinsing but at least they were cleaner. And they dried in ten minutes. I saw a sergeant give two gallons of water as a birthday present! We were issued with Egyptian onions, hotter than English ones; I ate them and never got desert sores, which were very painful, but I did get ringworm — I think the cause was lack of vegetables. In the desert visibility was wonderfully good, but it was not without its wildlife — scorpions, snakes, antelopes, jerboa (which wasn't really a rat). And at night there was a really black sky with brilliant stars. I never minded guard duty, although others got bored, because I had always been interested in astronomy and spent my time studying the stars.

The Germans treated POWs decently, they seemed to respect the British because they were good fighters. But Alamein was terrible for both sides. Alexander was the Boss and Monty was his Foreman. When Monty first came out to Egypt he had all ranks paraded for PT at 0600. He led them himself in shirt, shorts and plimsolls. Anyone who couldn't run two miles was sent back to UK. He kept Grades A1, A2 and A3 only, the rest were weeded out. He knew he was up against a formidable fighting force. No one liked Monty but we respected his generalship. There was not much left of 44 Div after Alamein, and we were pulled out — an eight-day lorry trip to Damascus. The loveliest sight I ever saw was when we came over the Hill of Galilee and saw the wonderful blue lake. When I saw the stones on that beach, I thought: Jesus may have walked on those stones here.

Attached to the 44th Infantry Division, not too long out from England, were the Royal Scots Greys (2 Dragoons). Captain Basil Miles was their MO. He enjoyed his time with them, their officers' mess being more intellectually stimulating than an RAMC one. He was with them during the long period when they were changing from horses to tanks; some officers were found to be unmechanisable. Their first task when they arrived in Egypt was to provide a screen through which the remnants of the Tobruk garrison could retreat.

> It was an undisciplined rout apart, I remember, from a Guards (Scots?) battalion who came past, shaved, properly dressed and each man with his rifle, which could not be said of the rest. Shortly before El Alamein our thermometer disintegrated from being left in the sun. Being technically a 'Scientific Instrument' we had to fill in a complicated form in quadruplicate — I imagine one for Division, one for Corps, one for Montgomery and one for Rommel! The listed price was I think 11 pence but for some inscrutable reason we had to add 10% and later subtract 10%. This comes to 10.89 pence which rounded up to 11 pence again. A nearby MO, falling into the spirit of this farce after a similar catastrophe, answered the question 'How Lost?' by replying 'chewed in half by a maniacal patient', which might have amused Rommel more than Montgomery who was short on humour.

No one of experience can fail to recognise distinctly British Army techniques here, but the rival armies were in many respects similar. For instance, Martin Ranft was called up for the RAD (Reichsarbeitsdienst or labour corps) in 1941 prior to being conscripted for the Army. The discipline was much more severe in the RAD.

> My first punishment was for leaving my locker open, when I had dressed hurriedly in the morning. My second was when the instructor was explaining a wheelbarrow to our group. I never knew it had so many parts. I was bored, so didn't listen. The instructor demanded: 'Who can repeat what I have said?' No one answered, so he picked on me. When I had to say I couldn't remember he went berserk. For 14 days he chased

me with fatigues like polishing his boots. I had a fortnight's leave at home and then I was called up for the Army. During recruit training in the artillery barracks at Altenburg there was heavy punishment for the slightest thing but now I listened to every word!

British Army recruit training was similar to that of the RAD, as many may remember. But sooner or later it all became serious. Captain Miles recalled:

And then, the start of the battle of El Alamein with the spectacular barrage and our mixed Brigade deployed ostentatiously to draw off the enemy armour from the north where the breakthrough was planned. The sick parade was smaller than usual, a sure sign of good unit morale. The first casualty we encountered was a Psychiatrist who had wounded a leg, which we splinted; he had been sent forward to get battle experience. Soon afterwards we got a bullet right through the side of our South African Harrington Mark II armoured car which we learnt to our surprise was only armoured in the front. Then, I remember a group of demoralised infantry, who had lost their sergeant, heading towards the rear. I got out and was able to persuade them to head west again.

Then, the shambles of this first night. Our Sappers had been unable to penetrate the second minefield so we were stuck more or less in a gap in the first where we were forced to remain as wounded kept being brought to us, instead of siting our Aid Post between the two gaps in the first minefield as planned. Our petrol and ammunition lorries were close behind us. Jerry soon pin-pointed the gap and I estimated that at least 25 shells landed within 50 yards and we could do no more than spend the night digging the wounded into slits in the sandy gravel, giving them morphine and attaching the appropriate label. That splendid American academic from Yale, who used to sit in his four-wheel-drive Dodge ambulance reading Chaucer through his thick myopic glasses, was superb, coming back time and again in his unprotected ambulance to pick up more wounded. These American volunteers, many Quakers, became proudly attached to the British units to which they were posted. He deserved a Mention. We had these Americans attached because our heavy ambulances invariably got stuck in the sand. I shall always remember our first, a Geologist from Harvard, who joined us in an area where there were silicified remains of a bygone forest. His very first words, before introducing himself, being 'Gee, the cellular structure is well preserved.'

The next morning, the second day of Alamein, Captain Miles went up to the adjutant, to learn the plan for the day. Ruefully, he recalled that he stood on the wrong side of the adjutant's tank, not realising that the French Foreign Legion had failed to secure the high ground to the south. Fragments of casing from an 88-mm shell punctured lung and liver; a splinter still remains less than an inch below his heart. He was given morphine and driven on a tank to an MO of the Rifle Brigade, and sent on a medical unit where, propped up, it was thought he was just paying a social call. Thence by hospital train to a Base Hospital, still very confused.

But I remember a screaming German prisoner who thought he was being given a lethal injection. I managed to get out of my bunk and, having some German, was able to reassure him that it was just morphine for his pain.

Captain Miles was on the 'dangerously ill' list for six weeks and was eventually medically downgraded. Then on to Salerno and the Italian campaign. In 1982 his right knee became inflamed and an X-ray showed three tiny shell fragments, one loose in the joint, which was extracted surgically, with no trouble since. He has no recollection of being hit there.

Lieutenant-Colonel D. L. A. Gibbs, commanding 1/6 Battalion of the Queen's Royal Regiment in 131 Brigade of 44 Division, was a regular officer.

> We were part of the southern flank of the 'Front' and the forces in that area were by their aggressive actions to make it appear to the enemy that the major effort and attempt to 'break out' was to be there at the southern end rather than in the area of Alamein village itself and the coastal strip. To that end repeated efforts and attacks were made in the first forty-eight hours or so of the battle to regain broad minefields lost to the enemy at Alam Haifa in order that the Armour could follow the Infantry through. These initial efforts failed on that first night and on the following night, 24/25 October. Twenty-four hours later my battalion and the 1/5 Queen's on our Brigade front were ordered to 'try again'. This entailed a very long and noisy night advance and attack — noisy because of the creeping barrage ahead of us, the exploding of mines in the minefields set off by the barrage shells, and the shattering explosions of the enemy defensive fire directed at us whilst we ploughed through the extensive minefields, attempting to keep up with the barrage. During this my batman and runner, Private Biggar, had a foot blown off, possibly by an exploding mine. It could as well have been me. One could do no more than give him morphia tablets from the 'First Field' dressing kit, leave him and tell him that the stretcher-bearers would pick him up. Much later I learned that this is what happened. He was duly repatriated and fitted with a new foot. It is when you have nothing to do, or to think about, that a battle becomes very much more frightening. We obtained our objectives beyond the minefields on the enemy side of them and reorganised as best we could — not easy in an open and featureless desert. I suppose it was partly my own

inexperience that 'put me in the bag' (as the saying goes) by the evening of 25th October following the attack. It has always been rather a mystery to me that I was awarded a DSO for it. I was probably rather further forward than I should have been, and I and a few others were isolated in the desert whilst the armoured vehicles, due to follow us up, were unable to break out of the minefields in our wake and thus we very shortly lost any support. We were extremely close up to the enemy forward defensive fire. I could hear the German orders to their guns quite clearly. If only our Armour had managed to follow us, the battle down on this southern flank would have been highly successful. After some eighteen hours of being shot up by German and Italian mortars and by German infantry guns (small pieces), I and a few others became prisoners of war.

This proved to be the pattern along most of the positions to be attacked, although the penetrations by the main attacking force in the north, made in the main by battle-experienced Dominion divisions, was greater. Generally, the Montgomery method was not working. Even the diversion scheme, with dummy pipelines, guns, tanks and dumps, was not working. Rommel soon spotted that the real *Schwerpunkt* was in the north, somewhat south of the coastal road which he — and Montgomery — knew was vital to him. In spite of the order to medical units to remove their Red Crosses and anyway concentrate medical resources obviously in the south, the give-away was the enormous concourse of vehicles which built up in the north, all in full view of the heights still held by the Germans. Montgomery called a conference of his corps commanders in the early hours of 25 October in order to instil a little 'ginger' into the Armour. It seemed as if General Freyberg of the New Zealanders and General Morshead of the

Australians had been right in their predictions before the battle of what the tanks could or would not do.

Meanwhile, the price of their failure was a POW camp for those fortunate enough to escape wounds or death. This comes as a tremendous shock, for after a time the Army becomes your mother, father and nurse, who thinks for you and provides all necessities including water (lacking in a desert, which circumscribes escape attempts). Colonel Gibbs did escape eventually from a POW camp in Italy, but this first night he was very cold in shirt and shorts and a single blanket provided now by his German captors.

> Our German sentries were fairly cock-a-hoop because, they said, Rommel who had been away in Germany ill, was now back in the desert in command of his armies and hence, they declared, the British would be once more and finally 'on the run'. We gazed at the starry desert night, which seemed strange enough from inside a large wire enclosure. In the morning early, after a cup of coffee, we were pushed into a lorry and a long journey via a desert track within the coastal strip began. From time to time our own Desert Air Force appeared in the skies and the Italian drivers and escorts pulled up, scuttled out of their vehicles, and lay down flat in the sand some way from the column. Prisoners were left inside! Eventually we were embarked in a Savoia Marchetti, a wooden-strutted aeroplane. Inside they were rather like a tube train, with passengers sitting facing one another. We were a small party of officer prisoners of war and much larger groups of Italian farmers and families and 'contadini'. I felt a friendly feeling towards the civilians, mostly farmers and peasants, because their appearance, manner and language took me back to the Italian Campagna with memories of pre-war days when we used to know the country fairly well, and liked its people. There were air gunners fore and aft and from time to time they became terribly excited and dashed about from one end

of the plane to the other, traversing their Breda automatics, presumably because of threats by our own fighters. I prayed hard that we landed unscathed in Italy, which we did at Lecce in the heel of Italy after a roughly 500 miles flight from Cyrenaica. Not until 8th December did my wife get a telegram to say I was a POW, not just 'missing'.

The 4th and 5th battalions of the Royal Sussex Regiment were virtually wiped out after being transferred from 44 Division to the north to help the tanks get forward. Donald Barker was an NCO in 5 Royal Sussex.

We were a new div out in the spring when Monty said to us 'A wooden cross for England is not a bad thing', and of course we all looked at each other and there were mutters of 'Up yours, mate!' But our platoon officer was dead keen, he came back off a course so as not to miss the battle. I was given a deserter in my platoon but when it came to battle he didn't run. We were mustered all through the day and then got the order to go through. There was a muddle. In front of us were dug-in Scottish troops and one trigger-happy bloke on our side fired at them. At first it was a slow, quiet advance to our front line and then over wadis to the Italians who were holding their front line. There were a few skirmishes. The Italian infantry were still shell-shocked, they were coming out, giving themselves up, and were sent back, hundreds of them guarded by one of our chaps with his rifle slung. It seems we pushed on too far and the tanks supposed to support us didn't turn up. A couple of Italian tanks worried us, then the big German tanks rolled in and their mortars knocked out so many that there were only a handful of our lads left. But if you're ordered to advance, you do. You don't stop to help casualties or even take much notice. There was a sergeant who had lost both legs. 'My legs don't 'arf 'urt!' It looked as if he didn't have legs, but you could hardly tell him that, so we comforted him. 'You'll be all right, they'll get you back.' By 10 in the morning there were very few of the battalion left, the whole of the battalion would have filled one lorry. In my platoon I was the only NCO left.... When I got back to Company HQ there was only the CSM and two men. The enemy were all round us, we were behind a ridge as the CSM said: 'We aren't going anywhere.' I was all right except for a little bit of shrapnel in the arm. The Germans were the infantry who go with the panzers, they were amazed to find the English had got this far.

The POW camp wasn't Butlins but in Italy, some men hanged themselves, conditions were so bad. The guards sang 'Lili Marlene' and we sang 'Land of Hope and Glory'. Then we were sent in cattle trucks to Lamsdorf in Silesia where we were shackled in revenge for what the Canadians did at Dieppe. But you get all sorts in the Army and we had some burglars who took off our fetters, so we only wore them for parades. Then there was the death march away from the advancing Russians. I got away by lying in a ditch and then walked west, finally walking towards the sound of guns and meeting soldiers with big tanks who spoke funny English. They said I was 'a Goddamn Limey'.

Private Eric Laker was with HQ Company of 4 Royal Sussex in 133 Infantry Brigade, formerly of 44 Division but now bussed north apparently to help 1 Armoured Division's tanks. It serves to date Donald Barker's account from the 5th Battalion, because the same incidents occur in the same order, including mistaken firing on 51st Highland Division and setting a truck ablaze. Oddly, this chaos in the sand escapes mention in many general's memoirs, but the official history of the Gordon Highlanders refers to 'The 4th Royal Sussex, lorried infantry of the 1st Armoured division' during the night of the 29th opening fire on the Gordons, killing or wounding several men and burning their petrol truck.

At 1830 hours on Tuesday 27th October we moved off from our place of rest — the start of the night attack. From the back of my closed truck we appeared to move most of the way through dense traffic, and the sandy dust was rising in thick clouds. Almost from the start the manoeuvre was a fiasco — unfortunately for us! We arrived at the appointed starting line at approximately 2215 hours, apparently 45 minutes late, for the preliminary barrage by the Corps Artillery had ceased at 2115. Another barrage had been started and been cut short again because we were still not there. Absolute chaos reigned. Officers were dashing here, there, and all over the place, trying to put their men 'in the picture', but owing to the rush instructions were perforce of a very abridged nature. At 2230 hours the barrage came down again and we had to be ready to go in at 2300 hours, when the guns ceased fire. For that 30 minutes one had to shout to be heard, and to add to the din Jerry returned a fraction of our fire with his mortars. One shell landed on one side of a carrier while I was approaching the other side and about five yards away. It rendered hors de combat one of the carrier crew and this blast sent me reeling.

When we were due to start, the guide, who should have led the battalion, could not be found. Finally we went off and with such a devil of a rush that I am sure lots of people never started. Our little party of Company HQ and about 8 signallers trailed along behind a line of trucks as we had been told, until we found it was the wrong line! We rectified this and made another start. Going steadily forward someone was blessed with the bright idea of fixing bayonets, so with a sinking heart I drew my 'tin opener' and affixed it to the end of my rifle in the approved manner. The fact that for a time we were mixed up with our 'A' Company and then with the 2nd battalion, our reserve battalion, was a mere nothing. We eventually got sorted out.

I may as well give the object of the attack at this point. The Rifle Brigade was supposed to have taken the position which was classed as a strong point. Apparently they had not done so, and the 88-mm guns there were proving an obstacle to our tanks. We were to go in with the design of putting out the 88s, hold the position until dawn, when our tanks would go through us and we would withdraw, our job done. That was what it was on paper! A hundred yards from the starting point we went at right angles through a long line of 'Swallows' and 'Crusaders'. Comforting sight. 'Don't be late in the morning' someone shouted to one of the crews. 'We'll be there about five — don't worry' came the answer.

On still more, and in the distance I could see a bright glow which as we approached turned out to be one of our English 3-tonners. It was the ration [*sic*] truck of the Gordon Highlanders, set on fire by our forward companies. Apparently the chaps had not been told to expect any of our own troops in front of them, in fact been told to shoot up anyone they came across. Consequently when they came up to a company of the Gordons they opened fire on them and inflicted severe casualties until the error was realised. All this while the 88s were cracking away in front of us and their tracer shells were singing overhead. Mortar and artillery fire was dropping among us as we went forward. Eventually we halted and dug shallow trenches for shelter from small-arms fire which was now whistling over. We got down in them and I even had a fairly respectable sleep. We were awakened by the Company Commander shouting that we were going forward.

The Gordon history suggests that the Sussex might have lost direction. The discrepancy of one day in the date between Laker's diary and that of the Gordon author is of no consequence, especially not during night attacks. Laker's diary was hand-scribbled when he had the chance, the keeper of the Gordons' war diary had been under fire for some days and doubtless needed sleep. The general trend of events shows that the area involved was that of Kidney Ridge (which was a depression, not a ridge, although kidney-shaped), which was south-west of Tel el Eisa past Miteiriya Ridge, and on the Gordons' map had the code name of 'Aberdeen' (from where many would have been recruited). After their tragic error the Sussex went forward again and Laker got a 'grand little automatic' out of a derelict Italian tank. Then they came to Italian trenches and stopped there.

It was now about dawn and we heard the tanks warming up in the distance. We saw a couple of Crusaders come up and lay a perfect smokescreen, but when it had cleared all our tanks had WITHDRAWN under cover of it. We did not worry unduly, thinking they were perhaps going through in a different place, but concentrated on keeping well down as the stuff was now coming over thick and fast. MG fire was singing about in goodly quantities also. At about 0900 hours we received the shock of our lives. I looked up and saw some of our fellows climbing out of their slit trenches with their hands up! One even had a white handkerchief tied to his rifle. I saw a tank that had come over the ridge, with others on the right of it. A fellow was sitting on the top with a nasty looking LMG which he was waving around in a most unfriendly manner, and walking beside the tank was a chap with a revolver. He was waving his hands around indicating to our fellows that they were to come to him and surrender. Then to my horror I saw a black cross on the front of the tank.

I am convinced that no man living can put into words what my feelings were at that moment.

Had our tanks been beaten back? Impossible! Had Jerry made a counter-attack? Question after question flashed through my mind as we sat seemingly frozen. I tried to think straight, but the truth was we were all a little dazed with the pounding we had received during the night and that morning. Slightly bomb-happy. The three of us climbed out of the trench, first putting on our small packs (and how glad I was of that later), and joined the crowd of our fellows now beginning to stream towards the German lines. The fact that we had to walk through a barrage from our own guns did not help matters. I could not help but notice how well the Hun tanks were dug in and being used as MG nests. Transport, etc. was very well dispersed, but at the same time there was very little of it — in fact very little of anything at all and I think our tanks could have gone through as a knife through butter. But of course that is only my opinion from what I saw.

They had to walk unescorted for four miles, stopped first for compasses (escape material), then a search for cigarettes (most of which were taken by a 'roughneck', but Laker managed to hang on to his haversack with his washing tackle in it), then halted by an Italian officer. 'I was relieved of my knife, fork, spoon and tin opener, but luckily I had just put my watch down my sock'. Then they were put into trucks and dumped apparently in the middle of nowhere, but surprisingly given biscuits and Italian bully beef.

> Several times during the afternoon we saw Bostons come over in formation and bomb objectives. We hung about until dusk, and it was during this time that the full realisation of what had happened came over me. I nearly cried in my misery, if I had been alone I think I would have done so.

After a few days of such travel, via Mersa Matruh, Tobruk, Benghazi and Tripoli, 'I prayed I might not wake up in the morning.' Benghazi was 'a beastly place' with a terrible reputation. 'The Commandant was raving about striking at everything and all and sundry with a whip, and several other officers carried whips.' After Benghazi the journey became even more nightmarish. 'To see the fellows fighting for bad biscuits, green with mildew, that had been thrown away by the Wops, was a horrible sight. Before very long I was glad enough to eat them myself — and be thankful for them. Is it any wonder that we do not love the Italians?' In Tripoli they were better treated and better fed, but then crammed into the hold of a ship whose previous cargo had been coal. Many had dysentery, others were now seasick, and the place was teeming with lice. They had to wait for several days before the convoy — four ships and a destroyer escort — could find an opportunity to slip across to Sicily. At Palermo they were marched through the streets to the railway station.

> We had to face our first crowd of Italian civilians, gaping curiously at us, many of them laughing or jeering, but the majority of us could look straight at them.

On their train journey up the beautiful west coast of Italy they had a glimpse of Vesuvius in eruption.

> During the stops at stations many trains of troops, German and Italian, passed us going south. The Germans were very friendly and generally wished us good luck.

Laker finished up working in the mines near Brux in Czechoslovakia, and when above ground being bombed by the RAF, the USAAF and the Red Air Force. The German overseers here were quite different to the fighting troops in Africa, and the Czechs when they took over struck Laker as being worse, like something out of the French Revolution. First by Dakota and then by Lancaster, he was flown home to England in May 1945.

Alamein seemed a long way away.

12: 'YOUR BRILLIANT LIEUTENANT'

By 27 October Rommel, having taken over again and divined that the main threat was in the north, was launching counter-attacks with the infantry of the 90th Light and tanks from both his panzer divisions plus the best part of two Italian divisions. In particular, he saw the attack on Kidney Ridge (which he called Hill 28) as a key point for his riposte, which explains what happened to the Highland Division and the Sussex regiments. He found Montgomery's 'hesitancy and caution' astonishing but his own situation dire. Lack of fuel for his tanks and other vehicles pinned him down to absolutely minimum movement and there was no hope for the near future as on the 26th had come the news that the tankers *Proserpina* and *Tergestea* had both been sunk by the RAF off Tobruk. The tanker *Louisiana*, 2,550 tons, had left Taranto on the 25th but was sunk on the way two days later, again by the RAF.

In this respect — the interdiction of Rommel's supplies by the RAF and the Malta submarines — Ultra was providing vital information. But it would be misleading to suggest that Montgomery was provided with every single piece of information he required. As early as 11 September Rommel had issued an appreciation which spelt out why he could not even fight an effective defensive battle. Neither the Enigma decrypts nor any other source revealed these key facts. Even the layout of the Axis defensive positions and his order of battle was incompletely known. A good deal of guesswork was still required, the information eventually coming not from Ultra at all but from RAF PRU, army ground patrols, occasionally from captured prisoners, and from actual contact with the fighting enemy who had so far, despite some British gains, battled Montgomery's soldiers to exhaustion.

Normal experience of battle (even of air raids) keys people up. Everything becomes sharp and clear through heightened faculties — this phase can be extremely enjoyable and thrilling provided that personally one does not get hit. The keying up phase cannot last and is succeeded by deep exhaustion, lassitude and depression worsened by lack of sleep, and the nerves become jumpy from continual dangerous noise. The battle is read far more through the ears than the eyes, and troops new to it must learn this alphabet of sound so vital to survival.

Montgomery now decided to withdraw whole formations from the battle, partly to rest and restore them for new exertions and sacrifices, but also to build up a battering ram of largely armoured divisions to break through regardless. As it was to be in Normandy later, he could afford to lose many hundreds of tanks and many of their crews too, but his superiority in infantry numbers was not all that great. When it was learned in England that the new, barely tried general was sending his soldiers down to the sea to bathe and sending his tanks to the rear after only a few days' fighting, there was both rage and consternation.

There were also a number of advisers around Montgomery who had begun to doubt the wisdom of battering away in the north where the enemy was strongest, Rommel having moved much of his armour there. They suggested that the new thrust be made further south, not to the Qattara depression area of course, but still in the north at a point where German and Italian formations met. Army boundaries are always weak points. This discussion came to a head on 29 October when the critical decision was made, at the instance of General McCreery, Alexander's Chief of Staff, and Brigadier Williams, Monty's intelligence officer. The day was critical in other respects, because it saw a 'trouble-shooting' visit to Eighth Army HQ by Churchill's Minister of State in the Middle East, Richard Casey, accompanied by General Alexander.

One tends to overlook the stresses of high command, but they were there in plenty at this time. Churchill was mindful of the perilous position of Malta and above all anxious to claim a British victory in the desert before the (largely American) landings planned for North Africa in just over a week's time. He cannot but have been worried by the threatened resignation of Sir Stafford Cripps, the Lord Privy Seal, because the war was not being conducted with the necessary vigour and imagination. Security prevented him from revealing the detail of the imminent landings in French North Africa, but there the security seemed to be shaky and the reaction of the French themselves doubtful, and also of the Spaniards in case they mistook the preparations for a move against Franco.

In these circumstances, news brought to him by Eden of what Monty was doing in the desert sent him into a rage, which he vented on Brooke, the Chief of the General Staff. Brooke himself, uncertain of the outcome of the desert battle and twitching with nervousness, nevertheless reacted stoutly, defending his protégé, and got the Prime Minister to tone down a tactless message to the Middle East, which had told Montgomery how to handle the tactical details of the battle. This was fortunate for Winston, who otherwise would have had to eat his words.

Brooke wrote to his wife on 29 October telling her that he had had another unpleasant day and a row with Churchill. After that, to support his case, Churchill said that he had called a Chiefs of Staff meeting for 1230 that day, which he had a perfect right to do. Previously Churchill had told his junior ministers of Montgomery: 'I don't think any of you would like the fellow.' But he had approved of his appointment to succeed the doomed 'Strafer' Gott. Now, complained Brooke, Monty had become MY Monty in Churchill's eyes. What was MY Monty doing, to allow the battle to peter out? Why was he fighting a half-hearted battle? Had we not got a single general who could even win a single battle? The Staff meeting would review the matter.

At the staff meeting, apart from Churchill and Brooke, were the former Boer War general, Jan Smuts, Eden the Foreign Secretary, Attlee, leader of the Labour Party and deputy to Churchill, and Oliver Lyttelton. Smuts supported Brooke and Churchill climbed down, claiming falsely that he had not previously discussed the matter with him.

This same day, at Eden's suggestion, Richard Casey, Alexander, and his Chief of Staff, McCreery, arrived at Monty's HQ just behind the battle front. In Montgomery's account, Casey asked if the battle was lost, and Monty replied that he was just about to win it and Casey should go away and not bellyache. Deliberately, he radiated confidence and certainty, although his original plan had failed. Casey was heard muttering, obviously uncertain of what to report to London, and was threatened by a senior officer with political retribution.

But already the fateful decision had been taken, to switch 'Supercharge', Montgomery's final attack to not just break in but break through, to the junction between the German and the Italians and away from the coastal sector where the Australians, assisted by the Rifle Brigade, had so very nearly succeeded. Montgomery was brought round to this plan by others, but did not give them much credit, taking most for himself, as this projected the image he required of the commander who, for once, knew what he was doing, whose plans always worked out as he had said they would and who thereby gave confidence to his soldiers, the men upon whom in the end all depended. Also this apparently boastful claim suited the Intelligence officers part of whose duty was to camouflage the fact that they were able to read within hours many of the messages the enemy commanders were making. All the know-all newspaper features of how Monty had the portrait of his opponent, Rommel, hung up in his battle caravan so as to try to divine his enemy's intentions were calculated inventions to cover up for Ultra. But during the actual battle it was the 'Y' service, monitoring the battlefield messages between enemy fighting units, which kept Montgomery best informed on a day-to-day basis.

In the very early hours of the same day, 29 October, Rommel wrote that he was pacing up and down, thinking about the decisions he must soon take. It was doubtful that the Axis army could resist much longer. The obvious thing to do was to forestall the enemy by pulling back to a defensive position well in the rear, thus imposing a delay, for the whole lumbering strength of the Eighth Army would have to be moved forward too. He ordered one last counter-attack. Then followed an obscure comedy of sometimes delayed and thus misunderstood messages between Rommel in the desert and the HQ in East Prussia to which Hitler had just returned from a visit to the Russian front.

The grim difference between Hitler's rages and Churchill's was that the British staff system allowed for some brake on extreme or unwise measures, whereas failure to carry out Hitler's wishes could bring ignominious death, as was also the case with his rival tyrant Stalin. In the beginning, as the record shows, the brisk 'off with his head' decisiveness of the Führer was a political public image belied by his inner often irrational fears and caution which he showed for instance during the all too successful campaign in France in 1940. But now, two years later, Adolf Hitler had convinced himself that he was the greatest military genius of all time. A glance at the map of Europe in 1942 will show the enormous territory conquered by the Wehrmacht under his increasingly erratic and irrational guidance. All Churchill had to show was loss and failure, except for the Battle of Britain which had given him his 'bulldog' image, and a few small Middle Eastern successes. But a wide sweep over the map could show Hitler's tremendous gains; and he was now determined that where the German soldier stood, there he would stay. There would be no retreats.

This was now to confront his commanders with a terrible dilemma. Some were to realise sooner than others that their leader, to whom they had sworn an oath of allegiance, cared nothing for the German people who existed only to serve him and his megalomania. He was a public murderer, but what were they? And now they knew what he was, what should they do? Each man has to answer the question for himself, when his time comes.

Hitler returned to his HQ at the Wolf's Lair in a gloomy forest in East Prussia and, reading Rommel's reports of his serious situation, at once sent off a 'victory or death' exhortation of a type favoured by none-too-intelligent tyrants, but not well received by the condemned. This signal was delayed in transit and Rommel received it only at noon on 3 November. He assumed it to be the reply to a long signal sent by his chief of staff, stating that Rommel intended to retreat at once. Rommel therefore cancelled his own orders for retirement on the grounds that as he had always insisted on unconditional obedience from his own men, so too must he obey even when the order was clearly wrong. In some fury he set in motion moves which might result in the destruction of the Afrika Korps. He was not alone in the Second World War, or any other war, in facing such a dilemma; nor did such problems occur only on the German side.

At the Wolf's Lair in East Prussia further delay and the resulting confusion in the sequence of messages resulted in a splendid Führer-rage. The message sent by Rommel's HQ did not ask the leader's permission to retreat, it announced it as a fact. The additional fact that Hitler had not been woken to receive this bad news — because a new officer coming on duty knew nothing of Hitler's command to stand fast and die to the last man — suggested to the Führer that he was part of an Army plot to turn retreat into a fact in spite of his own demand for a last stand. The officer was reduced to the ranks. Hitler hated and despised the German officer caste, but having delayed the retreat of the Afrika Korps by 24 hours, at last he agreed to a retirement after a message from Kesselring.

The passing of these messages and their subsequent decoding in England was the first hint that Churchill and his staff had that Rommel was in serious trouble and that after all General Brooke's Montgomery might be winning. Restless as usual, the Prime Minister wanted the church bells rung for a victory — his victory, as he saw it; but, cautious as ever, Brooke advised waiting until matters became completely clear. After all, British victories had been won before in the desert and as swiftly erased by Rommel. But there was to be no doubt about it this time.

Montgomery's final attempt to break through — Operation 'Supercharge' — proved to be aptly named. It was not lightly won, being aimed at the well-defended height of Tel el Aqqaqir, west of Kidney Ridge and south-west of Tel el Eisa.

Prior to 'Supercharge' the infantry, not much aided by most of the tanks, had engaged in what Montgomery called 'crumbling' operations to penetrate the web-like net of Axis defensive positions; it was bloody and unspectacular work. Bombardier Challoner recorded:

Day by day we continued to make slow and persistent progress but the gains had been limited until October 29th. Then the Australians decisively battered their way across a vast minefield and opened up a route wide enough for us to pass through. Our passage was strongly opposed. 88 mm shells landed close to us with all the ferocity of old and Stukas made some of the most audacious attacks we had ever known. We made only two miles of ground, but this small gain proved to be of vital importance. We were now in the position known as 'Woodcock' and it was from here that a further attack was launched on November 1st. Our barrage was afterwards described by the enemy as 'inhuman'. The graft that was entailed in getting the programme under way at short notice was also inhuman, and no galley slaves could ever have surpassed our work rate. Oblivious of time, we just worked ourselves to the limit, until we were punch drunk from the pounding of the guns and dazed with fatigue. Close to exhaustion though we were by the time the fire-plan was completed, we at least saw something to give us a feeling of satisfaction. Droves of shell-shocked and thoroughly demoralised soldiers from the other side were staggering through our lines. Their weapons they had thrown away, and some of them could hardly raise their hands to put them on their heads. They were surrendering to anyone who would lead them away from the scene of the dreadful shelling and the hell it had created. Groups of bedraggled Italians and gaunt-faced Germans — no matter what nationality — were shuffling along, with no semblance of order or discipline, being conducted by a single private or junior NCO. As he passed between our guns, one fierce wee Jock leading a mixed bag of these unfortunates seemed to be thoroughly browned off with the task. He roundly cursed the fates which had caused him to act as escort to such a bleeding shower of camel shit, as he called them, trudging through the hot sand 'just to put the ****** bairns to bed'. Some of them indeed were little more than bairns. They could not have been much more than seventeen and it made one wonder at what age their military training had begun. It was possible to feel a modicum of compassion for them. Mac read their thoughts differently. 'Better a live prisoner than a dead hero,' he said. 'I wouldn't mind changing places with them myself.' 'I think you will', said Len. 'A few days ago those chaps were the proudest soldiers in the world — and look at them now! A human being without pride is no human being at all'.

'Supercharge' was to be immediately preceded by an attack in the extreme north by the Australians under their formidable and aggressive commander, General Morshead, while the main blow at the junction between elements of 15 Panzer and part of the Italian Trieste Division was to be made by General Freyberg's New Zealanders, another well-tried force under a resolute and skilful commander. To make up Dominion losses, two British infantry brigades would in fact lead the New Zealand attack, assisted by two squadrons of Valentine tanks. Tom Witherby recalled:

> Valentine tanks fought with infantry throughout the battle. In my regiment, one squadron went out each night to support one or other of the infantry brigades. They could not be used by day, being too small. But, being with the infantry, they were never mentioned. My brigade, the 23rd, supported the

Australians who captured the road and railway below Tel-el-Eisa. Almost everyone was killed or wounded.

Behind the two leading infantry brigades would come the New Zealanders' 'cavalry', the 9th Armoured Brigade with its three regiments, the Wiltshires, the Warwickshires and the 3rd Hussars. And behind that battering ram would roll the 1st Armoured Division to exploit a breakthrough into open desert and meet the enemy's armour when it counter-attacked. The CO of the 3rd Hussars, Lieutenant Colonel Sir Peter Farquhar, suggested to Montgomery that the task given 9th Armoured Brigade amounted to suicide, given that the lanes driven through the minefields would be covered by a concentration of German anti-tank guns. Montgomery told him that he was prepared to accept 100 per cent losses both in vehicles and men.

This was to be an interesting foretaste of Operation 'Goodwood' in Normandy, where to obtain a breakthrough and save his exhausted and decimated infantry Montgomery lined up three armoured divisions one behind the other and sent them forward as a battering ram. There was considerable congestion and confusion, but a large break-in was achieved for the loss of some 300 tanks, all expendable, and many of their crews, more expendable then than infantry. The German armour corralled it off — but only just. The margin between a clean breakthrough and an extended break-in was small.

The infantry attack began early on 2 November. The 9th Armoured Brigade attack went in out of the dawn light with 132 'runners'. By the time the tanks had advanced through the infantry their strength had been reduced to 94; by the time they had completed their task there were 19 left. The brigade had lost 113 tanks (according to Montgomery in *Alamein and the Desert War*[14]). A 9th Armoured Brigade source quotes 128 tanks at the start, including the 33 Crusaders in 'A' Squadron, the 34 Shermans in 'B' Squadron and the 34 Grants in 'C' Squadron, plus no doubt a number of tanks with headquarters, with a total strength of 425 men. The number of tanks knocked out or lost in minefields was 102, with 240 men killed. If you add the wounded and missing, casualties approximated 90 per cent. For once, the armour had not let down the infantry. They had broken through, destroying some 40 dug-in tanks and anti-tank guns. Across the ground strewn with their wreckage, the leading brigade of 1st Armoured Division went through into the open.

Reginald Vine was a witness. He was serving with the Light Aid Detachment of the Wiltshire Yeomanry, whose task was to recover and repair such tanks as were not on fire or otherwise knocked out completely.

> This time we were supported by 600 guns and got through the minefields and in among the German gun emplacements. These gun pits without exception were full of dead. In my group we ran over the trails of the German guns to put them out of action. The German general 'Fireball' Stumme had died of a heart attack and he was succeeded as head of the Afrika Korps by General Ritter von Thoma. I saw him surrender with his general's bag. There were four POWs on my left, a lot of dead on the ground, and the barrage had shaken up a great dust cloud. We decided to have a brew-up. A distinguished looking chap, rather forlorn, came out of the dust cloud, wearing field uniform and equipment, not like a British brass hat. He looked quite a gentleman. I did not know who he was at the time, but Captain Singer (killed next day) told me it was von Thoma. I understood that the upper-level

---

[14] *Alamein and the Desert War*, edited by Jerek Jewell (Sphere Books, 1967).

Germans were getting browned off, saying this is hell, no one can stand it.

It seems that there was something odd about von Thoma's surrender, possibly his reaction to Hitler's order to fight to the end (in a hopelessly lost battle), for which he would have to give the orders condemning his men to suffering and death without adequate military reason.

Bombardier Louis Challoner of 2nd Royal Horse Artillery in 1st Armoured Division was above all impressed by the difference between what was happening now and his unpleasant experiences back in June and July under the previous management; these had included being bombed by the RAF and, on orders from above, firing 50 rounds per gun on a delegated target — which turned out to be South African (this was on 2 July, probably the occasion complained about by General Dan Pienaar to Denis Johnston of the BBC). In his pen-and-ink diary Challoner was critical of what he said was 'the continual failure during this period of the Command to keep in touch with its own forces.' He wrote also of the new management's method:

> Mr Stephenson (a junior officer) came to us and made it his habit to go round daily with the fighting maps and explain to us the position. What a difference this makes to morale only a gunner can tell; yet it should be obvious to the meanest intelligence that when men are ordered to fire, to retreat, to advance, to switch right and left without any explanation they very soon lose all interest and begin to think the war is a game the higher-ups play, in which they have no intelligent part.

Challoner was also critical of Rommel for his attacks against Auchinleck early in July when

The pursuing enemy harried by the RAF by night and by their own impetuous commanders by day had gone about twenty nights without any adequate sleep. Many of them overran our positions and were easily made prisoners.

But by 4 November, he wrote,

Now it was the turn of Rommel's men to be in disarray and they were in a far worse state than we had been. Some of their artillery units found themselves unexpectedly staring eyeball to eyeball with British, Australian and French infantry and surrendered on the spot. Wireless codes were being broken and instead of enemy units rendezvousing with each other, they were greeted by the British instead. Several ten-ton lorries, for instance, were scheduled to pick up remnants of the Pavia Division at Bir Khalda, but Scottish troops got there first and made an amazing scoop at no cost to themselves. The reception of the most recent prisoners was interesting. They were not granted the opportunity to display any truculence, which might have been overlooked by the tolerant patient English, for they were in the hands of the Scots who wasted no time showing them who were the masters. This seemed to mean that any valuables or assets which would be of no use to him as a prisoner, had to be handed over, with little hope of return. Many such captives handed over watches, fountain pens, cigarette lighters and suchlike in exchange for a swig from their captors' water bottle, but some of the Germans who had reasoned that they would be given water in any case, tried to hide their valuables under stones or in slit trenches, hoping to recover them later. When this incredible dishonesty was detected the fat was indeed in the fire, and the anger of the Jocks blazed up, but not so much as when some other prisoners, with deliberate contempt, smashed their possessions before the very eyes of their captors — rendering them useless, of course. It was doubtless a very brave demonstration of defiance, but a most imprudent one, as the Scots have always had a reputation for playing rough games with enthusiasm. On November 4 Aqqaqir was cleared so went on, taking a German MO and his vehicle prisoner. He did not seem to mind very much and we were only too pleased, as Medical Officers and their equipment were in short supply and we could have done with a few more of them, regardless of their source.

They were through into the enemy's back areas overrunning all who still stood and fought. Some of the RAF aircraft which kept droning over them in circles during the night contributed to the disorganisation of the defenders by jamming their radio communications, hoping in particular to harass the panzers. John Perry was a sergeant pilot of a Wellington of 162 Squadron employed on this duty on 24 and 27 October, and also during the final breakthrough on 1 and 2 November. It was a Special Signals squadron whose Wellington Ics were fitted with a wide-band radio jammer. An aerial 20 feet long lay under the fuselage and could be lowered in flight to a vertical position from the old 'dustbin' turret. They were not told much about the operations but were merely given a map reference and told to stay close to that area with the jammer operating. Each time they spent about four hours at 5,000 feet, jamming the frequencies used by the German tank crews, with the aim of stopping them using their radios for regrouping or forming up.

> We were told that the operations were very successful, and I believe this to be true as the German ground and air defences were very strong and determined to stop us operating. We did suffer some losses.

On 3 November, the Ultra transcripts had been read at the Foreign Office. On 4 November Brooke found a 'wildly excited' Churchill busy dictating messages to his peers, Roosevelt and Stalin, to the governments of the Dominions, and to various military commanders including Alexander in Cairo in which he referred not to 'your Monty' but to 'your brilliant lieutenant, Montgomery'. Brooke himself was now convinced by a message from Alexander that the 'vast victory' he had been looking for had actually happened. If Monty had failed as all the others had, Brooke felt that he would have had no option but to resign. As it was, the victory must help 'Torch', the invasion of French North Africa, as it would influence them to come in on the Allied side, and it should keep the Spaniards sweet also. And if 'Torch' was to be a success, then we could stop losing this war and start winning it, he noted cautiously.

13: ROMMEL PUTS HIS SHOULDER TO THE WHEEL

The battle which began on 23 October ended with Rommel's second order to retreat on the afternoon of 4 November. There was no pursuit, merely a follow-up. Montgomery's estimate that it would take ten to twelve days of hard slogging to cripple the Axis forces had been proved correct; similarly his estimate that it would cost his army (which included some French and Greek units as well as Dominion troops) some 13,000 casualties was close. Eighth Army losses were approximately 13,500 killed, wounded and missing, or slightly less than his British and Canadian armies suffered in the 1945 battle of the Reichswald, which lasted a good deal longer and saw the same methods employed — but in the context of bitter cold and vast floods rather than extreme heat and lack of water.

As cold figures these may be approved, but the costs were individual, to widowed girls and smashed and torn men, in days and weeks of agony, which is the reality of both victory and defeat.

Axis losses at Alamein totalled 7,800 killed and wounded (5,000 German, 2,800 Italian) and 27,900 prisoners (7,900 German, 20,000 Italian). A true total of 35,700. The losses in key items were 450 tanks and more than 1,000 guns. It has been estimated that the British ended the battle with a ten to one superiority in armour. Montgomery has been widely criticised both by generals and also informed outsiders for his failure to complete his victory by cutting off the retreating Afrika Korps by wide sweeps into the desert.

Neither Tom Witherby nor Louis Challoner supported the criticism. Tom wrote briefly:

> There was as vigorous a pursuit as possible, but there were thousands of prisoners to collect, the Australians were leaving, and the troops were almost dead with exhaustion.

Bombardier Challoner's comments were written soon after the battle:

> The Allies could, and no doubt should have done better; perhaps cutting off Rommel's main forces entirely, but several unexpected factors combined to assist the Axis powers. We were ourselves bogged down by a colossal rain-storm just after we had reached Guwala, and our plight was typical of that of other formations. The delay was catastrophic, for while we were struggling under appalling conditions, the Axis had reached a point where the weather was more favourable to movement and a great chance of decisively smashing up the opposition was lost.

For someone who was not there and anyway lacked experience of high command it is difficult to judge whether Monty was right or wrong. The Germans certainly thought him hesitant and cautious, but presumably he knew his army and its state of training best, and decided not to risk anything further. At Alam el Haifa he had stopped a German offensive (with small losses on either side), now he had defeated a German army in a set-piece offensive of his own — the first such British victory in the war. And the defeated army was never able again to attack in strength (except against 'green' American troops at Kasserine).

There was no real reason for Montgomery to risk anything, because the 'Torch' landings had begun on 8 November, so that Rommel had Allied armies front and rear. There was much bitter fighting ahead, but there was also an unexpectedly favourable result. Hitler, having refused to allow his Sixth Army to retreat from the Stalingrad trap, had decided to reinforce failure in North Africa. The massive Tiger tanks (the Mark VI) and the multiple rocket batteries which might have turned the tide for Rommel were now poured uselessly into the battle for French North Africa against three Allied armies. The eventual cost to the Axis was some quarter of a million men, dead, wounded or prisoner, almost as many as at Stalingrad. But it took until May 1943 for the Allies to achieve this.

Meanwhile, the further it advanced, the longer became the Eighth Army's communications; and as theirs lengthened, so Rommel's shortened. Montgomery's caution at least made sure that the tide could not now be reversed, as it had so often in the past. Eventually, all the old names appeared and fell into British hands — Benghazi on 20 November, Tripoli on 23 January 1943.

Susanna Agnelli, still a nurse in an Italian hospital ship, easily recognisable because it was painted white relieved only by the crosses, was in Tripoli almost at the end. One morning, as they approached the port, an explosion shook the hull. Putting on their life-jackets the staff went on deck to find it littered with broken glass and flakes of paint from the deckhead. Mines cannot tell a tanker's hull from that of a hospital ship. They were brought into port by tugs; in Tripoli there was utter confusion, but in a military vehicle Susanna recognised her brother Gianni. An elbow was bandaged but the wound was not serious — he had been shot by accident by his orderly. He refused a passage home in the hospital ship, but Susanna got a few hours off to be with him. They went out into the desert to the ruins of Sabratha, both of them in uniform, and sat on the broken columns eating dates. Then she went back to the ship and he drove off to Tunisia.

Martin Ranft was retreating with his artillery unit, which had had to leave its guns behind. When they reached Benghazi they saw a lovely green countryside, good to look upon after the raw desert. Here the unit got brand-new guns and half-tracks to tow them; but Ranft's gun never fired a shot — the RAF destroyed it. One plane flew so low that he could see the pilot, smoking a cigarette and waving. Jumping off a lorry to take cover, a sergeant landed in a bush and ripped his trousers — and a little skin, too. He shouted out: 'I'm wounded, I'm wounded!' This man had the biggest mouth, commented Ranft, and so he got a wound medal; but after the last battle he ran away.

It was in Benghazi during the retreat, with the road blocked, that Rommel appeared in an open, chauffeur-driven car, which went into the ditch. Rommel, now a Field Marshal, got out and said: 'Come on, boys, give us a push,' and put his shoulder to it himself. He was a smashing chap, one of the best, thought Ranft. If Montgomery had done that, remarked a British general, it would have been as a carefully calculated ploy for effect; but with Rommel it was just natural.

The war ended for Ranft in Tunisia, encircled by Americans to the west and the Eighth Army to the east. His unit's three remaining guns carried out their tasks from in front of a hill instead of by indirect fire from behind, which was usual. To their amazement, no one fired at them; and when they saw a spotter plane, all movement stopped. They finally surrendered to soldiers of an Indian division who were primarily interested in collecting watches.

Back near Oran, we marched through the night to a POW camp which was just wire — no huts, no water. The first morning, three men died from thirst. Water arrived only in the late afternoon. Then we were in an American Liberty Ship, a terrible 4-5 weeks passage in rough weather, packed into the cargo deck like fish in a box. Then we were taken back to Europe, to England, where I served a year working on a farm. I was demobbed in 1947 but my home was now in the DDR. I preferred to stay in England and went into business.

And what of the principal actors in the drama? Rommel was ordered back to Germany and was replaced in North Africa by General von Arnim. Monty went on to plan the invasion of Sicily and clashed with impatient, inexperienced American generals sure of their country's potential power. After a while Monty was called back to England to take charge of two invasion armies being formed there — the British Second Army and the Canadian First.

By that time I was serving in a rifle company of the Gordon Highlanders stationed in the Orkneys as part of the defences of Scapa Flow, the main British fleet base. Then, together with the Argylls, we were moved south to England to form part of the Highland Brigade in the new 15th Scottish Infantry Division. Monty came and looked at the new division but not our battalion and we were told that he was not happy with our state of training. This, one now sees, was all part of the standard Monty pep talk, strictly not to be taken seriously. At the time we did not take it seriously because it was clearly wrong. In one direction we had had too much training — sub-unit battle drill for instance — but in other ways we were completely ignorant. And that was the Army's fault, not ours. We did very little actual firing practice, which matters a great deal when one considers that only a tiny proportion of any army actually engages in anything so animal-like as fighting, and if this tiny minority cannot shoot then it is wasting its time.

We had naturally no idea of how to operate with tanks — indeed, I was a slight exception in that I lived in the south and had actually seen a few tanks — painted in desert colours, on flatcars and bound for Southampton Docks and North Africa. Up to now, the Army had made sure that was the nearest we had come to them.

As far as anti-tank weapons were concerned, these can be easily described — there weren't any. The Boys anti-tank rifle which I had carried when with the London Scottish had vanished, as it was of no use anyway, and people no longer pretended that rifle grenades or sticky bombs were a practical anti-tank defence. We had a great fellow-feeling for the unfortunate Hampshires in the First Army who had had to meet the formidable Tiger tanks, with seven inches of frontal armour it was said, and an 88-mm gun in the turret, with the pathetic inadequacies which were all that the British Army had provided them with. They fought bravely of course, but it was not war.

There were to our minds not nearly enough automatics. The Thompsons issued to us in the London Scottish for cliff patrols had now been replaced with the appalling Sten, the world's worst machine-carbine. If you wanted it to fire, it wouldn't; if you didn't want it work, it shot you in the foot. The rifles were the old short magazine Lee Enfields (mine was marked 1912), perfectly adequate even if British Army drill — which meant bashing the butt on the parade ground hard and often — was not calculated to improve a weapon. The bayonets were also 1914-18 and never seriously considered by us, regardless of what the brass hats might have thought. Without the bayonet, you could use a Lee Enfield to kill people up to 600-800 yards depending on your skill; with the bayonet attached, the aim was completely spoiled and a deadly rifle became simply a short pole with a knife on the end, enabling you to kill a nasty if he came within a couple of feet and hadn't shot you first.

The modern generation — and the promoters of the war at the time — might argue that we had a superior cause; but if I recall rightly a war poet wrote that our lot was to 'defend the bad against the worse'. How true to the feelings of many of us that was, particularly in the Gordons. The callous treatment of the men who survived the trenches of 1914-18 had gone deep, they had been cast on the scrapheap by a Parliament of the 'hard-faced men who had done well out of the war'. ABCA (Current Affairs) lectures about war aims and the shape of the world after the war always roused impassioned argument, unseemly in men many of whom were subsequently to die or be maimed. But we did think of what was to become of us if we survived. My family had not suffered in the inter-war years, but I felt as an unbearable agony what had been done to the generation of our fathers. To me it was then, and still is, the supreme atrocity of the twentieth century. And the perpetrators of it had taken us into another world war without, it appeared, real thought of how it was to be waged and with what weapons.

However, almost at the last hour, after Monty took us over, there was a remarkable change. Up to now, remember, the rare but mighty 2-pounder pop-gun had been too technical for infantry even to approach. Now, without warning, we were given a battery of 6-pounder anti-tank guns for our very own! And the PIAT for close-range anti-tank work, a personal spring-loaded weapon. And then began the exercises — or 'schemes' as they were called then — in which we were not only shown real tanks but were actually able to practise with them, firing live ammunition and plenty of it (which cost us two men killed the first time it was tried). But why had all this not been done before? The war had begun, after all, in September 1939 and now it was the autumn of 1943. Four years, and only now were we more or less up to the job. And only just in time, for now on the far side of the Channel, once more Erwin Rommel was waiting to dispute the way. We did not know then that he was soon to be murdered by his Führer, or the full iniquities for which that regime had been responsible.

A politician with ambitions to be the greatest war leader of all time had already written:

> The spirit of the broad masses enables it to carry through to victory any struggle that it once enters upon, no matter how long such a struggle may last or however great the sacrifice that may be necessary or what the means that have to be employed; and all this even though the actual military equipment at hand may be utterly inadequate when compared with that of other nations.

The nation he was referring to was Britain. The politician's name was Adolf Hitler.

For the struggles of the Eighth Army in the desert there could be no better epitaph.

SOURCES AND
ACKNOWLEDGEMENTS

I owe a debt of gratitude to the following:

The Trustees of the Imperial War Museum for access to some of the collections held in the Department of Documents at the museum:

Challoner, Bdr Louis, 2 RHA, 1 Armd Div[15]

Drew, Pte J. E., 18 DLI

Gibbs, Lt-Col D. L. A., OC 1/6 Queen's, 44 Inf Div

Laker, Pte Eric G, 4 R. Sussex, 44 Inf Div

Miles, Capt Basil E., MO R. Scots Greys, 10 Armd Div

Parry, Major David F., 57 LAA attd 50 Inf Div (Courtesy of Mrs Jean Parry)

Witherby, Major Thomas, 46 R. Tanks, 23 Armd Bde, 8 Armd Div[16]

Additional witnesses: British and Commonwealth Armies

Barker, Donald, 5 R. Sussex, 44 Inf Div

Beel, Tom F., 20th Batt, 2 NZ Div

Bettesworth, David, APO Tobruk

Burridge, Eric H., 8 Water Tank Coy RASC

Easthope, B., 577 Fd Coy RE, 44 Inf Div

Freeman, Albert Edward, 2 Cheshires

Gosington, William, Wksps 5 Bde, 4 Indian Div

Philbrick, Charles, 44 RTR, 1 Army Tk Bde, 2 NZ Div

Vine, Reginald, LAD, Wilts Yeo, 9 Armd Bde, 2 NZ Div

---

[15] Additionally the MS of 'Where Right and Glory Led', written jointly with the late Bdr Joe Nugent.

[16] Additional to personal communications over many years and assistance with this present book.

Williams, Bernard L., OC No 6 Field Surgical Unit

Additional witnesses: Royal Navy
Britton, Gus, Asst Curator, RN Submarine Museum, Gosport, Hants[17]
Crawford, Captain N. L. C., HM S/M *Upholder*
Forbes, James Reid, HMS *Sirius*, cruiser
Goldsmith, F., HMS *Belvoir*, Hunt-class destroyer
Henley, Victor, HMS *Glenroy*, infantry landing ship
Ogle, Howard, Malta and Alexandria dockyards.

Additional witnesses: Royal Air Force
Aircrew Association via K. J. Sutton for help in contacting the witnesses
Clark, Frank, A/Gnr, 38 Sqdn (Wellington torpedo-bombers)
Foulis, S/Ldr Michael, DFC, 38 Sqdn (Wellington torpedo-bombers). Documentation courtesy Ursula Kiernan
Grant, Charles, Nav., 39 Sqdn (Beaufort torpedo-bombers)
McGarry, Terence Arthur, Nav. 39 Sqdn (Beaufort torpedo-bombers)
Oldfield, Fred F., WT/Radar op 221 Sqdn (Radar Wellingtons)
Perry, John A., Pilot, 162 Sqdn (Wellington Ic)
Richards, 'Dickie', WT op, 233 Sqdn (Baltimores)
Roberts, Jack, Dvr, 145 Sqdn (Spitfires)
Sheppard, L. J., DFC Pilot, 260 Sqdn (Kittihawk fighter-bombers)
Taylor, H. A., Pilot, 38 Sqdn (Wellington torpedo-bombers)
Trotman Jack C., Nav, 272 Sqdn (Beaufighters)

---

[17] Gus, who served with the Malta submarines, was a fount of knowledge and advice.

Additional witnesses: *Wehrmacht (German Armed Forces)*
Manfred Rommel, Oberburgermeister of Stuttgart and Heinz
Becker, Verband DAK for help in contacting special witnesses
Bongartz, Arnold, L.-Flottilen
Drescher,   Hans,   Staffelkapitän,   5   Staffel   II.
Schlachtgeschwader 3
Heimberg, Helmut, Luftwaffe Feld Bn O.B.S.
Huber, Helmut, reinforcement in 'Esperia'
Pechmann, Heinz, sgt in anti-tank battery (88s)
Ranft, Martin, medium arty
Zwintscher, Helmuth, Uff, 'ITALLUFT' HQ

For assistance in contacting witnesses
The News, Portsmouth; and the *Hayling Islander*

For obtaining books
The Public Library, Hayling island; and David Bettesworth

For drawing the maps and diagrams
Maurice Young

For German translations
Ilse McKee

BIBLIOGRAPHY

Intelligence and Code/Cipher Breaking

British Intelligence in the Second World War, Vol I (1979) and Vol II (1981). Hinsley, Thomas, Ransom and Knight (HMSO).

Ultra and Mediterranean Strategy 1941-1945. Ralph Bennett (Hamish Hamilton, 1989).

The Hut Six Story: Breaking the Enigma Codes. Gordon Welchman (Allen Lane, 1982).

The Ultra Secret. F. W. Winterbotham (Weidenfeld & Nicolson, 1974).

Secret Intelligence in the 20th Century. Constantine Fitzgibbon (Hart-Davis, MacGibbon, 1976).

Very Special Intelligence: The Story of the Admiralty's Operational Intelligence Centre 1959-1945. Patrick Beesley (Hamish Hamilton, 1977).

Room 40: British Naval Intelligence 1914-1918. Patrick Beesly (Oxford University Press, 1984).

Rommel's Intelligence in the Desert Campaign. Hans-Otto Behrendt (Kimber, 1985).

Royal Navy

Unbroken. Alistair Mars (Muller, 1953).

HM S/M Upholder. Captain M. L. C. Crawford, DSC.

Staff History of Second World War Submarines, Vol II.

Our Penelope. Her Company (Harrap, 1943).

Malta Convoy. Peter Shankland and Anthony Hunter (Collins, 1961).

Royal Air Force

The Royal Air Force 1939-1945, Vol 1: The Fight at Odds. Denis Richards (HMSO, 1953).

The Royal Air Force 1939-1945, Vol 2: The Fight Avails. Denis Richards and Hilary St G. Saunders (HMSO, 1954).

The Desert Air Force. Roderic Owen (Hutchinson, 1948).

Middle East 1940-1942: A Study in Air Power. Philip Guedalla (Hodder & Stoughton, 1944).

The Air Battle of Malta: Official account 1940-1942. (HMSO, 1944).

Air Spy. Constance Babington-Smith (Harper, N.Y., 1957).

The Ship-Busters. Ralph Barker (Chatto & Windus, 1957).

The Ship-Hunters. R. E. Gillman (Murray, 1976).

Wellington at War. Chaz Bowyer (Ian Allan, 1982).

German Wehrmacht

Afrika Korps. Major H. J. Macksey, MC (Pan/Ballantine, 1972).

Rommel's War in Africa. Wolf Heckmann (Granada, 1981).

With Rommel in the Desert. Heinz Werner Schmidt (Panther).

The Foxes of the Desert. Paul Carell (Macdonald, 1960).

Rommel. Desmond Young (Collins, 1950).

Panzer Leader. Gen. Heinz Guderian (Michael Joseph, 1952).

Panzer Battles. Maj.-Gen. E. W. von Mellenthin (Cassell, 1955).

The Other Side of the Hill. B. H. Liddell Hart (Cassell, 1948).

The Fatal Decisions: The Battle of El Alamein. Lt-Gen. Fritz Bayerlein (Michael Joseph, 1956).

The First and the Last. Adolf Galland (Methuen, 1955).

The Italians

Alamein 1933-1962. Paulo Caccia-Dominioni (Allen & Unwin, 1966).

We Always Wore Sailor Suits. Susanna Agnelli (Weidenfeld & Nicolson, 1976).

The Ciano Diaries. Count Galeazzo Ciano (Heinemann, 1947).

The Allied Generals

Auchinleck. Philip Warner (Buschan & Enright, 1981).

Alex. Nigel Nicolson (Weidenfeld & Nicolson, 1973).

Alexander's Generals. Gregory Blaxland (Kimber, 1979).

Alanbrooke. David Fraser (Collins, 1982).

A Soldier's Story. Omar N. Bradley (Eyre & Spottiswoode, 1951).

Tobruk. Michael Carver (Batsford, 1964).

And We Shall Shock Them. David Fraser (Hodder, 1983).

A Full Life. Brian Horrocks (Leo Cooper, 1960).

Man of Armour. Ronald Lewin (Leo Cooper, 1976).

El Alamein. John Strawson (Dent, 1981).

Approach to Battle. Francis Tuker (Cassell, 1963).

Alamein and the Desert War. Ed. Jerek Jewell (Sphere Books, 1967).

Monty: The Making of a General. Nigel Hamilton (Hamish Hamilton, 1981).

Monty: The Man behind the Legend. Nigel Hamilton (Sphere Books, 1980).

A Field-Marshal in the Family. Brian Montgomery (Constable, 1973). *Nine Rivers from Jordan.* Denis Johnston (Verschoyle, 1953).

Soldiers

Desert Episode. George Greenfield (Macmillan, 1945).

Brazen Chariots. Robert Crisp (Muller, 1959).

The Gordon Highlanders 1919-1945, Vol V. Wilfrid Miles (University Press, Aberdeen, 1961).

Report My Signals. Anthony Brett-James (Hennel Locke, 1948). *Long Range Desert Group.* W. B. Kennedy Shaw (Collins, 1945). *Popski's Private Army.* Vladimir Peniakoff (Reprint Society,

1953). *The Fusing of the Ploughshare*. Henry R. Ritchie (Ritchie, Dunmow, 1987).

Top Hats in Tobruk. Kenneth Rankin (Rankin, Odiham, 1983).

Desert Rats at War. George Forty (Ian Allan, 1975).

(The last three books loaned and specially recommended as authentic by Dave Bettesworth who like many other Desert veterans will not accept works by a younger generation).

Politicians

The War and Colonel Warden. Gerald Pawle (Harrap, 1963).

Former Naval Person. Vice-Admiral Sir Peter Gretton (Cassell, 1968).

Miscellaneous

Dieppe. Terence Robertson (Hutchinson, 1963).

The Pacific War. John Costello (Collins, 1981).

Gunners at War. Shelford Bidwell (Arms & Armour Press, 1970).

The Guns 1939-45. Ian V. Hogg (Macdonald, 1970).

German Tanks of World War 2. Terry Gander and Peter Chamberlain (Patrick Stephens, 1975).

Tank: A History of Armoured Fighting Vehicles. Kenneth Macksey and John H. Batchelor (Ballantine, N.Y., 1971).

A NOTE TO THE READER

If you have enjoyed this book enough to leave a review on **Amazon** and **Goodreads**, then we would be truly grateful.
Sapere Books

SAPERE
BOOKS

Sapere Books is an exciting new publisher of brilliant fiction and popular history.

To find out more about our latest releases and our monthly bargain books visit our website:
saperebooks.com

www.ingramcontent.com/pod-product-compliance
Lightning Source LLC
LaVergne TN
LVHW051544080426
835510LV00020B/2842